The Raw Gourmet

Simple Recipes for Living Well

Nomi Shannon

alive
BOOKS
Vancouver

This book is dedicated to Douglas W. Shannon and Laura Jean Shannon
who are in so many ways my "raison d'être."

To Etta S. N. R. Norris, because she has always been there, and always will be.

To Brian Clement, a man who has succeeded in educating the public in a positive and loving way,
and who has given me wonderful opportunities to expand and grow.

And to Catherine June Manter for so wholeheartedly allowing me to be her lifestyle coach
on the physical plane, and who so lovingly coached me on a spiritual level.
I shall always be grateful for the lessons I have learned in our twenty-year friendship.

And God said, See I have given you every plant–yielding seed that is on the face
of all the land and every tree with seed in its fruit; you shall have them for food.
Genesis 1:29

alive
BOOKS

7432 Fraser Park Drive
Burnaby, BC   V5J 5B9
Canada
(604) 435-1919

Canadian Cataloguing in Publication Data
Shannon, Nomi
The raw gourmet

Includes bibliographical references and index.
ISBN 0–920470–48–3

1.Cookery (Natural foods) I. Title.
TX741.S52 1998   641.5'637   C98–910983–6

Food Stylist: Fred Edrissi
Art Director: Terence Yeung
Recipe Photographs: Edmond Fong

First Printing in March 1999
Second Printing in August 1999
Third Printing in April 2000
Fourth Printing in May 2001
Fifth Printing in November 2001
Sixth Printing in July 2002
Seventh Printing in January 2003
Eighth Printing in July 2004

Printed and bound in Canada.

Table of Contents

Foreword

by Brian Clement
Director, Hippocrates Health Institute

Living food is at the heart of any serious health seekers' lifestyle. After many decades of a society confused and lost as to what it should eat, common sense has finally prevailed.

Fresh non-cooked fruits, vegetables, nuts, seeds, grains and beans not only provide the maximum amount of nutrition, as Nomi will explain to you in this book, they can also be delicious gourmet delights that turn on your palate. Foods that are fun and foods that heal were once thought of as incompatible. Within these pages lives a tapestry of delectable, healthful recipes which will eradicate any former notion that you may have had.

When spending the time to prepare menus that make you well, you are not only building your body, but also elevating your mind and spirit. Nomi's heart, as well as the experience that she gained here at the Hippocrates Health Institute, really come through in this easy-to-follow, step-by-step book for better living. Without fail, you will raise your level of energy, lengthen the time you will be on this earth and enjoy your life much more by chewing and swallowing living food.

Our experience over several generations has been that the body not only likes, but requires the vitamins, minerals, protein, oxygen, enzymes and hormones that are in these non-cooked splendors. Tens of thousands of people worldwide have brought themselves back from the grips of death by fueling their body with this ultimate diet. For some of you this will become part of your lifestyle, for others, you will further embrace it and have this food be the way you eat. However far you go, you will gain enormous benefit from the simple act of following Nomi's guidance in this wonderful world of power-charged cuisine.

Preface

My goal in writing this book, is to get you "up and running" in the living foods lifestyle. Most of the recipes have been designed for ease, speed and simplicity.

Even more importantly, I hope this book will help spark your own creative forces when it comes to preparing life-giving food for yourself and others. In the beginning, you may want to use this book daily, but ultimately my wish is that you will create living foods with such ease that you will not need this book at all. Then you can give it to someone else who is interested in living life to the fullest by creating and maintaining good health. *L'chayim!*, which means "to life."

There are two categories of recipes in this book: Raw and Optimum Choice Raw. The Optimum Choice Raw recipes adhere to the tenets of the Living Food Program as originated by Ann Wigmore and furthered by Viktoras Kulvinskas, Herbert Shelton, Brian Clement and others. You will know when you see the Optimum Choice Raw symbol next to a recipe that it contains approved food and adheres to food combining principles. For a more detailed explanation of the pros and cons of food combining, and a detailed food combining chart, see page 201.

If you have chosen this lifestyle because you are ill, or are seeking an optimal cleanse, then use only the Optimum Choice Raw recipes. By experimenting with the food combining principles, including single-food meals (mono-meals), you will learn through experience what is best for your own metabolism and digestion.

To explore raw foods without many restrictions, go ahead and enjoy all the recipes.

Throughout this book there are references made to the "cleanse phase" or the "initial three-week cleanse." This is what you would do if you were to stay at one of the health institutes devoted to raw foods (see Sources, page 210).

If you want to introduce yourself to raw foods with a similiar three-week cleanse, follow the Optimum Choice Raw recipes or use the three-week menu plan at the back of this book (see page 204). By reading over this book carefully, you can create your own three-week cleanse without ever leaving home.

Look for the

Optimum Choice

Raw recipe symbol.

Introduction

A Healthier Way of Life

Most people would agree they should be eating healthy food. But, often, they don't know how to take the next step. "How do I do it?" is a common question, often followed by: "Isn't it a lot of work?" and "Isn't it boring?"

The purpose of this book is to introduce you to the healthiest food imaginable, and to show you how to prepare it in easy, delicious and interesting ways.

I was introduced to raw food over ten years ago by a holistic physician. At that time, I had serious digestive problems and felt ill no matter what I ate. For the first time in my life, I was gaining weight and had begun to develop an alphabet of maladies.

With my physician's encouragement, I began to eat about fifty percent of my food raw. Most of us already eat quite a bit of raw food, such as fruit, salads, coleslaw, and even smoothies, so I found it quite easy to expand on that theme. I carried around a pocket full of raw almonds for snacks. I began to feel better almost immediately.

But it wasn't until sometime later that I became really serious about eating raw food and went on a three-week one hundred percent raw food and juices program, including wheatgrass juice. I lost eleven pounds in fourteen days and couldn't believe how physically and mentally well I felt. It made me realize that the degenerative process was so very subtle and slow that I simply had forgotten how it felt to be healthy.

From that moment on, I embraced a raw food program, and over a matter of several weeks said good riddance to fibromyalgia, hypoglycemia, mood swings, allergic sinusitis, digestive disorders, including acid reflux, and in time rid myself of candida (a systemic yeast infection that has multiple symptoms). My physical, emotional and mental energy was so high—I had never experienced anything like it. It would be a lie to say that, in my mid-forties, I felt as though I were in my twenties again. I had never felt as good in my twenties.

Because of my passion for the remarkable effects of food on the body, it wasn't long before I was working as a health consultant at a world-renowned, alternative health institute in Florida. Called the

Hippocrates Health Institute, the center teaches the living foods approach to wellness and provides a three-week educational program devoted to cleansing and healing the body with natural, fresh, organic, uncooked, unrefined foods. A gift from nature, these foods provide the body with everything it needs to stay healthy and vigorous. It is a diet rich in enzymes and oxygen, both of which are lacking in processed foods, dairy products and meat.

At Hippocrates, I had the opportunity to meet people from all walks of life and from all over the world, ranging from average working-class people to movie stars, from young to old. Some were ill, others were healthy and wanted to learn how to maintain and improve their quality of life. During my years there, I saw profound improvements in people's health when they changed their habits and embraced a living foods lifestyle.

It was quite common to see drastic reductions in blood cholesterol levels, blood pressure and weight. I saw chronic infections dramatically heal and chronic headaches disappear. I saw insulin-dependent people able to substantially lower their insulin doses. People limped in with painful arthritis only to walk out with a huge reduction in pain. And just about everyone experienced high energy and greatly improved moods by the end of the three weeks. Time after time I was witness to gravely ill people reversing the course of their illness with perseverance and bravery, and becoming well again.

Although the living foods program is meant to be preventive, if people who have had such serious illnesses feel that they have cured themselves, just think what this program can do for you if you are relatively healthy. How much better to prevent rather than try to cure a problem.

What should you eat? Over the years wherever I go, the one question I hear the most is: "But what should I eat?" Whether you'd simply like to add more vegetable servings to your diet, or want to change your lifestyle in a more dramatic way, this book has been designed to answer that question. It includes recipes for all occasions, most of them very simple, so that you will be able to enjoy a variety of food with no more expenditure of time than in a traditional Standard American Diet (SAD) kitchen. Although you may find this hard to believe right now, once you get into the rhythm of raw food preparation you will likely spend less time in your kitchen than you did before.

You will see that a raw food diet can be as exciting and interesting as any other type of cuisine. The recipes in this book will give you the tools to prepare meals for all occasions that are tasty, nutritious and easy to make.

1 The Basics

It's Not All About Food

The most important thing to remember as you begin to change your lifestyle is this: Don't think it is all about food. Yes, what you eat is vital, but it is not the only thing to focus on. At least as important, and perhaps even more important than food, is exercise. You can't improve your health by sitting at home reading cookbooks and watching television! Keep moving. Or begin moving.

You Need Exercise

Seventy-five percent of all the good you can do for yourself by using the recipes in this book could be lost if you don't exercise. Walk, run, jog, use a trampoline, ride an exercise bike, join a water aerobics class or a mall walking group, use a hula hoop, go hiking, rollerblade, kayak, row, canoe, play basketball, play tennis, play volleyball, swim, play hockey,

climb stairs on your lunch hour— whatever you like. And if no form of exercise interests you, start doing something anyway and you will find that eventually you'll begin to enjoy it. If you are ill—too ill to exercise—do the most that you can; even visualizing your body going through the motions is good for you. Don't be afraid to ask for help if you need it to find a way to get your body moving. Finally, remember that laughing is good exercise, so lie on your back on the living room floor and fake a great big laugh. You will probably feel so silly that it will make you chuckle.

Think Holistically

As you move toward a cleaner lifestyle, analyze your mind, your body, your spirit, your attitude, the air you breathe, the water you drink, the food you eat, the clothes you wear, forces in the environment, toxins of the body, of the mind and of the spirit.

Many of us have grown up treating the body and the mind as separate entities. The mind, however, exerts influence down to the most minute cellular level. If you are chronically negative, fearful or angry, it matters little that you eat "perfectly," or even that you run marathons. Chronic emotional upset such as resentment, anger, grief, fear and depression restricts the regenerative capacity of the body.

While you are scrupulously attending to your sprouts and your waistline, don't forget the most important thing of all: the state of your mind. Positive feelings, thoughts, emotions and behavior are essential for optimum health.

Just Do It!

Eating living foods is not a religion. You don't need to make an intellectual decision about whether or not to believe in it. The only way to know if you will be greatly improving your life is try it for a fair amount of time and see for yourself. You don't even need to understand all the facts about enzymes and digestive processes in order to benefit from changing your habits. The bottom line is, like the sneaker people say: Just do it!

Why Eat Raw Food?

Eating a high-enzyme diet consisting of raw fruits and vegetables, sprouted seeds, nuts, grains and some seaweed will profoundly increase your chances of achieving optimal health.

Eating predominantly cooked food puts a tremendous strain on the body. To understand why this is true, you need to understand the role enzymes play. Enzymes are in the cells of every living plant and animal. It is enzyme activity that accomplishes all biological work from blinking an eye, to lifting a finger, to having a thought.

When we eat, we need enzymes to help digest the food. If the food we are eating is raw—whether it is a rutabaga, a carrot, a lettuce leaf or a trout—all the enzymes we need are right there in the food itself, ready to go to work for us.

If the food is cooked beyond 118°F (48°C), however, these naturally occurring enzymes are killed by heat, and our body must manufacture its own digestive enzymes to do the job.

Is this a problem? Raw fooders believe it is. The father of the food enzyme concept, Dr. Edward Howell, argued that when the body is busy digesting food, it is unable to divert the necessary energy to make the type of enzymes needed to do other tasks. There is a tug-of-war between the demands of the digestive system for a constant supply of digestive enzymes and the needs of the body for the metabolic enzymes vital for cleansing, healing and building. Without an adequate supply of metabolic enzymes, over time, we suffer.

What does this suffering look like? It looks like disease, indigestion, constipation, age spots, fatigue, lethargy, wrinkles, bad skin, declining eyesight, declining memory, mood swings, irritability, allergies, brain fog and candida. This decline in health is usually attributed solely to 'aging.' But it is really the result of two facts: Over time, the body loses its ability to manufacture enzymes (young adults have thirty times the enzymes of the elderly); and, when we eat food that is cooked, it forces our bodies to manufacture enzymes for digestion, instead of enzymes that could be used for healing. Ultimately, when we don't have enough enzymes to carry out the basic needs of life, we die.

The SAD (Standard American Diet) of meat, bread, dairy, processed and cooked foods, caffeine and alcohol is not only totally enzymeless, it also creates an acid state in the body which causes a variety of health problems. On the cellular level, our body needs to be in a predominantly alkali state to take in nutrients and oxygen efficiently and expel toxins.

Why Organic?

All truth passes through three stages:
First, it is ridiculed.
Second it is violently opposed.
Third it is accepted as being self-evident.

Schopenhauer

Until recently, people bought their groceries at their favorite supermarket and didn't think much about it. Now, more and more consumers are seeking out organic food—and with good reason. Environmental pollution has put more stress on our bodies than ever before in history. And chemicals never meant for human consumption may be found in every step of the food chain.

There has been an exponential growth in the use of artificial fertilizers and pesticides since World War II. Farmers are applying ever-increasing amounts of chemicals to our crops. One of the things these chemicals do is kill the micro-organisms that would normally break the soil down to release plant nutrients. This is one of the reasons that food grown today is less nutritious than it was even twenty years ago.

When you read the packaged food labels in any supermarket, you will see that a profusion of chemicals have been developed to preserve food and prolong shelf-life, even though no one knows what will happen with those chemicals in the human body over time or from generation to generation.

Based on this evidence, more and more people are coming to the same conclusion: To enjoy optimal health we need to seek out the most nutritious, natural, chemical-free foods we can find—and this means buying as much organic as possible.

Guide to Using This Book

To help you make the recipes in this book, here are descriptions of some of the commonly used methods.

Soaking Nuts, Seeds and Grains for Use in Recipes

The following directions are for the preparation of nuts, seeds and grains for use in recipes such as pie crusts, nut and seed loaves, soups, dressings and gravies. Soaking and sprouting times for nuts, seeds, grains or legumes that are going on to be jar- or soil-sprouted can be found in the sprouting chart beginning on page 194.

Depending on the amount of nuts or seeds called for, one quart or one gallon jars (1 or 4 liter jars) are excellent for soaking. With the exception of sunflower seeds (see below), once the nuts or seeds have been soaked and drained, they are ready to use in the recipe. Alternatively, the jar may be covered and placed in the refrigerator for a short time until you are ready to prepare the recipe.

Almonds, cashews, sunflower seeds, sesame seeds and flax seeds should be soaked in twice the amount of water (1 cup nuts or seeds to 2 cups water). They can be covered or uncovered, in or out of the refrigerator. If you live in a particularly warm climate, it is a good idea to refrigerate those nuts and seeds that require longer soaking times. The minimum soaking time is eight hours and the maximum is twelve hours, after which time the nuts or seeds should be rinsed, drained and used in the recipe or refrigerated. Pine nuts and pumpkin seeds need only a short soaking time, from twenty minutes to four hours. Pecans and walnuts will not sprout, but are soaked in some recipes. Each recipe gives the recommended soaking time.

Depending on the recipe, hulled sunflower seeds may be soaked or they may be sprouted for three to four hours after soaking. A few recipes call for unsoaked or ground sunflower seeds. Each recipe will state how to prepare the seeds.

To sprout sunflower seeds, after rinsing and draining the soaked seeds, leave the jar inverted on the kitchen counter for three to four hours. Rinse thoroughly, being careful to remove the skins that float to the surface. The seeds will then be ready to use in a recipe.

To soak grains, measure, then wash them thoroughly in several changes of water. Soak them in twice the amount of water (1 cup grain to 2 cups water). Drain if necessary and they are ready to use.

Soaking Dried Fruit

The soaking time is given in each recipe. If the recipe calls for four to twelve hours, soak the fruit in twice the amount of water (1 cup fruit to 2 cups water) in a jar in the refrigerator. When the soaking instructions call for for five to thirty minutes, soak with just enough water to cover the fruit. It is not necessary to refrigerate the fruit during the short soak period. Before discarding the soak water, check to see if it is incorporated into the recipe.

Sprouting

See sprouting chart, page 194.

A Note On Cucumber

When a recipe calls for cucumber, if it is organic and unwaxed, assume the peel stays on it unless the recipe indicates otherwise.

Directions for Preparing Raw Foods

Cut in chunks: Pieces that will fit in a processor or blender or juicer.

Coarsely chopped: Pieces that are no larger than one square inch (2.5 square centimeters), with many of them smaller. Pieces do not need to be the same size.

Chopped: Smaller than coarsely chopped (approximately ⅓–½ inch or 1 centimeter) and more-or-less equal in size.

Finely chopped: Smaller than chopped.

Diced: Means a precise cube is important. Pieces should measure from ⅓–½ inch (1 centimeter).

Minced: The smallest chop obtainable; often used for garlic and ginger.

Slivered: Long thin pieces, for example red pepper strips that are 4–5 inches (10–12.5 centimeters) long and ¼-inch (0.5 centimeter) thick.

Julienne: Like a sliver in that it is long and thin, but a more precise, squared-off kind of cut—also called matchstick. A julienne can be achieved by hand or with a mandoline (see equipment, page 191).

Shred: Usually created with a machine, but a wide shred can be achieved with a hand grater. A shred would be the thinnest possible piece that is at least 1-inch (2.5 centimeters) long.

Grate: Smaller than a shred—and small bits rather than long shreds; normally made with a hand grater.

Torn: Used for greens such as spinach; should be broken into bite-sized pieces.

Chiffonade: Cut in thin strips or ribbons. Most commonly used in this book for basil.

Ten Raw Food Kitchen Essentials

When you're starting out with any new type of cuisine, it takes some time to learn the "tricks of the trade"—the little shortcuts and strategies that save time and make food preparation a breeze. Here are ten tips that will help you become faster and more efficient in your raw food kitchen, so you have time for all the other things that are important in your life.

1. Always keep at least two jar-sprouted items in your refrigerator. (See sprout chart, page 194, for directions on how to grow sprouts in a jar.) Whether they're lentil sprouts, alfalfa sprouts or green pea sprouts, you'll be glad to have them on hand for using in salads or placing at the bottom of a soup bowl.
2. Always have sunflower sprouts and buckwheat lettuce on hand. (See sprout chart, page 194 for directions on how to grow sprouts in the soil.) The most economical way to have them available is to grow them yourself. But, if that is not possible, consider buying them at a health food store or through a grower. Some growers will ship them directly to your home. (See sources, page 207.)
3. Keep a jar of almonds soaking in the refrigerator. Change the water every day and they will keep, ready to use, for five days.
4. Mix up a big batch of your favorite Basic Pâté each weekend and add different flavors to vary the taste during the week. (See Basic Pâté recipe, page 136, for instructions.) Remember to begin the

Metric Conversion Chart	
Imperial	**Metric**
1 inch	2.54 centimeters
1 ounce	28.35 grams
1 pound	0.45 kilogram
1 teaspoon	5 milliliters
1 tablespoon	15 milliliters
1 cup	250 milliliters
16 fluid ounces	0.47 liter
32° Fahrenheit	0° Celsius

Note: Conversions in this book from imperial to metric are not exact. They have been rounded to the nearest standard measure for convenience. To prepare the recipes exactly as they were intended, follow the imperial measures.

sprouting process on Thursday or Friday night. Also, make up enough of your favorite salad dressing to last you one week. Keep ingredients like tahini, oil, lemons and onions on hand so that you can whip up dressings quickly.

5. Keep sauerkraut in your refrigerator. (See sauerkraut recipe, page 49, for instructions.) Once made, this tasty food will last for many weeks. It is a healthy addition to many recipes and makes a great condiment or side dish.

6. Always have assorted greens, root vegetables, red peppers and parsley in your refrigerator, so that you can "throw together" a meal quickly. Whether you shop each night on your way home from work, or go to the farmer's market twice a week, buy the best, freshest organic produce you can find that day and use it very soon after purchasing.

7. Pre-wash all your produce before putting it away. Having to wash and dry your vegetables for each meal is very time consuming. For one or two people, bags of pre-washed organic baby lettuces containing a variety of greens are convenient and waste-free.

8. Make a large salad every night for dinner, using the freshest ingredients possible. Make enough to use for lunch the next day. Keep your dressing on the side so the salad will stay fresh and crisp.

9. Keep a piece of fresh ginger root in your refrigerator, and another piece in a plastic bag in the freezer. If you are out of fresh ginger, you can flavor foods and make tea by grating in a little frozen ginger. Note that you should never let frozen ginger thaw.

10. To maintain freshness and for convenience, keep the following foods stored in your freezer: shelled nuts, seeds, dried fruits, carob, coconut, grains, all dried herbs and spices (keep them in their glass or plastic containers), and a dozen ripe, peeled bananas in plastic bags. If you do not have room in your freezer, store the shelled nuts, seeds and bananas in the freezer, and the rest in the refrigerator.

2 Breakfast

Rather than starting your day with a traditional "big, hearty, breakfast," the living foods concept prolongs your fast. By taking in nourishment with fruit or juice you are on some levels continuing your fast, as the body quickly and easily processes this simple food. When the body is relieved of the complex burdens of digestion, assimilation and elimination, it is able to attend to such important functions as cleansing, healing and building.

The best breakfast during the initial cleanse stage is either a green drink, made by juicing green vegetables, or a very light serving of fruit, preferably one type of fruit at a time. This is called a mono-meal. If you are avoiding sugar, then put off eating fruit until the maintenance phase of the program. (See the chapter on juicing for Green Drink suggestions.)

If you are eating fruit, the best way to start your day is with watermelon juice, including some of the rind, or with a piece of watermelon, drinking one or two ounces (30 or 60 grams) of the juiced rind as a starter. If you cannot obtain organic watermelon, do not eat the seeds or the rind. The reason for eating watermelon is that it digests rapidly and easily when eaten alone, as it always should be, and has excellent alkalizing and diuretic properties.

A typical breakfast plan for the initial three-week cleanse consists of the following: watermelon juice for five days of the week; citrus such as oranges and grapefruit for one day; other types of melon such as honeydew and cantaloupe for one day. (Then repeat for two more weeks.)

For the most part, the following breakfast recipes are suggestions if you are in transition, or if you have been following a raw food program for some time and are ready for the maintenance phase, in order to preserve your newfound health and vitality.

Awesome Applesauce 🌿

Why eat cooked, commercially colored applesauce from a jar when this raw, enzyme-filled applesauce is so easy to make and so delicious? Put every part of the apple through the juicer except the stem. If you are preparing the sauce for an infant, or if you must use non-organic apples, peel and core them before putting them through the juicer.

In a heavy-duty juicer, using the blank screen, put the apple pieces through the machine and into a bowl. Stir in the cinnamon. Eat immediately. Serves 1.

1–2 whole organic apples, cut in chunks

Dash cinnamon (optional)

Banana-Papaya Pudding 🌿

Smooth, creamy and filling, this pudding is also delicious with two pitted prunes or figs blended in. The variation with tahini is particularly popular. When you make this pudding, don't throw away the papaya seeds. They can be dried and used to flavor other dishes such as Squash Noodle Salad (see recipe, page 86).

Put the payaya in a blender and blend just enough to break up the fruit. Add the banana; blend until smooth. Eat immediately. Serves 1.

½ ripe papaya (approximately 1 cup), peeled and seeded

1 banana, peeled and cut in chunks

Variation 1: Add 1–2 tablespoons almond butter; blend.
Variation 2: Add 2–3 teaspoons raw tahini; blend.

Bananafanna

This smooth and creamy mixture is both filling and tasty.

See soaking instructions, page 5. In a blender, combine the cashews with water and blend until smooth. Add the banana gradually, continuing to blend until smooth and creamy. Serves 1–2.

1 cup cashews, soaked 8–12 hours

¼–½ cup water

1 banana, peeled

Variation 1: Pour Bananafanna over 1 cup sliced strawberries or blend with strawberries.
Variation 2: Use almonds instead of cashews.

Melon Dream ❦

3–4 cantaloupe or honeydew melons

This is an unusual treatment for cantaloupe or honeydew melon. Because the seeds from the melon are used, the meal will be very rich in oil. It is important to strain the mixture thoroughly, as the outer coat of the seeds is rough, and can be very irritating to the digestive tract. You can also make a delicious soup by mixing cut-up melon with some of the melon seed sauce in the blender or food processor. Remember to eat melon alone, and not to mix different kinds of melon at one meal.

Cut the melons in half. Scrape out the seeds, separating them from the stringy membranes, and put the seeds in a blender. Cut the fruit of the melon into chunks. Add enough melon chunks to the seeds to be able to liquefy it all. Let the blender run for a very long time to be sure the seeds are pulverized. The amount of time depends on your blender. If you own a Vita-mix, 4–6 minutes will do; other machines will take longer. Then strain the mixture through linen or several layers of cheesecloth, several times. You will wind up with an orange or green sauce that is extremely rich and is delicious served over the remaining fruit. Serves 8.

Sprouted Wheat and Raisin Cereal

¼ cup raisins or 4 dates, soaked 8–12 hours (reserve soak water)
1 cup sprouted wheat
Chopped apple (optional)

If you like warm cereal for breakfast, gently heat the raisin water. How can you tell when the water is the right temperature? Dip your finger in it. You should be able to let your finger sit in the water without any discomfort.

See soaking instructions, page 5. In a blender, combine the wheat, raisins and enough of the reserved soak water to allow the blender to operate. Blend, adding additional soak water to achieve desired consistency. Place in a cereal bowl and top with additional chopped dates, raisins or some apples. Serves 1.

Fruit Compote

½–¾ cup dried fruit, soaked 8–12 hours
Water

Dried fruit is a very concentrated food that should always be soaked prior to eating. The sugar content is very high, so use this compote only as an occasional breakfast treat. Use any combination of fruit—prunes, apricots and figs are all good choices.

In a small bowl combine the fruit with enough water to cover, plus one inch. Refrigerate 8–12 hours. The compote will be ready to eat in the morning. Serves 1.

Melon Dream

Almond-Sunflower Cereal

½ cup almonds,
    soaked 8–12 hours

¼ cup sunflower seeds,
    soaked 8–12 hours

4 tablespoons raisins,
    soaked 8–12 hours
    (reserve soak water)

Soaking the almonds and the sunflower seeds begins the sprouting process. They will double or more in size overnight and the fats and proteins in them will begin to change to simpler, easier-to-digest components.

See soaking instructions, page 5. In a blender, combine the almonds, sunflower seeds, raisins and enough of the reserved raisin soak water to allow the blender to operate. Blend until smooth. Add the raisins, blending quickly so the fruit remains chunky. Eat as is or pour over fresh seasonal fruit. Serves 2.

Oats with Almonds and Dates

¼ cup almonds,
    soaked 8–12 hours

½ cup raw whole oats,
    soaked 8–12 hours

2 pitted dates or 2 figs,
    soaked 8–12 hours
    (reserve soak water)

½ banana, peeled

Dash cinnamon

Finding raw oats can be a challenge. Apparently, whole raw oats turn rancid quite quickly, so the companies that supply it are steaming the oats after harvest. The euphemism they use is "stabilizing." This is not a good thing, because steam reaches 212°F (100°C) and will destroy all the enzymes. Ask your suppliers, but don't be surprised if they don't really know that this is happening. You can be fairly sure that any oats in a grocery or health food store have been treated in this manner. (See sources, page 207, for suppliers that carry truly raw oats.) This is a delicious and hearty recipe but if you can't get raw oats, don't indulge in it too often. Instead, try this recipe with other whole raw, soaked grains such as barley, kamut or spelt.

See soaking instructions, page 5. In a blender, combine almonds, oats (drain, if necessary) and dates with their soak water. Blend until smooth. Add the banana and cinnamon and blend quickly. Eat immediately. Serves 1.

Variation 1: Use 2 tablespoons soaked flax seeds in place of the almonds, and an apple or another fruit (cut in pieces) in place of the banana.

Variation 2: Use 1–2 tablespoons raw tahini or almond butter in place of the almonds.

Multi-Grain Mélange

If you prefer, rather than just soaking the grains which begins the sprouting process, you can let them sprout, then make the cereal. Try adding some chopped apple or more raisins, or any fruit in season.

See soaking instructions, page 5. In a blender, combine the wheat, rye, barley and oats with raisins and the raisin soak water. Blend. Serves 1.

**2 tablespoons wheat,
soaked 8–12 hours**

**2 tablespoons rye,
soaked 8–12 hours**

**2 tablespoons barley,
soaked 8–12 hours**

**2 tablespoons oats,
soaked 8–12 hours**

**2 tablespoons raisins,
soaked 8–12 hours
(reserve soak water)**

Oats with Almonds and Dates

Hearty Buckwheat Breakfast

4 tablespoons raisins, soaked 8–12 hours (reserve soak water)

¾ cup sprouted hulled buckwheat

Sprouted buckwheat is the softest of all the sprouted grains, and does not need to be blended. Rinse the buckwheat frequently as it sprouts if you wish to minimize its slippery texture. (See sprouting chart, page 194.) For a warm cereal, heat the raisin soak water slightly, being sure not to let it go beyond 118°F (48°C), in order to preserve the enzymes.

See soaking instructions, page 5. In a bowl, mix the sprouted buckwheat with the raisins and enough of the raisin soak water to achieve desired consistency. Serves 1.

Six-Grain Cereal With Fruit

½ cup whole six-grain cereal, soaked 8–12 hours

2 dates soaked 8–12 hours, pitted (reserve soak water)

1 apple, chopped

2 tablespoons coconut (optional)

If you have trouble finding a wholegrain blend of six or seven cereals (many come ground) then make up a blend yourself from the bulk section of your health food store. Keep the mix in your freezer, as grains go stale fairly quickly. Suggested grains to use: wheat, spelt, kamut, rye, oats, quinoa and barley. Or, perhaps you can ask your favorite supplier to make it up for you. The easiest way to pit dates is to soak them first. Then, simply pull them apart by hand and discard the pit.

See soaking instructions, page 5. In a blender, combine the cereal, dates and date soak water, and blend until smooth. Add the apple, and blend again. Stir in coconut. Top with raisins or seasonal fresh fruit. Serves 1.

Hearty Buckwheat Breakfast

3 Juices & Blended Drinks

Juicing extracts the juice from a fruit or vegetable, leaving the pulp behind. The big benefit of juicing is that you can consume large amounts of nutrients and digest and assimilate them quickly. After all, it is a lot easier to drink eight ounces (250 milliliters) of liquid, than to try to consume three pounds (1.5 kilograms) of food! Juicing also gives your digestion, assimilation and elimination systems a rest from the constant work they do while still taking in some nourishment.

Juicing should not take the place of eating. While it is possible to go on lengthy juice-only fasts, you cannot sustain yourself on juices alone. (For more information about extended juice fasts, refer to the Bibliography, page 215.) You must consume fiber to keep your digestive tract healthy.

Blending breaks down the food in order to make it easier to eat and to make it taste better. Some examples of blended food are raw applesauce, banana-papaya pudding and spinach mousse. Blended food contains all the original fiber. Smoothies are an example of a combination of juicing and blending.

The Green Drink 🌱

½ **tray sunflower sprouts**

⅓ **tray buckwheat sprouts**

5–6 ounces (150 milliliters) green vegetable juice (see note)

Garlic or ginger or onion or fresh herbs (optional)

In a perfect world, this is the juice we would drink every day. As a matter of fact we would drink ten to fourteen ounces (300 to 400 milliliters) of it twice daily. It is served every day at the Hippocrates Health Institute in West Palm Beach, Florida. Make this drink an integral part of your routine, especially if you are dealing with serious illness. Use it for a mid-morning and mid-afternoon "pick-up" and use it in conjunction with wheatgrass juice, definitely not in place of it.

The ultimate juice is made of fifty percent juice from sprouts and fifty percent juice from green vegetables. In the beginning, if you find this juice unpalatable, add a small amount of carrot juice until your taste buds become accustomed to the flavor. Most people enjoy this drink when it is made with fifty percent celery juice.

Soil-grown sprouts are commonly planted in cafeteria trays or nursery flats.

In a heavy-duty juicer, using the juicing screen, juice the sprouts. If the pulp is still wet, put it through again, or place it in a linen bag and press out the remaining juice. Yield should be 5–6 ounces (150 milliliters) of sprout juice. Mix with an equivalent amount of green vegetable juice and add garlic, ginger, onion or fresh herbs, if desired.

Note: Celery, cucumber, kale, spinach, cabbage, edible weeds or any other dark green vegetable are all good juice choices.

Wheatgrass Juice 🌱

A number of books have been written about wheatgrass juice and its benefits. (*See* bibliography, page 215, for the names of some.) It is considered to be a cleansing and healing substance. Wheatgrass juice should be consumed on its own and on an empty stomach. Typically you would take one ounce (30 milliliters) in the morning and evening, and work up to 3 to 4 ounces (100 to 125 milliliters) a day. There are many topical uses for wheatgrass as well. If you sincerely want to experience a cleanse, include wheatgrass as an important part of your routine. Once you feel that you are well and are on a maintenance program, it is not as important to use wheatgrass every day. Many people continue to use it twice a week, but listening to your body is the best advice.

Making wheatgrass juice requires a specific kind of juicer. Please see descriptions of juicers in the Sources section of the Appendix.

Watermelon Juice

Watermelon juice is highly recommended during the initial three-week cleanse. If the watermelon is organic, juice some of the green rind (about a two-inch or three-centimeter square piece) and the seeds along with the pink flesh. As all juices are rapidly digested and assimilated, you can eat as soon as thirty minutes later, if you feel like it.

Watermelon juice is alkalizing and is a natural diuretic. Limit your consumption to six to ten ounces (200–300 milliliters) because of the high sugar content. If you are ill, or have sugar-related health issues such as diabetes, candida, hyperglycemia or hypoglycemia, do not include watermelon juice as part of your diet.

If you have normal blood-sugar levels, in-season watermelon is a wonderful way to begin a weight-loss program. You will feel full, its diuretic properties will allow you to shed retained water quickly and by following a raw food program, you will begin to lose unwanted weight.

Fruit Juices

The most popular fruits to juice either singly or in combination are oranges, apples, pears and grapes. Take advantage of seasonal fruits such as cherries, strawberries and cranberries. If you are interested in additional fruit juice recipes and combinations, consult the juicing books mentioned in the Bibliography (see page 215).

Cucumber Juice

Like watermelon juice, cucumber juice is a natural diuretic. It is best used in combination with other vegetables for a tasty drink, although many people love their cucumber juice "straight up." The challenge is to find unwaxed cucumbers. If the skin is waxed, the cucumbers must be peeled, thereby losing some valuable nutrients. In the summer, pickling cucumbers abound and they are wonderful juiced. Long English cucumbers are sold in many markets encased in plastic wrap. They are also good juiced, although not as sweet as the little pickling cukes.

3–4 pickling cucumbers will yield about 6–8 ounces (200–250 milliliters) of juice.

Carrot, Beet, Red Pepper, Spinach and Parsley Juice

Pineapple-Grape Ambrosia

1 whole pineapple, skinned
1–2 pounds (0.5–1 kilogram) organic red grapes
2 tangerines or 1 orange, peeled
1 lemon, peeled

The season for organic grapes is brief but the wait is worthwhile when you taste this delicious sweet drink. Be sure to thoroughly wash the grapes first.

In a heavy-duty juicer, using the juicing screen, put the pineapple, grapes, tangerines and lemon through the machine and into a bowl. Drink as is, or dilute it with water. Refrigerate. The ambrosia will keep for 1–2 days. Makes 1½–2 quarts (1½–2 liters).

Carrot Juice Controversy

Carrot juice is by far the most popular vegetable juice at juice bars. While it's delicious, both carrots and beets contain higher levels of natural sugars than other vegetables and some living foods experts suggest that you avoid all sugars, even natural ones. At some health institutes, carrot juice and beet juice are not served at all.

On the other hand, extremely well-respected people in the alternative health field strongly advocate the use of large quantities of carrot juice, especially if disease is present. The eminent and well-loved father of iridology, Dr. Bernard Jensen, DC, reportedly used copious amounts of carrot juice and raw goat's milk along with green drinks, to save himself from very serious illness. He has long recommended this practice to his patients.

The Reverend George H. Malkmus also feels that he saved himself from grave illness with carrot juice and raw food, and is reaching out to thousands of Christians with this information through his health ministry in North Carolina.

Dr. Norman W. Walker, the pioneer of juicing and juicing equipment, claimed that he completely recovered from a liver weakness by drinking large amounts of carrot juice.

There have also been many cases where restricting any type of sugar seems to be beneficial. Since the Hippocrates Health Institute first began in Boston in 1963, thousands of people feel that they have healed themselves of illness with green drinks and wheatgrass juice, and by avoiding the higher-sugar juices. These health proponents believe that sugar feeds certain conditions such as cancer, candida and pancreatic deficiencies. The bottom line is that you need to find your own way and come to your own conclusions in this matter.

If you choose to follow the specific Living Foods Program as presented at several living foods health institutes and in this book, carrot or beet juice is recommended only as a sweetener in the Green Drink that this program recommends.

Pineapple-Grape Ambrosia

Tomato Juice Supreme 🌿

**8 ounces (250 milliliters)
tomato juice (3–5 tomatoes,
or one pound (500 grams)
of tomatoes)**

1 tablespoon lemon juice

Dash liquid aminos

Pinch pepper

Dash dulse flakes

The tomato is a fruit and as such is best eaten alone. It's refreshing for breakfast, although you should wait at least twenty minutes before eating anything else, to allow for proper digestion. To maximize the taste and nutritive value, use only local, vine-ripened, in-season tomatoes.

Plain tomato juice is also perfectly delicious.

Combine the tomato juice, lemon juice, liquid aminos, pepper and dulse powder. Serves 1.

Juice Combinations

It is difficult to make a juice that tastes bad. Try some of these combinations or invent your own. Use strong flavors like parsley, garlic or spinach in small amounts and be sure that your vegetables are fresh and well washed. (Whoever came up with the concept of "using food up before it goes bad" needs to be informed that wilted vegetables contain wilted nutrients.)

- Carrot, Celery
- Carrot, Celery, Parsley
- Carrot, Celery, Beet, Parsley
- Carrot, Celery, Spinach, Parsley
- Carrot, Celery, Beet, Spinach, Parsley
- Carrot, Beet, Red Pepper, Spinach, Parsley
- Carrot, Beet, Red Pepper, Cucumber, Parsley
- Carrot, Cabbage, Celery

- Carrot, Cabbage, Celery, Alfalfa Sprouts
- Carrot, Cabbage, Parsley
- Celery, Spinach, Red Pepper, Cabbage
- Celery, Spinach, Red Pepper, Cucumber
- Carrot, Cabbage, Celery, Parsley
- Carrot, Cabbage, Celery, Sprouts, Parsley
- Carrot, Cabbage, Celery, Spinach
- Carrot, Sprouts, Celery, Parsley
- Sprouts, Celery, Parsley
- Cucumber, Carrot, Parsley
- Cabbage, Spinach, Cucumber, Carrot
- Cucumber, Sprouts, Parsley

Other foods to use include: all greens, beet greens, buckwheat lettuce, butternut squash, dark leaf lettuce, dandelion greens, dill, edible wild weeds, fennel, garlic, ginger, green beans, Jerusalem artichokes, jicama, kale, kohlrabi, leeks, onions, parsnips, radish, rutabagas, scallion, sweet potatoes, Swiss chard, sunflower sprouts, tomatoes, turnips, turnip greens, watercress and zucchini.

Blending

If you own a powerful blender, you can enjoy blended rather than juiced drinks. What is the difference? With blending, all the fiber is left in. For example, your favorite salad combination can go into the blender with a bit of juice. Depending on how much juice or other liquid you use, this blended food can be served either as a drink or as a soup. Any vegetable or fruit juice can be blended with 1–2 cups of sprouts.

Sprouted Juice Drinks

You can give any juice or smoothie a big nutrition boost by blending them with some sprouts.

In a blender, combine the juice with the sprouts and the lemon juice; blend until smooth. Drink immediately. Serves 1.

Note: For juice, consider pineapple, apple, tomato, carrot and carrot/celery. For sprouts, try alfalfa, clover, buckwheat and sunflower sprouts, or any combination of them.

1–2 cups freshly made juice (see note)

½–1 cup sprouts (see note)

Dash lemon juice

Nut Milks

Nut and seed milks can take the place of dairy milks in many instances. They are superior to soy milk products because all soy products are cooked and are difficult to digest. Nut milks make an excellent drink, and their richness and sweetness can be altered depending on your taste and need. They can serve as a base for soups and smoothies, and can also be used in gravies and sauces. Nut and seed milks are often used by body builders to increase their calorie and protein intake and by people who are underweight to help build themselves up.

Although almonds and sesame seeds are by far the best nutritional choices for milk, other nuts and seeds can be made into good milks also. Soaked sunflower seeds make a nourishing milk. You can also use soaked pecans, walnuts, cashews or a combination of any of these. Try adding a tablespoon of flax seeds with other nuts and seeds for a thicker milk. For a sweeter milk, use dates, raisins, maple syrup, stevia or vanilla. Follow the ratio in the almond and sesame milk recipes: one cup nuts or seeds to three to six cups water.

Almond milk can serve as a milk substitute in recipes or as a nourishing drink on its own. Blanch and peel the almonds for easier digestion. These recipes require you to strain the milk through a very fine strainer or cotton cheesecloth. Note that if you are making almond milk for a young child, the almonds should definitely be peeled first and the milk should be strained at least twice.

After straining, you are left with a pulp that can be used in cookies, crackers, Halvah (see page 184), soups or dressings. Use the pulp the same day or discard it.

Basic Almond Milk 🌿

**1 cup almonds,
soaked 8–12 hours
6 cups pure water**

Once the almonds have soaked overnight, it is important to discard the soak water and to rinse the almonds. All nuts and seeds contain growth inhibitors so that if the nuts and seeds are briefly moistened they won't sprout prematurely. This is nature's way of protecting them and gives them a better chance to grow under the right conditions.

The first time you make this milk, be sure to taste it after the first half is made. If it is not "rich" enough, you can change the ratio of nuts to water at that time. Simply place the nut milk you have just created back into the blender with the remaining almonds and repeat the process. This will reduce your yield by half and give you a much richer milk.

See soaking instructions, page 5. Place half of the almonds and half of the pure water in the blender. Blend for 3 minutes or longer. You want the almonds blended as finely as possible. Strain the mixture through cheesecloth or a fine strainer into a jar. Repeat the process for the second half. Refrigerate. If you want a richer milk, use less water. This milk will keep for 2 to 3 days. Yields just over 6 cups.

Sweet Almond Milk

**½ cup almonds,
soaked 8–12 hours
5 dates, soaked 8–12 hours,
pitted (reserve soak water)
3 cups water**

See soaking instructions for nuts, page 5. Place the dates in a bowl or jar and cover with 3 cups water. Refrigerate and let soak 8–12 hours. In a blender, combine the almonds, dates and date soak water and blend well. Strain. Refrigerate. For a richer milk, use more almonds. This milk will keep for 2–3 days. Yields 3 cups.

Quick Almond Milk

**1–2 tablespoons raw almond
butter, or more to taste
1 cup water**

This recipe is a quick solution when you need almond milk for a recipe, but it is not recommended for everyday use. Almond butter is made from unsoaked almonds so you do not have the benefit of a nut that has begun its sprouting process, nor have the growth inhibitors been eliminated.

In a blender, combine the almond butter with water. Blend until smooth. Refrigerate. Use this milk within 1 day. Yields 1 cup.

Sesame Milk 🌿

This drink is a delicious way to increase your intake of those extremely nutritious seasame seeds. The milk can also be made from sprouted sesame seeds. (Use 1½ cups.) (See chart, page 194, for sprouting instructions.) Be sure to carefully strain the milk, as the solids are irritating to many people. If you like a sweeter taste, add dates, maple syrup, honey or stevia.

See soaking instructions, page 5. In a blender, combine the sesame seeds with water. Blend thoroughly. Strain twice, carefully. Add sweetener if desired. Refrigerate. This milk will keep 2–3 days. Yields 2½–3½ cups.

1 cup hulled sesame seeds, soaked 8–12 hours

2–3 cups water

Dates or maple syrup or honey or stevia (optional)

Quick Sesame Milk

This quick sesame milk takes advantage of tahini—a butter made from hulled sesame seeds. Use this milk if you find the roughage from sesame seeds irritating, even when the milk has been strained. Raw tahini makes a very nutritious milk.

Be sure your tahini—and all your nut butters—are raw. If you can't find raw products, consult the Sources section (see page 207) to find a mail-order supplier. You will usually save money on nut butters from mail-order sources.

In a blender, combine 2 tablespoons tahini with water. Blend thoroughly and taste. Add additional tahini and blend again for a richer milk. Add sweetener if desired. Refrigerate. This milk will keep 2–3 days. Yields 1 cup.

2–4 tablespoons raw tahini

1 cup water

Dates or maple syrup or honey or stevia (optional)

Grain Milks 🌿

Sprouted grains are another excellent source of non-dairy "milks." You get the benefits of the live enzymes, along with carbohydrates and proteins in an easy-to-make and easy-to-digest milk. Grain milks can be used in the same way as nut and seed milks—as a beverage or as a base for gravies, soups and dressings. It's also used by body builders for strength, stamina and building muscle. (See chart, page 194, for sprouting directions.)

Make your grain milks from one or a combination of sprouted grains. If you're using oats, be sure to buy the unsteamed variety. If you're using unhulled grains, be sure to strain them well.

In a blender, combine as much grain and water as your blender can safely accommodate (start with 1 cup grain and 2 cups water). Blend for at least 3 minutes. Strain twice through a fine mesh strainer. Continue blending in batches until complete. Refrigerate. Keeps 1 or 2 days. Yields 7–8 cups milk.

Note: Good choices include quinoa, wheat, kamut, amaranth, millet, teff, spelt and oats.

3 cups sprouted grain (see note)

6 cups water, or more

Smoothies

Smoothies are not served at any of the living food health institutes. Even the best smoothies are very high in sugar and usually don't follow the principles of good food combining. On the other hand, you could make far worse nutritional choices. If you do decide to start your day with a smoothie, mix in any supplements you may be taking. Smoothies are quick and easy to make, taste wonderful, and all you need is a blender.

Use a base of fresh juice that has just been made in your juicer, like fresh apple, grape or pineapple juice. As an alternative, use a good brand of bottled juice. (There are no live enzymes in bottled juice because of the heat involved in pasteurization and bottling.) Look for a juice that is organic and has no preservatives, additives or high fructose corn syrup. Apple juice is a popular base and grape, cranberry, pineapple and other varieties also work very well.

Next you need a variety of fruit. Keep some on hand in the freezer, cut in chunks and ready to use. Bananas are simple—just peel, put them in plastic bags and keep in the freezer. Other good fruits to have on hand are strawberries, blueberries, raspberries, boysenberries, mangos, papayas, peaches and pineapple. Buy them in quantity, in season, and freeze them in ready-to-use portions.

You can find pre-prepared fruit in the freezer section of health food stores. It may not always be organic, but it is often prepared without any preservatives or additives.

One or two dates can be used for sweetness, or a frozen banana, cut in chunks, for thickness and substance.

Fruit and Berry Smoothie

1 cup apple juice
1 handful frozen mango chunks
2 large frozen strawberries
4 tablespoons frozen blueberries

This smoothie will be so thick you can eat it with a spoon! If you want to keep the sugar and the calories down, reduce the juice by half and replace it with water. Add any supplements—for example, bee pollen or blue-green algae—in the apple juice at the very beginning. This recipe is also delicious using grape or cranberry juice as a base.

In a blender, combine the apple juice and mango chunks. Blend until smooth. Add the strawberries one at a time and blend until smooth. Add blueberries; blend until smooth. You may have to tilt the entire blender (not just the container) in different directions for the blades to get all the fruit blended in. Serve immediately. Serves 1.

Variation 1: Replace the apple juice with cranberry juice and replace mango with ½–1 frozen banana, cut in chunks.
Variation 2: Replace apple with grape juice, and use the following fruit: handful of frozen papaya chunks, 2 frozen strawberries, ½–1 frozen banana, cut in chunks.

"Milk" and Fruit Smoothie

You can make variations of this drink by adding 2–3 dates, blueberries or other frozen fruit.

In a blender, combine the milk, banana and strawberries. Blend until smooth. Drink immediately. Serves 1.

1 cup grain milk or nut or seed milk
1 frozen banana, cut in chunks
2 frozen strawberries

Carob Shake

For an old-fashioned, "soda-fountain" type of treat.

Place dates in a small bowl with just enough water to cover. Let them soak 20 minutes; drain. In blender, combine the dates, nut milk, banana, carob powder and vanilla. Blend until smooth. Drink immediately. Serves 1.

3–4 dates, pitted, soaked 20 minutes
1 cup nut or grain milk
1 frozen banana, cut in chunks
3–4 tablespoons carob powder
Dash vanilla (optional)

Frozen Vanilla Bliss

This smoothie tastes like dairy soft-serve ice cream, only better. Not only is it a great way to start your day but it also makes a healthy snack. Use more tahini if you are a body builder or if you are trying to increase your fat, protein and calorie intake. Body builders might try one cup of water, four tablespoons of tahini and two frozen bananas. Add carob or fruit to this recipe—let your imagination run wild!

In a blender, combine the water, tahini, banana and vanilla. Blend until thick and smooth. Serve immediately. Serves 1.

¾ cup water
2 tablespoons raw tahini, or more to taste
1–2 frozen bananas, cut in chunks
Dash vanilla (optional)

4 Vegetables & Salads

We've all experienced restaurant salads made of tired lettuce, a slice of stale onion, a ghost of a tomato slice and maybe, if we are lucky, two shreds of red cabbage with a flood of chemical-laden dressing.

To avoid salad being just another pallid and dull side dish, think of salad making as an art. Seek to obtain the highest possible nutritional value from your salads while making them a feast for the eye as well as the palate.

The body obtains its nutrients more easily from a finely grated carrot than it does from a whole carrot because it has been partially broken down for you. So you will become a study in grace and speed as you break down your food into slivers, dices, minces, juliennes, gratings, purées, juices, blends, pâtés, loaves, mousses and soups. You can do a lot of this by hand—but if you own some kitchen appliances you will appreciate them.

It is possible to eat one hundred percent raw food if you own a grater, a good knife and a blender. With these three vital pieces of equipment, you can get along well for many months. With the right attitude, you can do it with whatever equipment you have. Trust yourself. If you are a bit appliance deficient, live simply for now and go to garage sales to find what you need! It's more important for you on the physical, emotional and spiritual planes to prepare your food with love and appreciation than to own every gadget ever created.

The best salad of all is the one you assemble in minutes from all the great food you have on hand. Consider the recipes in this book as guidelines, a starting point for your creativity. A list of what to keep on hand for easy raw food preparation can be found in the Grocery Guide (see page 211).

In traditional food preparation, the salad is treated as a side dish or as an appetizer. With raw food, the distinction between a main dish and a salad is blurred. Many of the salads and vegetable dishes in this book can easily be served as a main dish. You can also savor one flavor at a time by serving single-vegetable recipes as side dishes. Enjoy green beans almondine, beets, carrots, corn on the cob, squash, greens and more. For quick meals, parties or 'brown bag' lunches, simplicity is best. Cut up fresh vegetables like carrots, cauliflower, broccoli, celery, green beans, jicama, turnip, red pepper, yellow pepper, sweet potato or yam rounds, whole radishes, daikon radish rounds, parsnip rounds, mushrooms, beets, turnip, rutabaga, squash, whatever is fresh and delicious that day. Arrange the vegetables attractively on a bed of lettuce and serve them with a dip of hummus, Notmayo! (page 118) or one of the pâtés.

Just because you are eating all raw or predominantly raw food now doesn't mean you have to take in all your vegetables as salad! Take your favorite salad or pâtés, top it with dressing or sprouts and roll it up in a large cabbage or lettuce leaf. Or, take a tasty filling and stuff it into a pepper or avocado half, onto a piece of celery or into a hollowed-out cucumber or zucchini half.

Remember, too, that sprouts are the most important component of living food because they are filled with more live enzymes and energy than any other food. To optimize their benefit include sprouts at every lunch and every dinner. Even when you see a recipe in this book that does not contain sprouts, assume that they should be served as an accompaniment. All your meals can be presented on a bed of sunflower and buckwheat sprouts, or served with a side of them. Make eating sprouts a habit for the rest of your life. Remember, it isn't what you do once in a while that helps you; it's what you make a habit of that sustains you.

Each type of sprout has its own characteristics; eating an ever changing variety of them is in your best interest. Always have sunflower and buckwheat sprouts available. Sunflower sprouts are an excellent source of highly digestible protein and enhance your energy. Buckwheat lettuce is high in lecithin. Sesame seed sprouts are high in bio-available calcium. Cabbage sprouts, like cabbage itself, benefit the digestive tract. Fenugreek helps dissolve mucus and benefits the lymphatic system. A salad consisting entirely of sprouts either tossed together or in separate, lovely piles is a wonderful meal. Dress them and enjoy them, and savor how truly beneficial this meal is for you.

Ensalada 🌿

6 cups assorted sprouts and
greens
½ cup chopped zucchini
½ cup fresh corn
½ cup diced red pepper
¼ cup chopped scallions
Dressing

This is a nice basic salad. Start with the sprouts and greens and vary the rest with the best you can find in season.

In a large salad bowl, combine the sprouts and greens, zucchini, corn, red pepper and scallions. Toss. Serve with your favorite dressing or just toss with a bit of lemon juice and oil. Serves 4–6.

Edible Wild Greens

3 tablespoons flaxseed oil
Juice of 1 lemon
3 tablespoons chopped onion
1 teaspoon liquid aminos
Pinch ground celery seeds
Chives or parsley (optional)
6 cups assorted edible wild
greens, torn

As a treat not only for your digestive system but for your spirit of adventure as well, take a walk on the wild side and forage for your own greens! Even city dwellers can learn to identify edible wild greens in parks and out-of-the-way places. Locate an herbalist in your area to take you and some friends on an edible food walk. Look for dandelion, poke, dock, marsh marigold, ferns, yellow rocket cress, young milkweed shoots, pigweed, mustard, purslane, wild celery, nettles, horseradish and fennel. There are dozens of edible flowers to add color and flavor to your food as well. Nasturtium, orange blossoms, red clover, rose petals and rose hips, geraniums, squash blossoms, fennel, honeysuckle, lilac, violet, pansy, Johnny jump-up are just a few. (See Bibliography, page 215 for books about edible wild foods.)

In a small bowl, using a wire whisk or a fork, combine the oil, lemon juice, onion, liquid aminos, celery seeds and chives until the dressing becomes as thick as heavy syrup. In individual salad bowls, place the greens. Top with the dressing. Serves 3.

Mixed Salad Greens

1 avocado, chopped
1 scallion, chopped
1 clove garlic, minced
3 tablespoons lemon juice
1 teaspoon liquid aminos
3 tablespoons flaxseed oil
(optional)
6 cups mixed salad greens
Sprouts

Remember those green leafy things you walk by at the grocery store because you don't know what they are or what to do with them? Well, stop a minute and look them over. You can combine greens in salad for a new taste, or use them in any of the recipes that call for spinach, such as Spinach Mousse or Spinach Soup.

Look for turnip greens, mustard greens, mizuna, arugula, Belgian and curly endives, radicchio, watercress, kale, chard, escarole, collard greens and beet greens at your local market. Be sure to include some bitter greens such as the endives, dandelion and radicchio to enhance the health of your liver and gall bladder.

In a small bowl, mash the avocado with a fork. Mix in the scallion, garlic, lemon juice and liquid aminos. Thin with additional lemon juice or oil until the dressing has the consistency of a thick, smooth purée. On individual plates, place the greens. Ladle the dressing over the greens. Serve with sprouts on the side. Serves 2–3.

Spinach and Mushroom Salad

Spinach and Mushroom Salad 🌿

Dehydrated mushrooms (see page 61) are a tasty alternative to fresh mushrooms in any tossed green salad. The dressing rehydrates the mushrooms and they lend a wonderful, earthy taste to the salad.

In a large bowl, combine the spinach, mushrooms, shallots, basil, red peppers and pine nuts. Toss well. Pour French Dressing over the salad and toss again. Serve immediately. Serves 4–6.

1 large bunch spinach (1 pound (500 g), chopped
2 cups thinly sliced fresh mushrooms or 1 cup dehydrated mushrooms
2 shallots chopped (or 1 small red onion)
½ cup chopped basil
2 red peppers, chopped
4 tablespoons pine nuts
½ cup French Dressing (see recipe, page 99) or dressing of your choice

Basic Hippocrates Mix 🌿

There are no rigid rules but it is good to have guidelines. If you wish to follow the living food philosophy, you will always need sprouts on hand. If you are preparing for one to two people, a bag of ready-mixed organic baby greens can be your base, then add whatever else you want for variety. Washing your greens in advance is a tremendous time saver. When you get them home, wash, spin dry and store them in airtight containers. Then it will only take a matter of minutes to throw together a salad.

There are many recipes to choose from or you can make them up as you go. Find your favorite healthy combinations and enjoy. Here is an example of a popular salad base.

In a large salad bowl, combine the sunflower sprouts, buckwheat sprouts, lettuce, peppers, cucumber and onion. Toss together and top with more sprouts such as alfalfa, clover, mung, lentil, fenugreek, green pea. Use any dressing, or serve the salad plain. Serves 4–6.

2 cups sunflower sprouts
2 cups buckwheat sprouts
2 cups torn dark leafy lettuce (greenleaf, redleaf, romaine)
1 cup chopped red peppers
1 cup chopped cucumber
Chopped onion, to taste
Sprouts

Curried Lentil Salad 🌿

Use this salad for either a quick and simple lunch or as an excellent side dish for a more elaborate meal. This salad also makes a tasty filling for an avocado or pepper half.

In a small bowl, mix the liquid aminos, lemon juice, garlic and curry. In a separate mixing bowl, combine lentils and onions; toss. Pour dressing over the lentils; toss again. Serves 2–4.

2 teaspoons liquid aminos
1 tablespoon lemon juice
1 clove garlic, minced
1 teaspoon curry powder, or to taste
2 cups sprouted lentils
½ cup chopped onion

High-Spirited Sprout Salad

1 cup sunflower sprouts

1 cup buckwheat sprouts

1 cup radish sprouts

1 cup mung sprouts

½ cup diced cucumber or zucchini

½ cup chopped scallions

½ cup diced red pepper

2 tablespoons chopped parsley

2 tablespoons liquid aminos or tamari

1–2 tablespoons cold-pressed, extra-virgin olive oil (optional)

Of all food, sprouts contain the highest amount of living enzymes. For optimal nutrition, eat some every day. If you prefer to use your favorite dressing with this salad, eliminate the liquid aminos and the oil. If you would like it to be a more substantial meal, toss in a handful of pumpkin seeds.

Use three or four different sprouts in this salad. Try mung, adzuki, lentil, radish, sunflower, buckwheat, clover or pea.

In a large salad bowl, combine the sunflower sprouts, buckwheat sprouts, radish sprouts, mung sprouts, cucumber, scallions, red pepper and parsley. Toss together. Pour the liquid aminos and olive oil over the salad and toss again. Serve on bed of baby greens. Serves 4.

High-Spirited Sprout Salad

Spicy Sprouted-Grain Salad 🌿

Rye berries or kernels are delicious grains that are soft and chewy once they have sprouted. Try this recipe with other sprouted grains to find your favorites—spelt, kamut, quinoa, wheat, buckwheat or hulled barley can all be used. If you want to flavor this salad with a dressing, eliminate the liquid aminos, ground cumin and cayenne.

In a large salad bowl, combine the sprouted rye, scallions, red pepper, sprouted peas, carrots, parsley and basil. Toss together. Add the liquid aminos, ground cumin and cayenne and toss again. Serves 4–6.

2 cups sprouted rye
1 cup chopped scallions
1 cup chopped red pepper
1 cup sprouted peas
½ cup shredded carrots
2 tablespoons chopped parsley
1 tablespoon chopped fresh basil (or 1 teaspoon dried)
4 teaspoons liquid aminos
1–2 teaspoons ground cumin
Cayenne, to taste

Exotic Sprout Salad 🌿

This salad brings you a wonderful assortment of flavorful sprouts. If you can't find fennel, substitute celery. And for a change of taste, you can replace the lemon juice with either celery or fennel juice.

In a bowl, combine the sprouts, red pepper, fennel, lemon juice, liquid aminos, ginger and 5-spice powder. Toss thoroughly and serve on a bed of buckwheat sprouts. Serves 3–4.

2 cups assorted sprouts: mung, lentil, pea, clover, sunflower, buckwheat, etc.
¾ cup chopped red pepper
⅓ cup finely chopped fennel
¼ cup lemon juice
2 tablespoons liquid aminos
2 teaspoons minced ginger root
1 pinch Chinese 5-spice powder or cinnamon

Beet Surprise 🌿

A rich, creamy blend. Use a food processor or salad shooter to shred the beets. Serve with a green salad and sprouts.

In a small bowl, mix the beets, onion and Notmayo! Toss. Serves 3–4.

4–5 beets, finely shredded
2 slices mild onion, minced
½–¾ cup Notmayo! (see page 118)

Long-Tail Rye Salad 🌿

3 cups sprouted rye
2 tablespoons cold-pressed,
  extra-virgin olive oil
5–6 green olives
¼–½ cup sauerkraut
  (see recipe page 49)
1 small clove garlic, chopped
Juice of ½ lemon
Dash liquid aminos, ground
  cumin, paprika and cayenne
4 tablespoons chopped
  cilantro
1 slice onion, cut in chunks
  (or more to taste)
2 scallions, chopped
½ cup coarsely chopped
  red pepper

This recipe was born the day some long-forgotten rye was discovered sprouting in the cabinet. The tails were one and a half inches long! They were rinsed and allowed to sprout a bit longer to give the grain that had dried out a chance to grow a tail also. By then, some of the tails were two inches (five centimeters) long, and there were a few that seemed ready to walk out the door!

Rye tastes wonderful with a tail between ¼–1½ inches. It is at its most nutritious when the tail length is between ¼–¾ inch. Once your sprouts have reached the length you desire, place them in the refrigerator to slow down their growth until you can work with them.

Other sprouted grains can be used for this salad. Try sprouted barley, kamut, spelt, wheat quinoa, or buckwheat.

In a food processor, combine the rye, oil, olives, sauerkraut, garlic, lemon juice, liquid aminos, cumin, paprika and cayenne. Pulse until the olives are uniformly fine and well combined, scraping down the sides of the processor several times. Add the cilantro, onion, scallions and red pepper. Pulse until the red pepper is chopped uniformly fine. Serves 4.

Variation 1: Add 1 tablespoon caraway seeds. For more intense flavor, grind them first in a clean coffee grinder.
Variation 2: Add 1½ cups sprouted lentils. Serves 5–6.
Variation 3: For chili, add 1½ cups sprouted adzuki beans or northern white or pinto beans. Serves 5–6.

New York Rye Salad 🌿

2 cups sprouted rye
2 cups seeded and diced
  cucumber
2 cups chopped red pepper
⅔ cup finely chopped onion
¼ cup chopped cilantro
3 tablespoons lemon juice
2 teaspoons fresh grated
  ginger root
2 tablespoons liquid aminos
1 teaspoon ground cumin
1 teaspoon caraway seeds or
  ½ teaspoon ground
  caraway seed
Pinch cayenne

Sprouted rye makes a tasty and hearty salad. For a different effect, combine the ingredients in a food processor and pulse-chop quickly, until the vegetables are in small bits and the rye is broken up. The wonderfully intense New York rye bread flavor comes from the caraway seeds. Use a clean coffee grinder to grind the caraway seeds.

In a medium-size salad bowl, combine the rye, cucumber, red pepper, onion, cilantro, lemon juice, ginger, liquid aminos, cumin, caraway seeds and cayenne. Toss thoroughly. Let the flavors blend for at least 1 hour before serving. Serves 4–6.

Red Cabbage-Caraway Slaw

This is a highly flavored dish. If you enjoy this salad, try the same method using Asian Sauce and experiment with different vegetables. This dish will keep for 4–5 days in the refrigerator.

In a bowl, combine the cabbage and onion; toss. Sprinkle the caraway seeds, liquid aminos and sea salt evenly over the vegetables. Knead and toss the salad, crushing the vegetables in your hands for 5–6 minutes.

Variation: For a more intense flavor, cover the salad with a plate and place a water jug or brick on top for additional weight. Allow the salad to marinate at room temperature for 2–6 hours. Remove the weight; refrigerate or serve. Serves 4.

6 cups thinly sliced red cabbage

1 large onion, sliced very thin

1 tablespoon caraway seeds

2 teaspoons liquid aminos

1 teaspoon sea salt

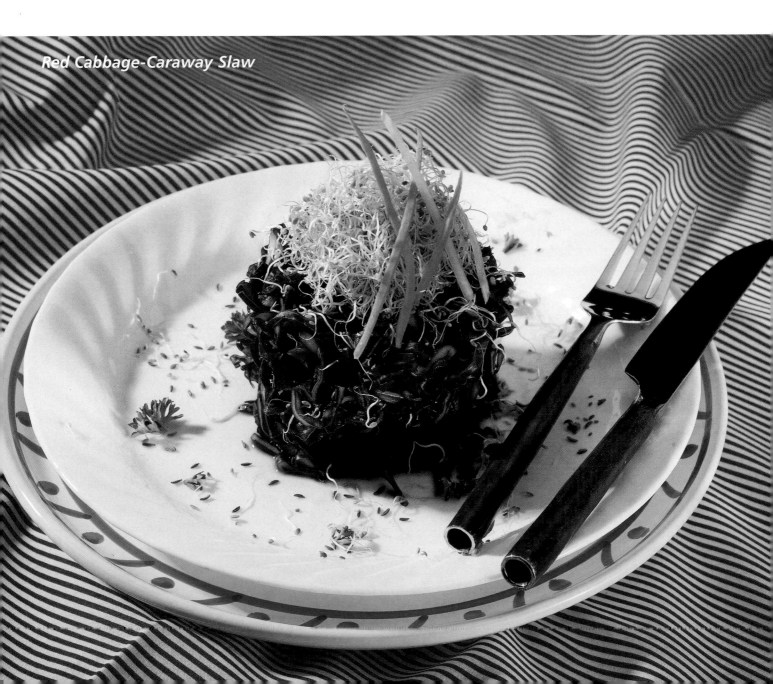

Red Cabbage-Caraway Slaw

Cabbage Roll-Ups 🌿

1 large cabbage leaf
½ avocado, cut in chunks
2 olives, chopped
Lentil, pea and/or fenugreek sprouts
Lemon juice
Liquid aminos
Dulse flakes
Slivered red pepper
Sprouts

A cabbage leaf makes a great "sandwich" for any filling. Softening the cabbage makes it easier to roll the filling up in it. Any guacamole, pâté or salad recipe would be delicious stuffed in a cabbage or lettuce roll.

Soften the cabbage leaf by putting it in a dehydrator for 10 minutes or dipping the whole leaf in hot water until soft; set aside. In a small bowl, mash the avocado with a fork and add the olives, sprouts, lemon juice, liquid aminos and dulse to taste. Place the mixture on the cabbage leaf. Top with red peppers, sprouts and any other vegetables you have on hand; roll up and enjoy. Serves 1.

Ten-Minute Blender Cole Slaw 🌿

1 small head red or green cabbage, cut in chunks
1 red pepper, cut in chunks
1 slice onion, cut in chunks
2 large carrots, cut in chunks
3 tablespoons cold pressed, extra-virgin olive or flaxseed oil
3 tablespoons lemon juice
1 teaspoon prepared mustard
1 teaspoon caraway seeds
Pinch sea salt
2 teaspoons maple sprinkles, date sugar or equivalent stevia (optional)

It's better to make coleslaw by hand or with a food processor because some nutrients are lost in the water that this blender method requires. But if you don't own a food processor or don't have time to chop by hand. You will still obtain many of the important nutrients from the cabbage.

Place enough cabbage, red pepper, onion and carrots in a blender, so the container is ½ full of vegetables. Add cold water to within 1 inch (2.5 cm) of the top. Blend for 2 seconds only. Pour into strainer and drain well, then place the drained vegetables in a large bowl. Repeat this process until all the vegetables have been blended.

In a small bowl, whisk together the oil, lemon juice, mustard, caraway seeds, salt and maple sprinkles. Pour over the vegetables, toss thoroughly. Serves 4–6.

Cabbage Roll-ups

Colorful Coleslaw

Colorful Coleslaw 🌱

Cabbage is considered a powerful therapeutic food all around the world. Many studies have linked eating cabbage with a reduction in cancer, especially colon cancer. And cabbage juice has been proven to help heal ulcers. Science has shown so many benefits from cabbage that it makes sense to eat some almost every day.

In a bowl, combine the red and green cabbages, carrot, red pepper, scallions, parsley, lemon juice, water, maple sprinkles, oil, dried red pepper and liquid aminos. Toss thoroughly. Let the flavors mingle for at least 1 hour before serving. Serves 4.

2 cups thinly sliced red cabbage

1 ½ cups thinly sliced green cabbage

1 carrot, grated

1 red pepper, slivered

4 tablespoons chopped scallions

4 tablespoons minced parsley

¼ cup lemon juice

3 tablespoons water

1 tablespoon maple sprinkles, date sugar or equivalent stevia (or more to taste)

1 tablespoon extra-virgin olive oil (or flaxseed oil)

1–2 teaspoons dried red chili pepper

Dash liquid aminos

Tip-Top Turnip Salad 🌱

An under-used and under-appreciated vegetable, turnip contains calcium and potassium. The juice of turnip greens contain more calcium than an equal amount of milk! So when you prepare this salad, save the greens and use them in mixed vegetable drinks. This salad keeps well in the refrigerator for a few days. Daikon radish can be substituted for the turnip. For a nice change, use fennel juice instead of the lemon juice.

Serve this salad over a bed of sprouts or baby greens.

In a serving bowl, combine the turnip, parsley, celery, scallions and red pepper. Toss together. Add the lemon juice and dulse flakes and toss again. Taste and add stevia or maple syrup, if desired. Serves 2.

1 cup shredded turnip

¼ cup chopped parsley

¼ cup chopped celery

2 scallions, finely chopped

1 red pepper, finely chopped

Juice of ½ lemon

1 tablespoon dulse flakes

1 teaspoon maple syrup or stevia (optional)

Fiery Carrots

1 tablespoon extra-virgin olive oil

2 teaspoons tamari

1 tablespoon minced garlic

1 tablespoon minced ginger root

½ teaspoon dried red chili pepper

½ teaspoon cayenne pepper

1–2 tablespoons water, if necessary

3 cups grated carrots

Carrots are good for you and readily available. They are fun to munch on "as is" but if you don't have a habit of doing that, try a few of the simple grated carrot recipes in this book and when you find your favorite, eat it often.

In a small bowl, whisk together the oil, tamari, garlic, ginger, chili and cayenne. Add additional water if necessary to achieve desired consistency. Place the carrots in a large bowl and pour the dressing on top. Serves 4.

About Sauerkraut

The place of fermented foods in a living food diet has evolved over the years. Many raw fooders make a fermented beverage from wheat berries and fermented pâtés out of nuts or seeds. But people sometimes have had negative reactions to these homemade fermented foods, in part because unwanted strains of bacteria occasionally grow in the medium.

As well, people who suffer from candida-based illnesses (a systemic yeast infection that is tenacious and difficult to overcome) historically have not had positive reactions to the fermented drinks and nut and seed cheeses. It appears that non-protein foods are safer to ferment. As a result, many alternative health experts now say that health benefits from fermentation are best derived from only the occasional use of raw sauerkraut. This is of course subjective, because many people sincerely feel that they derive great benefits from eating all types of fermented food. If you are confused by some of the differing approaches the bottom line is, has, and always will be the same: listen to your body.

Raw sauerkraut is used much like the delicious Korean fermented cabbage dish called kimchee—as a condiment served with the main meals of the day. Sauerkraut is also a component of several recipes, as you will see. Aside from providing important enzymes, the fermentation process creates bacilli that encourage intestinal health.

Raw sauerkraut is fun to make and the best part is that it lasts for a very long time in the refrigerator (up to two months) so you can make a large batch. If you have checked the price for raw sauerkraut at the health food store you will see how much money you can save by making it at home. Also, although the label may say 'raw', if the jar was sterilized or the food pasteurized it surely isn't raw anymore. And if sterilization and pasteurization did not occur, you should wonder if the sauerkraut was kept cold at all times during its transport to the store.

Be sure that you buy organic cabbage to make sauerkraut. Cabbage is a highly treated crop and the thought of mincing it up and letting it sit in its own juices, including dangerous chemicals, isn't very appealing or healthy. It would be better not to make sauerkraut at all than to make it out of cabbage that is not organic. Fortunately, sauerkraut isn't just made out of cabbage anymore! You can make many different types of vegetable "krauts," as the variations, below, demonstrate. Additional fermented food recipes can be found in books by Ann Wigmore and by Viktoras Kulvinskas, both of whom are well-known raw food pioneers.

Red or Green Sauerkraut 🦎

Use the cabbages soon after buying them. As they age they tend to dry out and you need the moisture from the cabbage to make evenly fermented sauerkraut.

While making sauerkraut, you can make a few pickles. Just slice a cucumber into one-quarter-inch (one-half centimeter) slices and combine the slices in a single layer while layering the sauerkraut. If your container is large enough you can do a few layers of cucumber. Make sure there is no wax on the cucumber.

Remove 3–4 of the large outer leaves of the cabbage; reserve. Chop the cabbage into pieces and put it through a heavy-duty juicer with blank screen. If extra juice is extracted, add it to the mixture.

In a gallon (4 liter) glass jar or ceramic crock (a crock pot ceramic liner is perfect), layer the following: 1 inch (2.5 centimeters) of grated cabbage, 8 of the apple slices, 2–3 inches (5–7.5 centimeters) of cabbage and half of the seaweed. Continue with another layer of apples, 2–3 inches (5–7.5 centimeters) of cabbage, seaweed and cabbage again. Press down with your hands as you make the layers. Cover the final layer with the reserved outer leaves and weigh it down with a water-filled plastic bag or a heavy plate. Cover the jar and the weights with a clean towel and let the sauerkraut sit for 3–7 days, until the cabbage develops a "tangy" taste. Skim any foam off the top of the sauerkraut and carefully transfer the fermented cabbage to clean jars. Discard the apples and reserve the seaweed for use in salads. Seal the jars tightly and store them in the refrigerator.

While the cabbage is fermenting, it can have quite a strong odor. It is best to allow it to ferment outside of the main area of your home.

Variation 1: For mixed kraut, place 1 cabbage, 3 carrots, 2 medium-sized beets, 1 slice onion and 1–3 cloves garlic through a heavy-duty juicer with the blank screen. Stir in 1–2 teaspoons caraway seeds (optional) then layer the cabbage in a crock with apple and seaweed, following the directions above.

Variation 2: For vegetable kraut, place 6 large carrots, 4 beets, turnip (or parsnip or rutabaga) to equal half the amount of the carrots, 1 small onion and garlic to taste through a heavy-duty juicer with the blank screen. Stir in 1–2 teaspoons caraway seeds (optional) then layer the cabbage in a crock with apple and seaweed, following the directions above.

1 head red or green cabbage, organic

1 apple, cut into 16ths

Seaweed (wakame or other), several large pieces

Corn 'n' Cabbage

Corn 'n' Cabbage

This recipe is a favorite at the Hippocrates Health Institute. It looks great when the cabbage is diced the size of corn kernels. Garnish this salad with a few rings of dehydrated red peppers and onions. If you are preparing food for one or two people, make half the recipe.

In a mixing bowl, combine the corn, cabbage, lemon juice, oil, liquid aminos and cinnamon. Toss thoroughly. Let the salad marinate for at least 1 hour then toss again. Pour onto a large platter and garnish. Serves 6.

3 cups fresh corn kernels
3 cups red cabbage, diced
2 tablespoons lemon juice
2 tablespoons extra-virgin olive oil
1 tablespoon liquid aminos
½–1 teaspoon cinnamon or pumpkin pie spice

Brilliant Cabbage Rolls

This is a very attractive way to serve greens and it is limited only by your imagination! The cabbage needs to be softened to allow for flexibility in rolling. There are two ways to do this. The best way is to put the individual leaves you are planning to roll in the dehydrator for about five to ten minutes, or they can be dipped in hot water just long enough to be pliable. The trick is to have the water hot enough to slightly wilt the leaves but not hot enough to kill all the enzymes in the leaf (although you will inevitably lose some enzymes with this method). These rolls are fun to serve with Hot Mustard Dip (page 120), or Asian Sauce (page 112).

This recipe calls for rolling up the cabbage and greens with the aid of a sushi mat, which may be purchased at an Asian supermarket or through gourmet suppliers and catalogs. It is little more than a square of wooden spindles that allows you to place the cabbage leaf on it and roll it up evenly and tightly. Follow the instructions that come with the sushi mat. If you don't have a mat, just place the ingredients on a clean, dry, flat surface and roll them up by hand.

Overlap the cabbage leaves on a sushi mat. Place the spinach leaves at the edge of the roll nearest you. Add some fennel and basil leaves. Top them with a line of carrot or red pepper. Tightly roll the cabbage leaf, pulling the mat toward you as you roll to ensure sufficient tightness. Slice the roll into ½-inch (1 cm) pieces or cut each roll in half at a sharp angle and serve. If necessary, use a toothpick to hold the larger rolls together. Serves 1.

2–3 large green cabbage leaves
3–4 spinach leaves (or other greens)
A variety of vegetables such as fennel, baby greens, sprouts, basil
Carrot or red pepper strips

Cucumber–Fennel Salad

Cucumber-Fennel Salad ❧

As always, if the cucumber isn't waxed, don't peel it! Many of the nutrients are in the peel and just under it. The basil and fennel create an unusual taste combination that is light, refreshing and different enough to stimulate your taste buds.

In a small bowl, combine the fennel, cucumber, basil, red pepper, sea salt, and lemon juice; mix. Taste and adjust for any tartness with a drop of stevia. Let the flavors blend for one hour or overnight. Toss again before serving. Serves 2–3.

1 cup finely chopped fennel
1 cup finely chopped cucumber
¼ cup shredded basil
¼ cup finely chopped red pepper
Pinch sea salt
A few drops of lemon juice
1–2 drops stevia (optional)

Tomato-Cucumber Summertime Salad ❧

This is a classic summertime favorite. Eat it alone or with other fruits or fruit-vegetable combinations. It also works well as a dressing for leafy greens and sprouts, too.

Combine the tomato, cucumber and onion in a small bowl. Sprinkle salt and pepper evenly over the mixture and toss. Allow the flavors and juices to blend at room temperature for 1–2 hours, stirring occasionally. This salad keeps several days in refrigerator. Serves 2–3.

1 cup diced (seeded) tomato
1 cup diced (seeded) cucumber
2 teaspoons minced onion, or more to taste
¾ teaspoon sea salt
Dash fresh ground pepper (optional)

Fresh Dilled Cucumber ❧

Wait for the delicious little local "pickling cucumbers" that are available in the summer. In some sections of the country, they are called Kirbys. They are never waxed because you can't make pickles with waxed vegetables! Or, look for European hot-house cucumbers, the kind that come tightly wrapped in plastic; they are never waxed either.

Place the tahini in a small bowl, gradually mix in the lemon and water. Add the dill. Pour over the cucumbers. Let the flavors blend for one hour or more before serving. Garnish with a sprig of dill. Serves 4.

⅓ cup raw tahini
½ cup lemon juice
2 tablespoons water
4 tablespoons minced fresh dill
2 medium cucumbers, thinly sliced

Fresh Dilled Cucumber

Mexicali Corn Salad 🌿

This simple little salad goes well with Mexican food.

In a small bowl, combine the corn, red pepper, scallion, cilantro, olives, lemon juice, olive oil, liquid aminos, cumin and cayenne. Toss together. Serves 3–4.

2 cups fresh corn kernels
¾ cup chopped red pepper
½ cup chopped scallion
¼ cup chopped cilantro
4–5 green olives, sliced
2 tablespoons lemon juice
2 tablespoons extra-virgin olive oil
1 tablespoon liquid aminos
½ teaspoon ground cumin
Pinch cayenne, to taste

Mexicali Corn Salad

Cinnamon and Orange-Glazed Carrots 🌿

4 carrots, thinly sliced in rounds

2 tablespoons orange juice (or lemon juice)

1 tablespoon maple syrup

1 tablespoon extra-virgin olive oil (or flaxseed oil)

½ teaspoon cinnamon

It is very important to slice the carrots paper thin in this recipe. A machine works best for this.

In a bowl, combine the carrots, juice, maple syrup, oil and cinnamon; toss. Serves 4.

Near East Cucumber Salad 🌿

2 medium cucumbers, very thinly sliced

2 tablespoons lemon juice

1 clove garlic, pressed

1 tablespoon tamari

1 teaspoon sesame oil

This is one recipe where it is better to use a machine. The cucumbers need to be more thinly sliced than you can usually do by hand.

In a small bowl, combine the cucumbers, lemon juice, garlic and tamari. Toss. Chill in the refrigerator for several hours. Just before serving pour the oil over the salad and toss. Serves 4–6.

Julienne of Carrot and Zucchini 🌿

2 carrots, julienned

1 zucchini, julienned

2–3 teaspoons extra-virgin olive oil

1 clove garlic, minced

2 teaspoons dulse flakes

Dash liquid aminos

This simple dish is at its best when the vegetables are sliced into very long, thin strips. You can make the strips with a gadget that can be found at country fairs. It looks like a poor man's mandoline (See Equipment List, page 191). It has scary-looking razor-sharp blades which you drag the vegetable across. A similar machine with V-shaped blades is occasionally advertised on TV and can be found in some kitchen gadget stores. Pulling the carrot and zucchini across the cutter the long way rather than on their ends creates 4–6-inch strips. Even if you are slicing by hand, try to achieve this effect.

If you are using a mandoline don't watch television or have a conversation at the same time. These pieces of equipment are sharp and dangerous and require one hundred percent of your attention!

Combine the carrots, zucchini, oil, garlic, dulse and liquid aminos in a bowl. Toss. Serves 2–3.

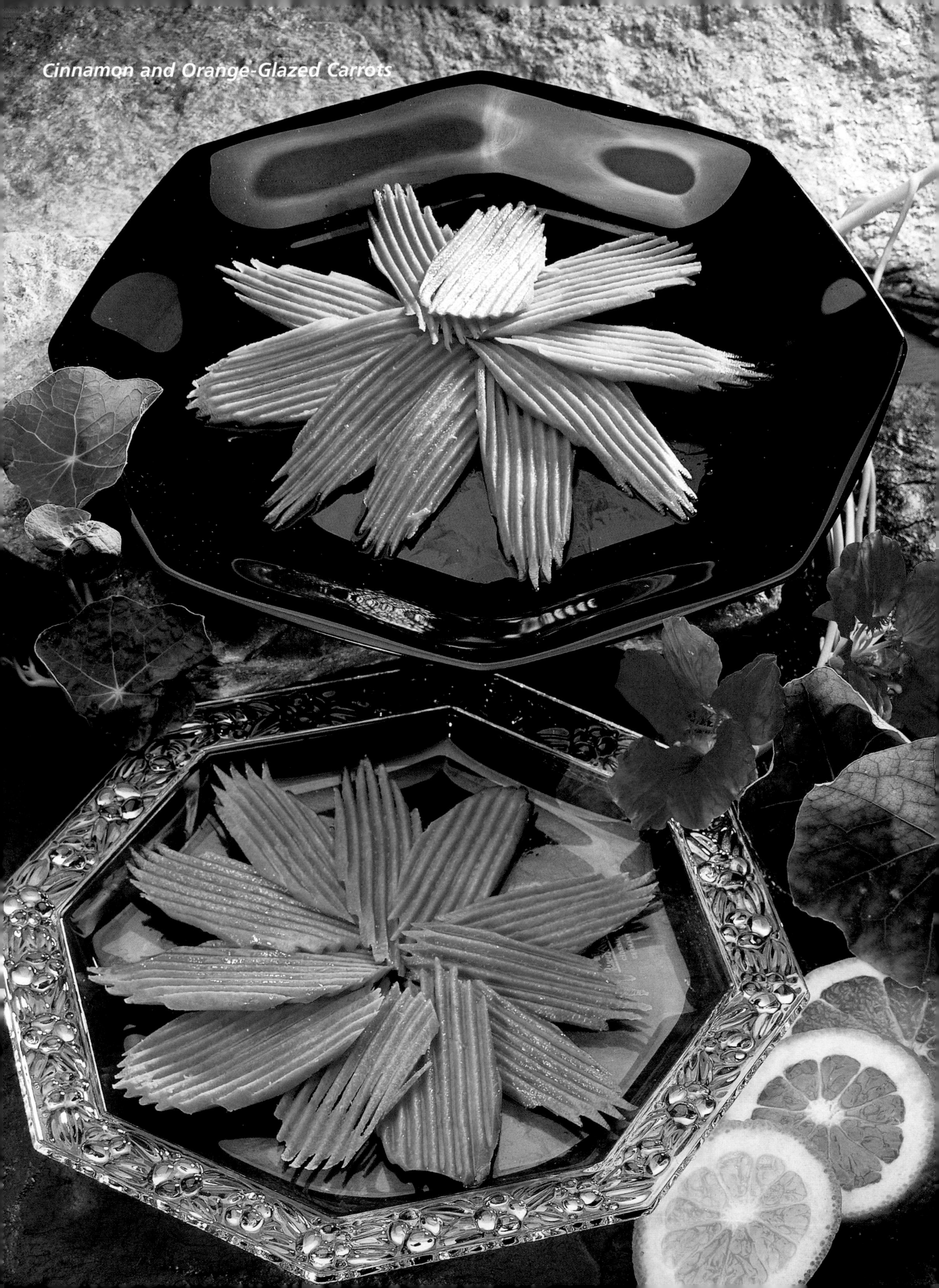
Cinnamon and Orange-Glazed Carrots

Julienne of Carrot and Zucchini

Minty Cucumber Salad ❦

Cucumber is an alkalizing food. It is considered to have a purifying effect on the digestive system, and is very beneficial to the skin. For a refreshing lift, lie down with a cucumber slice over each eye for a few minutes or rub a slice over your face after cleansing to tone and purify your skin.

If your cucumber tastes bitter, slice it, place it in a bowl, sprinkle it with sea salt and set a weight on it. A plate with a gallon (4 liter) water jug on top or a zip-lock bag filled with water works well. Leave the cucumber at room temperature for two hours, rinse it lightly and pat dry, then proceed with the recipe.

Fresh mint is, of course, best to use with this recipe, but dried mint (five teaspoons) will work if you have time to allow the flavors to blend.

In a small serving bowl, combine the cucumbers, mint, parsley, lemon juice and oil. Toss together. Taste and add stevia if desired. Chill the salad for several hours or overnight. Toss again before serving. Serves 2–3.

2 cups chopped cucumbers
⅓ cup finely chopped mint
2 tablespoons chopped parsley
1 tablespoon lemon juice
1 tablespoon extra-virgin olive oil or grapeseed oil
3 drops stevia or 1 teaspoon maple syrup (optional)

Minty Cucumber Salad

Green Beans Almondine

Green Beans Almondine 🌿

Did you know that there are no longer any commercial string beans? Scientists have genetically altered the vegetable that grandma used to sit on the porch stringing, for a bean without the inconvenience of a string. Now they are all called green beans. One wonders what else was altered when they eliminated the string.

Here's a raw version of an old stand-by with a crunchy new twist.

In a large salad bowl, combine the green beans, mushrooms, almonds, oil, liquid aminos and herbs and toss together lightly. Serves 5–6.

Variation 1: Try this recipe without the oil and liquid aminos and use Asian Dressing (see recipe, page 116) or another favorite.

1 pound (500 g) green beans, sliced
2 cups sliced mushrooms
1 cup dehydrated, flavored almonds (see page 88) or plain soaked almonds.
2 tablespoons extra-virgin olive oil
Dash liquid aminos
1 teaspoon favorite dried herb

Garlic Green Beans 🌿

This recipe works equally well with broccoli. If you are a garlic lover, this simple treatment works with almost anything.

In a small serving bowl, combine the green beans, garlic, oil and salt; toss. Cover the bowl and let the flavors blend for at least 30 minutes. Toss again. Sprinkle Gremolata on top of the beans just before serving. Serves 5–6.

3 cups slivered green beans
3 cloves garlic, thinly sliced, or to taste
2 tablespoons extra-virgin olive oil
Pinch sea salt
Gremolata (see recipe, page 115)

Dehydrated Mushrooms

Keep some of these mushrooms on hand because they make any salad special. Experiment with soaking the mushrooms in different marinades like Asian Sauce (see page 112) or Lemon-Tamari dressing (see page 112), without the oil.

Remove the stems and cut the larger mushrooms into chunks. Leave any smaller mushrooms whole. Place the mushrooms in a bowl and cover them with the liquid aminos; let sit for 5–30 minutes. Drain. Dehydrate the mushrooms until all the moisture is removed. Store the mushrooms in an airtight container in the refrigerator.

Mushrooms
Liquid aminos or tamari or marinade of choice

Yellow Squash Finocchio 🌿

1½ cups thinly sliced yellow squash (slice by hand)

2 cups cilantro, chopped

½ cup chopped red pepper

Fennel purée (see recipe, page 102)

Yellow squash is also called crookneck. Try to find little ones three to four inches (7.5 to 10 centimeters) long. They are melt-in-your-mouth tender. With the summer squashes a good rule of thumb is the smaller the vegetable, the tastier it will be.

The Italian word for fennel is *finocchio*. While any dressing works with this recipe, the fennel purée gives it a gourmet flair.

In a bowl, combine the squash, cilantro and red pepper. Toss. Add enough fennel purée to moisten the salad and toss again. Serve the squash on individual salad dishes topped with more fennel purée. Serves 2.

Buckwheat Snacks 🌿

2 cups hulled buckwheat groats, soaked 6 hours

Liquid aminos or tamari

Lemon juice

Seasonings of choice (optional)

A great little snack for those times when you have the munchies. You can chew on these snacks with a clear conscience, knowing they are much better for you than chips. Toss a handful of them in your salad for a different taste. Sunflower seeds can be treated in the same way; soak them in water for 4 hours.

See soaking instructions, page 5. In a shallow dish, combine the drained groats with enough liquid aminos and lemon juice to cover. Add any other spices, such as garlic, to taste. Marinate for about 1 hour. Drain. Place the groats in a dehydrator on a teflex sheet and dehydrate for 2–4 hours or until dry and crunchy. Store buckwheat snacks in an airtight container.

Note: If you do not have a dehydrator, an afternoon in the sun will give the same results or you can place the buckwheat in a warm oven, although that is less desirable. To reduce the slippery texture, drain and rinse every 30 minutes for the first few hours of soaking, if possible.

Asparagus Salad

If you've never tasted raw asparagus, you are in for a treat. Asparagus is high in vitamin A, especially in the green tips. This is a tasty combination of vegetables, but feel free to use whatever is in season. Serve with Asian Dressing (page 116) or one of the red pepper juice-based dressings.

In a salad bowl, combine the asparagus, onion, zucchini, red pepper and sprouted peas. Toss. Serve with the dressing of your choice. Serves 4.

1 pound asparagus, cut in ¾-inch pieces

1 small onion, thinly sliced

1 small zucchini, thinly sliced

1 red pepper, slivered

½ cup fresh or sprouted peas

Asparagus Salad

Stuffed Avocado Delight

Stuffed Avocado Delight

This stuffed avocado recipe is quick and easy; you can prepare it in less than five minutes. Of course, you will need to have the sauerkraut already made up (see recipe, page 49). As a quick lunch, plan on one avocado per serving. As an appetizer, use half an avocado per person.

Lemon juice preserves and slows down the oxidation of food. Sprinkling the avocado all over with lemon juice the moment that it is cut will keep it fresh and green.

In each avocado half, place 2 tablespoons of sauerkraut, one olive and a handful of sprouts. Splash the avocados with lemon juice and liquid aminos. Sprinkle with dulse flakes. Place on a bed of baby greens and sprouts.

1 avocado, halved and pitted
Lemon juice
¼ cup sauerkraut
2 green olives
Sprouts
Liquid aminos
Dulse flakes
Greens and sprouts

Avocado-Sprout Salad

Avocados consist mainly of high-quality fat. They contain no starch, very few carbohydrates and are high in minerals. Since calories from fats take longer to digest than calories from complex carbohydrates, avocados will satisfy your hunger quickly which prevents overeating. Avocados combine well with everything except proteins and melons. When making this recipe, use whatever sprouts you have handy in your refrigerator.

In a small bowl, combine the sprouts, celery, onion, carrots, red pepper, lemon juice and dulse. Toss thoroughly. Add the avocado and mix gently. Serve on a lettuce leaf. Serves 2.

2 cups sprouts
½ cup diced celery
½ cup diced red onion
½ cup thinly sliced carrots
1 red pepper, diced
4 teaspoons lemon juice
2 teaspoons dulse flakes
1–2 avocados, diced

Finocchio Salad

Finocchio is the Italian word for fennel. It has a delightful anise or licorice-like flavor.

Arrange the greens in a bowl. Place the diced fennel and red pepper rings on top of the greens. Pour ⅓ cup French Dressing over the salad. Serve the remaining dressing on the side. Serves 4.

2 cups mixed baby greens
3 cups diced fennel
½ red pepper, cut in rings
½ cup French Dressing
  (see page 99)

Kale and Hearty

Kale and Hearty

Kale is a marvelous source of chlorophyll and contains twice the amount of beta carotene as a serving of spinach! Along with the other leafy green vegetables, kale is also an excellent source of calcium. Save a few kale leaves to add to the next juice you make.

The magic of this recipe is that the mushrooms rehydrate with the marvelous taste of the marinade. If you do not have time to prepare the dehydrated mushrooms and nuts, plain mushrooms and nuts will work too.

In a large salad serving bowl, combine the kale, onions, red pepper, sweet potato, garlic, ginger, lemon juice, oil, liquid aminos and dehydrated mushrooms. Toss. Let the salad sit at room temperature for 1–2 hours. Toss again just before serving and top with the nuts or seeds.

Note: To blanch kale, tear into bite-sized pieces, removing the stems. Place the leaves in a sieve, and pour 2 or 3 cups of water that has been brought to a boil and cooled for 1 minute over the kale. Drain. To speed up the draining process, roll up the kale in a clean dishtowel for a few minutes. Serves 5–6.

5 cups kale, torn, blanched (see note)

½ cup thinly sliced onions

½ cup chopped red pepper

1 cup grated sweet potato

1 teaspoon minced garlic

1 teaspoon grated ginger root

½ cup lemon juice

2 tablespoons extra-virgin olive oil

2 tablespoons liquid aminos

1 cup dehydrated mushrooms (see recipe, page 61) (optional)

Handful dehydrated almonds or pumpkin seeds (see recipe, page 88) (optional)

Hijiki Salad

Hijiki is seaweed that looks like thick black threads. It is often served in Japanese restaurants. Seaweeds contain many minerals and trace elements, some of which are not found in land vegetables and they are all high in the B vitamins. Four ounces (100 g) of hijiki contains 1400 mg of calcium. If you soak and drain the hijiki, it doesn't need to be cooked and the flavor will be mild.

If you are not using the Optimum Choice Raw recipes, toasted sesame oil provides a more intense Asian flavor than raw sesame oil. Heated or refined oils are not recommended because they are harmful to the body (see page 110).

In a small bowl, combine the hijiki, oil, lemon juice, tamari, dried chili pepper and maple syrup. Allow the flavors to blend for a few minutes before serving. Serves 2.

Note: To soak hijiki, place in small bowl and cover with warm water. Let soak for 30 minutes; drain. Cover again with fresh warm water and let soak another 30 minutes; drain.

1 cup hijiki, soaked (see note)

2 teaspoons sesame oil

2 teaspoons lemon juice

1 teaspoon tamari or liquid aminos

¼ teaspoon dried red chili pepper

2 teaspoons maple syrup (optional)

Slivered Veggie Chop Suey 🌿

2 cups thinly sliced bok choy, both leaves and stems

1 cup green beans, slivered

1 cup snow peas or snap peas

1 cup mung sprouts

1 cup sunflower sprouts

1 cup clover sprouts

1 cup thinly sliced mushrooms

¼ cup chopped cilantro

1 red pepper, slivered

1 small zucchini, slivered

1 small red onion, finely chopped

2 carrots, slivered

2 stalks celery, peeled and slivered

2 cloves garlic, minced

2 tablespoons sesame oil, or more to taste

2 tablespoons tamari

2 teaspoons ginger juice or 1 tablespoon minced ginger root

4 pieces of nori, cut in ½-inch (1 centimeter) strips

Almost any vegetable works in this recipe. The secret lies in making the longest and thinnest slivers that you can. They will pick up the taste of the seasonings and are fun to eat and easy to digest. It is worth the effort!

If you want to make a one-dish main course, add two cups of soaked pumpkin seeds, sunflower seeds or almonds. (Soak pumpkin 2–4 hours, sunflower or almonds 8–10 hours following guidelines on page 5).

In a large salad bowl, combine the bok choy, beans, peas, mung sprouts, sunflower sprouts, clover sprouts, mushrooms, cilantro, red pepper, zucchini, onion, carrots, celery, garlic, sesame oil, tamari and ginger juice. Toss well. Just before serving, top the salad with the strips of nori. Serves 6–8.

Marinated Mushrooms 🌿

1 pound mushrooms, cleaned and trimmed but left whole

½ cup extra-virgin olive oil

Juice of 2 lemons

2 cloves garlic, pressed

6 peppercorns (whole or crushed, whichever you prefer)

½ teaspoon sea salt

These tasty morsels go very fast. They make a great condiment for a large meal or serve them as an appetizer, arranged on a platter with a toothpick in each one.

In a bowl, whisk together the oil, lemon juice, garlic, pepper and salt. Add the mushrooms. Let sit at room temperature for several hours, stirring occasionally, then cover and refrigerate. These mushrooms will keep for several days. Serves 6–8.

Lemon Cups 🌿

How can anything this simple taste so good? These adorable stuffed lemons are a great side dish with a main course of sprouted sunflower pâté. Use more lemon if you like, and if it is too tart for you add a touch of maple syrup or stevia.

The recipe works best when the carrots are grated very fine. Use whatever grating method you have that will give the best results. A heavy-duty juicer without a screen makes the finest grate but be sure to exercise extreme caution while using it, and keep children out of the way. Do not leave the machine set up without a screen in it.

In a small mixing bowl, toss the carrots, lemon juice, zest and oil. Taste. Sweeten if desired with maple syrup or stevia. Fill the lemon halves with the carrot mixture. Serves 4.

2 cups very finely grated carrots
1 tablespoon lemon juice, or more to taste
1 teaspoon grated lemon zest
1 teaspoon extra-virgin olive oil or walnut oil
Stevia or maple syrup (optional)
4 lemon halves, after juicing

Lemon Cups

Rainbows in Ribbons

Rainbows in Ribbons 🌿

This recipe is visual dynamite; make it when you want to impress someone. Tying the scallion in a knot or bow takes a bit of fussing but the results are very worthwhile. Rainbows in Ribbons also looks beautiful placed on a platter that has been decorated with squiggles of Fennel and Lemon Purée (see recipe, page 102) or Spinach-Avocado Sauce (see recipe, page 95).

Color is important in this recipe. Experiment with winter squash, yellow and orange peppers, broccoli stems, celery, jicama and zucchini.

In a small bowl, mix the lemon juice, liquid aminos, oil and ginger; set aside. In a shallow dish, combine the carrots, parsnip, red pepper, daikon, broccoli and scallions. Pour the dressing over the vegetables and let the salad marinate for 30–60 minutes. Drain well, pat dry with paper towels. (Save the marinade to use as a dressing in another recipe.)

Working on a cutting board, divide the vegetables into 4 equal piles, making sure that each pile has variety of colored vegetables. Place each pile on a scallion and tie, as you would a ribbon, making a knot or a bow. (It is easier to make a scallion "ribbon" if you cut the scallion in half, lengthwise, to within 1 inch from the end. Then, open the scallion so that it is twice as long as before.) Garnish the bundles with a sprig of parsley, cilantro, radish sprouts or edible flowers. Serves 4 as a side dish or placed on top of a salad.

Note: You can also make ribbons from fresh lemon grass (tuck an edible flower into the knot) or large chives. Maybe you will be lucky enough to find some perfect chives with the flowers still on them at the farmer's market.

½ cup lemon juice

2 tablespoons liquid aminos

2 tablespoons extra-virgin olive oil

2 teaspoons grated ginger root

2 carrots, sliced into very thin 5-inch long julienned strips

1 parsnip, sliced into very thin 5-inch long julienned strips

1 large red pepper, sliced into very thin 5-inch long julienned strips

1 5-inch piece of daikon radish, sliced into very thin 5-inch long julienned strips

1 5-inch broccoli stem, sliced into very thin 5-inch long julienned strips

4 scallions, green part only

Sweet Potato Salad 🌿

This is a rich and exotic lunch or main course. The dressing is protein based, and the yam is a starch.

Stir the orange zest in the dressing; set aside. In a small bowl, combine the sweet potato and red pepper. Add the dressing; toss. On 4 serving plates, place a bed of sprouts; mound the salad on top. Garnish with chopped vegetables of your choice. Serves 4.

1 teaspoon grated orange zest (optional)

1 cup Indonesian Yum-Yum dressing (see page 117) or Gado-Gado (see page 117)

2 cups peeled, grated sweet potato or yam

1 cup finely chopped red pepper

Sprouts

Chopped vegetables

Rainbow Salad 🌿

3 cups finely shredded red
cabbage

1 cup snow peas, cut in long
slivers

½ cup slivered red pepper

½ cup slivered yellow pepper

½ cup slivered daikon radish

Sunflower sprouts

Asian Dressing (see page 116)
or Ginger-Lime Dressing
(see page 121)

1 tablespoon sesame seeds

Eating rainbow-colored foods is felt by some to support the balance of the seven chakras of the body. By choosing food of many colors, you are ensuring a wide variety of nourishment not to mention extraordinary visual appeal.

In a mixing bowl, combine the cabbage, peas, red pepper, yellow pepper and daikon; toss together. On a large serving platter or on individual plates, arrange the vegetables on a bed of sunflower sprouts. Top with dressing and garnish with a sprinkle of sesame seeds. Serves 4–5.

Summer Squash Provençale 🌿

3 cups assorted baby greens
(or substitute romaine
lettuce)

1½ cups sunflower sprouts

1 small summer squash
(either yellow crookneck or
patty pan), shredded

1 small firm zucchini,
shredded

1–2 cups guacamole, with
1 teaspoon dried oregano
added

1 red pepper, finely chopped

3 tablespoons fresh basil, cut
in long thin strips (see note)

¾ cup fresh or sprouted peas

½ cup alfalfa or clover
sprouts

¼ cup organic, sundried
Greek olives

This is a layered salad that works well as a luncheon dish. The salad looks attractive, contains a lot of nourishing ingredients and is filling on its own.

For the best effect, shred the vegetables with either a salad shooter or a mandoline. As you prepare each vegetable, place it in a separate container until you are ready to assemble the salad. Use your favorite guacamole recipe (see page 127) or vinaigrette as a dressing and add one teaspoon oregano to either. Serve the salad with an additional layer of firm, diced tomatoes, if you like.

On individual dinner plates, layer the ingredients as follows: greens, sunflower sprouts, squash, zucchini, 2–3 tablespoons dressing; red pepper, a few basil strips, sprouted peas, alfalfa sprouts and olives. Top with the remaining basil strips. Serve additional dressing on the side. Serves 2–3.

Note: To make basil strips, stack several basil leaves of similar size in a little pile. Starting at one long side, gently roll the leaves into a tight cylinder. Slice very thin strips with a sharp knife at a slight angle (you can discard the first thin slice as it contains the stems). This technique, called a chiffonade, will yield many thin attractive strips quickly. To mince the strips, simply chop them finely lengthwise. Prepare basil just before using, as in some combinations it will blacken.

Rainbow Salad

Popeye's Secret 🌿

1 cup Notmayo! (page 118), or any thick and creamy dressing
1 clove garlic, pressed
1 pound (500 g) spinach (large bunch), roughly torn up
¼ cup coarsely chopped onion
1 tablespoon fresh mint (or 1 teaspoon dried)
2 tablespoons pumpkin seeds or chopped almonds

The days of being forced to "eat your spinach" are over! A great recipe that is high in iron, this dish is somewhere between a soup and a salad. It is a cool and refreshing meal that allows you to eat generous quantities of spinach; each serving contains the equivalent of three cups! Served with sprouts, this recipe makes a great lunch or a side dish for dinner.

In a food processor, combine the Notmayo! and garlic and process thoroughly. Add the spinach and onion and pulse-chop until they are evenly cut up. There should still be distinct pieces of spinach, not a purée. Serve the mixture in bowls and top with mint and seeds or nuts. Serves 2–3.

Over the Rainbow Salad 🌿

To make this beautiful salad, simply place mounds of jewel-colored vegetables next to each other. It hardly needs any dressing due to the moistness created by the fine grate but any type of dressing would be a good accompaniment. If you are making a quick lunch for yourself, use a hand grater and work directly onto your plate. For a big crowd, use a large, attractive serving plate and place the mounds of gem-colored vegetables on it as you make them. Experiment with different colored vegetables and different grating systems. This recipe works very well with a heavy-duty juicer without the screen (warning: keep your fingers away, you could do serious damage to yourself), although you may have to put some of the mixture through twice. You can also use a food processor or mandoline. The quantities and vegetables will be up to you.

- White grated vegetables: daikon radish, jicama (peeled), Jerusalem artichoke, turnips or parsnips
- Orange grated vegetables: carrots (best choice), squash (peeled), yams (peeled)
- Red grated vegetables: beets
- Other suggestions: cabbage, celery root, rutabagas, sweet potatoes (peeled), broccoli stems.

Mound the grated vegetables on a plate or mix the vegetables together. For a party presentation, use a large, shallow ceramic bowl. Place mounds of jicama, butternut squash, daikon radish, carrot and beet around the edge of the bowl. In the center, put fresh corn kernels. Place chopped parsley or cilantro between each pile. Place black olives around the corn in a circle. Sprinkle each vegetable with a little lemon juice. Put a dash of paprika on the corn. Serve a dressing of your choice on the side. Grate the beets last to avoid coloring other vegetables pink.

Over the Rainbow Salad

Confetti Salad 🌿

2 carrots, shredded

1–2 parsnips, shredded

1 rutabaga, shredded

1 turnip, shredded

1 3-inch slice daikon radish, shredded

2 cups mixed baby greens (packaged greens)

2 cups sunflower sprouts, cut up

1 cup kale, torn and blanched (see note)

1 cup slivered red pepper

1 cup slivered green cabbage

½ cup cucumber rounds, cut in half

¼ cup chopped parsley

¼ cup sliced celery

2 scallions, finely chopped

1 large shallot, finely chopped

Juice of 1 lemon or lime

2 tablespoons dulse flakes

2 tablespoons grated unsweetened coconut

Party-size Asian Dressing (see page 116)

A festive and unusual-tasting salad, this dish is good for a crowd and also stays fresh for an amazingly long time. Perhaps this has to do with the staying power of the root vegetables. By shredding and dispersing root vegetables throughout the salad, their energy seems to be transferred to the more perishable ingredients. Tossing the salad in lemon or lime juice also helps to preserve its freshness. Other good vegetables to use for the base are celery root and winter squash.

If you can, use a salad shooter or mandoline to shred the vegetables because the sharpness of the blades results in a shred that is firmer and more defined than shreds from a hand grater or a food processor.

Serve the dressing on the side so that any leftover salad will keep fresh longer.

In a very large salad bowl, combine the carrot, parsnip, rutabaga, turnip, daikon, greens, sunflower sprouts, kale, red pepper, cabbage, cucumber, parsley, celery, scallions and shallot. Toss well. Sprinkle the salad liberally with lemon juice. Toss thoroughly. Top the salad with half of the dulse. Sprinkle the coconut flakes over the other half. Decorate with red pepper or daikon radish rounds. Serve with Asian Dressing on the side. Serves 10–12.

Note: To blanch kale, tear into bite-sized pieces, removing stems. Place the leaves in a sieve, and pour 2 or 3 cups of water that has been brought to a boil and cooled for 1 minute over the kale. Drain.

Celery Root Salad 🌿

1 celery root, peeled and shredded

1 cup vinaigrette or Notmayo! (page 118)

Like some people, celery root (also known as celeriac) is homely on the outside, but beautiful on the inside. It has a delicate taste that is well worth adding to your recipe repertoire. The best way to peel celery root is to cut it into large pieces first, then slice off the outside. This same advice goes for the hard squashes such as butternut or hubbard squash. Use a salad shooter, food processor or mandoline to shred the root.

In a small bowl, combine the shredded celery root and dressing. This salad can be served right away or left to marinate for 1–12 hours. Serves 4–6.

Confetti Salad

Orange Carrots

4 cups shredded carrots

4 tablespoons orange juice,
  or more to taste

3 tablespoons lemon juice

1 tablespoon extra-virgin
  olive oil

¼ cup minced scallions

¼ cup minced parsley

1 tablespoon grated orange
  zest

1 teaspoon grated lemon zest

½ teaspoon ground cumin or
  curry powder

Pinch cayenne

Pinch sea salt

4–6 orange halves, after
  juicing

Kids enjoy seeing this dish served in a halved orange, lemon, red pepper or avocado. Adjust the seasonings for a child's tastebuds. Use fewer scallions, no ground cumin or curry, and, if you wish, add a spoonful of maple syrup or other sweetener.

Use your favorite method to shred the carrots: a heavy-duty juicer with no screen, a salad shooter, food processor or hand grater.

Place the shredded carrots in a large bowl; set aside. In a blender, combine the orange juice, lemon juice, oil, scallions, parsley, orange and lemon zest, cumin, cayenne and salt. Blend thoroughly, adding more orange juice or lemon juice to taste and to achieve the desired consistency. Pour the mixture over the carrots and toss. Use the carrot mixture to stuff half an orange, lemon, red pepper, or avocado. Serves 4–6.

Orange Beets

3 cups grated beets

Juice and grated rind of
  1 orange

1 tablespoon maple syrup
  (optional)

1 tablespoon extra-virgin
  olive oil

Pinch sea salt

Here is a quick way to dress up beets for a side dish. It only takes a few minutes to make this grated dish, and the benefits of beets are worth far more than the time taken to prepare them. This recipe is fun to serve in orange cups.

In a small bowl, combine the beets, juice, rind, maple syrup, oil and salt. Toss together. Let the flavors blend for a few minutes before serving. Serves 6.

Curried Winter Squash

3 cups grated winter squash
  or turnip or daikon radish
  or a combination

2 tablespoons extra-virgin
  olive oil or grapeseed oil

2 teaspoons curry powder

1 tablespoon lemon juice

1 tablespoon liquid aminos or
  tamari

2 tablespoons minced onion
  (optional)

Hubbard, butternut, acorn, golden delicious, turban (also called buttercup) and pumpkin are the most common winter squashes. The combination of curry and orange-colored squashes makes a wonderful, warming combination. Gently heat this dish in the top of a double boiler to bring out the sweetness of the squash and the contrasting pungency of the curry.

In a mixing bowl, combine the squash, oil, curry, lemon juice, liquid aminos and onion; toss. Let the flavors blend for 30 minutes. Toss again. Serves 4.

Ginger Beets

Beets are high in vitamin A and help cleanse the liver. If you are making several dishes at once with your salad shooter, grater or food processor, do the beets last. That way, you won't have pink vegetables and you won't need to stop to disassemble and wash any equipment.

In a small bowl, combine the beets, ginger, maple syrup, tamari and lemon juice; toss. Let the flavors blend for a few minutes before serving. Serves 4.

2 cups grated beets

2 teaspoons grated ginger root

1 tablespoon maple syrup (optional)

1 tablespoon tamari

1 teaspoon lemon juice

Ginger Beets

Hijiki-Yam Medley 🌿

1 cup hijiki, soaked for 30 minutes (see note)

2 cups grated yam or sweet potato

4 tablespoons dehydrated sunflower or pumpkin seeds, or soaked seeds (optional)

1 tablespoon sesame oil

2 teaspoons grated ginger

2 teaspoons tamari

Pinch cinnamon

Asian dressing can be used instead of the ginger, oil and tamari. If you are using the Optimum Choice Raw recipes, don't use the sunflower or pumpkin seeds.

In a small serving bowl, combine the hijki, yam, seeds, ginger, oil, tamari and cinnamon. Gently toss the ingredients. Serves 3–4.

Note: To soak hijiki, place in a small bowl and cover with warm water. Let soak for 30 minutes; drain. Cover again with fresh warm water and let soak another 30 minutes; drain.

Vegetables à la Grecque 🌿

Try the following vegetables served à la grecque. Use your favorite vegetable or a combination.

Asparagus

Broccoli florets

Carrots

Cauliflower florets

Celery, sliced

Celery root, grated

Cucumber slices

Daikon radish

Fennel, sliced

Green beans

Mushrooms, many varieties

Onions

Parsnips

Peppers, sliced

Rutabagas

Summer Squash, thinly sliced, or slivered

Sweet potatoes, sliced

Turnips

Winter Squash, thinly sliced, or slivered

Basic French Dressing, to cover (see recipes, pages 99)

In traditional cooking, Vegetables à la Grecque is a recipe for preparing whole or chopped vegetables. It calls for boiling then cooling them in a mixture of well-seasoned oil and water or wine. Very fine results can be achieved adapting this method to raw food preparation.

Marinating vegetables in your favorite vinaigrette or French dressing is easy, especially with several dressings to choose from (see recipes, page 99). Whether you blanch the vegetables first or leave them raw depends on you. Blanching results in fewer live enzymes but it does soften the vegetables, allowing them to soak up more of the flavor from the marinade. Blanching also heightens the color of the vegetable, which can sometimes be important in a presentation. You may prefer to blanch some vegetables like asparagus and broccoli, however, blanching is not recommended if you want to stick to the Optium Raw Choice program.

Slice, dice, sliver or grate the vegetables of your choice. If the vegetables are small enough, leave them whole. (Mushrooms and asparagus will marinate well if left whole.) Place the vegetables in a bowl and cover them with the vinaigrette of your choice. Marinate for a minimum of one hour or covered in the refrigerator overnight. Serve either drained or undrained.

Hijiki-Yam Medley

Vegetable Chop Suey 🌿

1 cup almonds, soaked 8–12
  hours, then chopped
1 cup sunflower sprouts
1 cup pea sprouts
½ cup mung bean sprouts
½ cup adzuki bean sprouts or
  soy sprouts or lentil sprouts
½ cup parsley, finely chopped
1 red pepper, slivered
2–3 broccoli stems, peeled,
  cut in long thin strips
4 scallions, cut in long thin
  slivers
1 stalk celery, slivered
4 nori sheets, cut in thin
  strips
Asian Dressing (see page 116)
Hot Mustard Sauce (optional)
  (see page 120)

For best results, prepare all the vegetables in long thin strips. The taste of the pea sprouts and mung bean sprouts in combination with your favorite Asian-flavored dressing all add up to a definite "chop suey" experience, only raw.

Pea sprouts are dried green peas that have been sprouted in a jar and then planted in soil like sunflower, buckwheat or wheatgrass. They take two weeks to mature, but they are worth the effort.

See soaking instructions, page 5. In a large salad bowl, combine the almonds, sunflower sprouts, pea sprouts, mung bean sprouts, adzuki sprouts, parsley, red pepper, broccoli, scallions and celery. Toss. Top with the nori strips. Serve Asian dressing on the side. For variety, you could also serve Hot Mustard Sauce. Serves 4–6.

Variation 1: For a more traditional Asian flavor, substitute cashews for the almonds (although this is not as healthy an alternative and should not be used if you are following the Optimum Choice Raw recipes).
Variation 2: When they are in season, substitute 1 cup slivered snow peas for the broccoli or add them to the existing recipe.

Salad Russe 🌿

1 cup cubed carrots
1 cup cubed turnip
1 cup cubed celery root
1 cup cubed beets
1 cup cubed sweet potato or
  yam
1 cup fresh raw or sprouted
  peas, blanched (see note)
Garlicky Dressing or other
  vinaigrette (see recipe,
  page 103)
Notmayo! or any thick
  dressing (optional)
  (see recipe, page 118)

This dish is a little unusual because the vegetables are dressed in two steps. First they are marinated, then drained and combined with a thick and creamy type of dressing. This technique results in an interesting blend of flavors. Cubing—which means cutting into equal size squares—rather than grating the vegetables gives the meal a different texture.

In a medium-sized bowl, combine the carrots, turnip celery root, beets, sweet potato and peas. Top with the Garlicky Dressing and toss to coat thoroughly. Marinate the ingredients in dressing for 3 hours to overnight. Drain. Serve as is, or mix the salad with enough Notmayo! to bind the ingredients together.

Note: To blanch peas, place the peas in a 2-cup measure and pour water that has been brought to a boil and cooled for one minute over them. After 45–60 seconds, pour the water off and plunge the peas into cold water. Drain and add peas to the recipe.

Gazpacho Salad

You can serve this salad two ways: either toss all the ingredients together or serve it as a layered salad. For a layered salad, choose a straight-sided glass salad bowl, like a footed trifle dish. Measure the volume of the dish and fill it as close to the top as possible. This recipe yields approximately ten cups, without the tomatoes. If your bowl is a lot bigger, increase the amounts in the recipe accordingly.

If you are not following the Optimum Choice Raw recipes, you might wish to add two cups of seeded, chopped tomatoes. Layer them on top of the cucumber.

For a layered salad, combine the parsley and cilantro, and set aside. In a straight-sided glass bowl, layer the vegetables in the following order: onions, peppers, celery, ½ of the parsley-cilantro mixture, corn, cucumber, remainder of the parsley-cilantro mixture. Pour dressing over the salad just before serving. Serves 5–6.

1 cup chopped parsley
1 cup chopped cilantro
1 small red onion, finely chopped
2 red peppers, finely chopped
2 stalks celery, finely chopped
2 cups fresh corn kernels (approximately 2 ears)
2 medium cucumbers, finely chopped
½–1 cup Basic French Dressing. variation 1 (see page 99) or Ginger-Lime Dressing (see page 121)

Gazpacho Salad

Asian Salad

Asian Salad 🌿

Using vegetables that have been introduced to the American palate from Asia is a rewarding culinary adventure! Most metropolitan areas have an Asian market where you can explore the vegetables, spices, dried mushrooms and whatever else the market carries that will fit in with your dietary choices. Try to use as many "typically" Chinese or Asian vegetables as you can in this recipe, along with some of your more familiar favorites.

Choose the two cups of assorted vegetables for their color and variety. Some good choices would be carrots, peppers, green beans, sweet potato rounds, broccoli florets, crimini mushrooms, onions or scallions.

As with all of the recipes in this book, feel free to alter, increase, decrease, substitute, delete and otherwise change this recipe to suit your fancy. This is an idea book, not a rule book.

In a large salad bowl, combine the bok choy, cabbage, bean sprouts, mushrooms and assorted vegetables. Toss. Pour some of the dressing over the salad and toss again. Allow the flavors to blend for 1 hour before serving. Leave additional Asian dressing on the side. Toss again before serving. Serve on a bed of greens or sprouts. Serves 4–6.

2 cups bok choy, leaves torn up or sliced, stems thinly sliced

1 cup sliced Chinese cabbage (also called Napa cabbage)

2 cups mung bean sprouts

1 cup dehydrated black or shitake mushrooms, soaked and thinly sliced

2 cups assorted vegetables

Double recipe of Asian Dressing (see page 116)

Potted Greens 🌿

It can be a challenge to take in enough bio-available calcium, and a salad of the most calcium-rich greens can be difficult to eat because many of them are quite tough. Breaking down the greens in the food processor is a wonderful way to render them palatable and opens up a whole new way of preparing highly nourishing food.

Spinach, collard greens, Swiss chard, beet greens or a combination can be substituted for kale. Kale and collard greens can be lightly blanched, the other greens are naturally more delicate and do not need to be softened. People who are used to eating one hundred percent raw food will enjoy this dish without blanching the kale.

In a food processor, combine the kale, onion, mushrooms, lemon juice and liquid aminos. Pulse-chop until the vegetables are uniformly chopped. Add the tahini and cumin and process until thoroughly mixed. It is not necessary to make a purée. Serves 4–5.

Note: To blanch kale, tear into bite-sized pieces, removing the stems. Place the leaves in a sieve, and pour 2 or 3 cups of water that has been brought to a boil and cooled for 1 minute over the kale. Drain.

1 bunch kale, torn up, lightly blanched (optional) (see note)

1 cup chopped onion

2 cups sliced mushrooms

2 tablespoons lemon juice

1 tablespoon liquid aminos

½ cup raw tahini

1 teaspoon ground cumin

Rootey-Tootey Salad 🌿

1 cup grated carrots
1 cup grated turnips
1 cup grated beets
1 cup chopped cabbage
1 cup fresh corn kernels
Juice of 1 lemon
Dash favorite seasoning
(optional)

Use your favorite method to grate the vegetables. Serve them in a mound placed on salad greens or sprouts. Serve your favorite dressing on the side, or toss it with the salad before serving.

In a medium-sized serving bowl, combine the carrots, turnips, beets, cabbage and corn. Pour the lemon juice and seasoning on top; toss. Serves 4.

Squash Delight 🌿

2 cups acorn or butternut
squash, shredded
½ cup finely chopped red
pepper
2 tablespoons lemon juice
1 tablespoon tamari or soy
sauce
2 teaspoons honey or maple
sprinkles or stevia
1 tablespoon grated ginger
root
Pinch Chinese 5-spice powder
(optional)

A lot of people are surprised that squash can be eaten raw. In fact, raw squash is an excellent, hearty food that can be enjoyed in many ways.

In a bowl, combine the squash and red pepper; toss. In a small bowl, mix the lemon juice, tamari, honey, ginger and 5-spice powder. Pour the dressing on the squash and toss. Allow the flavors to blend for 30 minutes. Serves 2–3.

Squash Noodle Salad 🌿

1 cup spaghetti squash
strands
1 tablespoon papaya seeds
1 teaspoon grated ginger
root
A few drops extra-virgin olive
oil or sesame oil
A few drops tamari
Pinch sesame seeds

Spaghetti squash does not need to be cooked to create the wonderful little strands that people love. Scrape the raw insides with a fork, and you will produce strands. Discard the dark orange, thread-like fibers that are mixed in with the seeds—they aren't as tasty as the flesh of the squash. To make one portion, just cut a pie-shaped wedge out of the squash and scrape off what you need.

The unusual aspect of this recipe is the papaya seeds. Scrape the seeds from the fruit and allow them to dry out a little before you use them in this recipe. They are spicy and peppery and add a different taste and crunch that is fun. This recipe is also good with Asian Dressing (see page 116). If you prefer, add some of the papaya seeds to the dressing and blend or try it with Gado-Gado dressing (see page 117), not an Optimum Choice recipe..

In a small bowl, toss the squash, papaya seeds, ginger, oil, tamari and sesame seeds. Serves 1.

Rootey-Tootey Salad

Dehydrated Onion Rings and Red Peppers

2 onions, thinly sliced

4–6 red peppers, thinly sliced

A tightly sealed bag of onion rings and red peppers is a good staple for your pantry. Not only do these snacks taste delicious, they dress up any recipe. Since dehydrator temperatures vary, and vegetable size and moisture content aren't consistent, dehydrator times cannot be given accurately.

Place the onion and red pepper slices on dehydrator trays and dehydrate until crisp.

Dehydrated Nuts and Seeds

2 cups nuts or seeds, soaked 8–12 hours

Tamari or liquid aminos

Garlic, pressed (optional)

Spices and herbs (optional)

This method will work with any of the nuts and larger seeds. Almonds, cashews, pecans, walnuts, sunflower and pumpkin all work well. Dehydrated nuts and seeds add a delightful texture and taste to a salad.

See soaking instructions, page 5. Dry the nuts with a towel, then place them in a shallow pan and pour tamari over top. (Add garlic, spices or herbs to the tamari, if desired.) Depending on how strongly seasoned you want the nuts to be, soak them anywhere from 30 minutes to 24 hours, turning them once in awhile. Drain the nuts well and place them in a dehydrator; dehydrate until very crunchy, 12–24 hours. Store dehydrated nuts in an airtight container in the refrigerator.

Note: In theory, dehydrated foods do not need to be refrigerated. In practice, however, unless they are totally dry, with no moisure in them, the nuts can spoil if stored without refrigeration.

Zucchini Zalad for Two 🌿

This salad has become a favorite among raw fooders and omnivores alike. Adding sauerkraut gives it a complex, hard-to-define flavor that gets rave reviews and requests for more. Finely chop some of the seaweed from the sauerkraut process and add it to the salad, too. If you don't have any sauerkraut on hand, make this recipe anyway; it is still a very tasty dish. It's especially wonderful served on a bed of sunflower greens and topped with clover or alfalfa sprouts.

In a small bowl, combine the zucchini, red pepper, sauerkraut, olives, garlic and basil. Toss thoroughly. Add the liquid aminos, dulse and lemon juice and toss again. Add the avocado and mix gently. Serves 2.

1 zucchini, slivered
½ cup chopped red pepper
4 tablespoons sauerkraut, or more to taste
4 or 5 green olives, chopped
1 small clove garlic, minced
2 basil leaves, chopped, or more to taste
1 tablespoon liquid aminos
2 tablespoons dulse flakes
1 tablespoon lemon juice
½ avocado, cut in chunks

Zucchini Mexicali 🌿

Serve this "hot" and pretty salad as a side dish on a bed of sprouts or as a stuffing in a red pepper. It looks attractive on the plate and its intense flavor works well as a condiment. Flavor the salad with jalapeno, garlic and cilantro according to your taste. Remember to use caution with jalapeno peppers—they can be mild or devilishly hot!

In a small bowl, combine the zucchini, onion, red pepper, jalapeno, cilantro, garlic, coriander, liquid aminos and lemon juice. Toss together; adjust the seasonings. Serves 2–3 as a side dish.

1 medium zucchini, finely chopped
¼ red onion, finely chopped
½ red pepper, finely chopped
½–1 jalapeno pepper, minced
¼ cup finely chopped cilantro
1 small clove garlic, minced
Pinch ground coriander seed
Dash liquid aminos
Dash lemon juice

Dried Root Vegetables 🌿

Thinly slice any of the root vegetables or hard squashes including sweet potato, yam, beet, turnip, rutabaga, parsnip, daikon radish or butternut squash.

Soak the slices in a mixture of tamari or liquid aminos and your favorite flavoring, such as garlic, ginger root, herbs or spices. Soak for 30–60 minutes. Drain.

Place the slices in a dehydrator and dry them out then use them as chips with dip. You can let them dry out just a bit to bring out their natural flavor or allow them to become hard "chips".

Variation: Dehydrate unmarinated vegetables. Briefly marinate the dehydrated vegetables in lime juice, then rehydrate them.

5 Fundamental Flavors

Soups • Sauces • Gravies
Dressings • Marinades
Spreads • Dips • Toppings

In traditional SAD (Standard American Diet) cuisine, the taste of food is enhanced by combining flavors, for example, by pairing potatoes with onions and garlic, or cinnamon with apples, then cooking it all, allowing the flavors to meld.

Great schools of cooking have developed over the centuries, each bringing its particular slant to the world. French cooking, known for its rich and flavorful sauces, brings taste and style to food. There is the fire of Cajun food; the subtlety of Asian cuisine; the comfort of Italian food; and the pleasure of down-home, turkey-stuffing-and-apple-pie American cooking. Each cuisine incorporates a wide variety of flavors, and raw cuisine is no different.

You will bring your favorite flavors to raw food preparation, just as you do now with traditional food preparation. As a matter of fact, when food is not broken down by cooking, which heightens the taste of food, flavoring becomes even more important. As a raw foodist you will not have to eat only salads for the rest of your life. You can eat

magnificently on a one hundred percent raw diet and never once eat what you now think of as a salad.

More than other styles of food preparation, you will rely on the kinds of flavors in this chapter to keep your meals fun, interesting, and, if you like, gourmet. Now, more than ever before, dressings, sauces, gravies, soups, dips, marinades and toppings will take on a new importance.

This chapter offers dozens of taste influences from American to Asian to Italian and Mexican. You will find flavors that range from garlic to citrus to fiery and more. These recipes are easy to make and their flavors will provide the taste and fun that are so important.

Perhaps you are wondering why one chapter contains both soups and dressings. In raw cuisine, most soups can also serve as dressings, either as is, or with the addition of an ingredient or two. You are achieving flavor, not by cooking for hours on a stovetop but by breaking food down into purées, sauces and dressings and bringing these mixtures to your loaves, pâtés, salads and soups.

How long does raw food preparation take compared with traditional cooking? Once you are used to it, you will most likely spend less time in the kitchen. However, if you were eating out three times a day before, you will of course be spending more time in your kitchen preparing the healthiest food available.

Soup satisfies in countless ways. First of all, soup is delicious and nutritious. Secondly, unlike traditional cooking, you can make fabulous soup in less than fifteen minutes! Once you know the basics, you cannot make a mistake when "throwing a soup together." You need little more equipment than a grater and a good blender. Soup makes a delightful lunch, carried to work in a thermos. Soups are so fast, simple and tasty that you will want to make them regularly. And, as you will see in the following recipes, it is easy to use soup as a dressing for your sprouts and salads.

By developing a repertoire of great-tasting dressings to enhance your salads, you are also enhancing your chances of making a permanent lifestyle change. Most of the bottled and packaged salad dressings on the market will not contribute to your health. And all the best intentions in the world will come to nothing if the food you eat doesn't taste great. Even the staunchest raw foodist will tire of naked sprouts.

What can you do to ensure that you enjoy raw food? First of all, give yourself time. Many people find that after eating raw food for three weeks or so, their taste buds seem to change, and what was once merely palatable has now become delicious.

Be willing to experiment. Go beyond that safe splash of olive oil, squeeze of lemon and favorite herb. Try lots of these recipes and then make up your own. A pile of sprouts and greens becomes something else entirely when covered with a creamy avocado dressing or exotic Asian dressing or a rich Notmayo! Once you've found a few dressings you like, always have some made up and ready in your refrigerator. (See The Ten Raw Food Kitchen Essentials, page 7, for more helpful hints.)

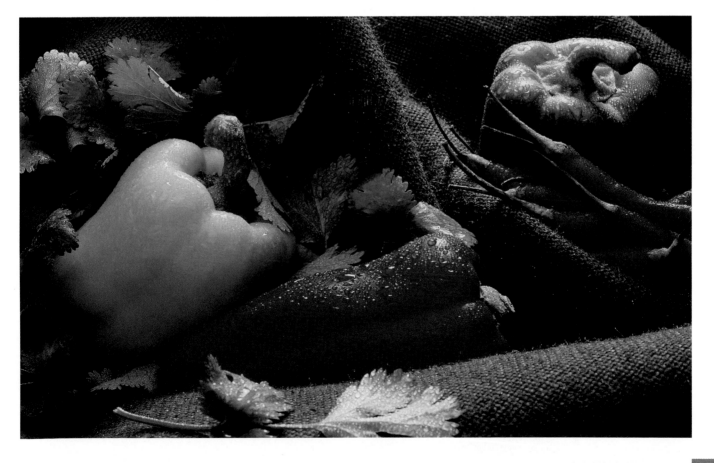

Marvelous Mushroom Soup

Sauce • Soup • Gravy

½ **cup water**

¼ **cup almond butter**

1 ½ **cups quartered mushrooms**

1 **tablespoon liquid aminos**

1 **pinch sea salt**

4 **tablespoons finely chopped mushrooms**

This is a great holiday recipe and it also makes a memorable soup that is rich enough so that a half cup provides a single serving. As a rich and thick gravy it has a heavenly mushroom flavor. Use it on loaves, pâtés or burgers, or drizzle it over stuffed mushrooms. For best results, choose the tastiest mushrooms you can find—crimini work very well and shitake mushrooms have proven health benefits. If you like, warm the soup or gravy over low heat or a double boiler until it is warm (not hot) to the touch.

In a blender, combine the water and almond butter, and blend. Add the quartered mushrooms, liquid aminos and salt. Blend until smooth. Pour into individual bowls and top with the chopped mushrooms. Yields 1 cup.

Marvelous Mushroom Soup

Spinach-Avocado Soup 🌿

Soup • Dressing • Sauce • Dip

One serving of this bright, vibrant green soup contains three full cups of spinach. It's full of nourishment! The soup can handle a lot of herbs—so be creative. Give it a pesto flavor with generous amounts of basil or a Mediterranean flavor with garlic and oregano. Or substitute other greens for some or all of the spinach. Try wild greens, escarole, chard, kale or beet greens.

In a blender, combine the spinach and water; blend. Add the cucumber, avocado, liquid aminos, lemon juice, parsley, garlic, basil and scallion. Blend until smooth, diluting with water if necessary to achieve the desired consistency. Taste and adjust the seasonings. Serves 1.

For dressing: Add 1 tablespoon lemon juice, 2–3 tablespoons extra-virgin olive oil and spices to taste.
For dip: Thicken with additional avocado.

3 cups torn spinach
½ cup water
½ cup coarsely chopped (seeded) cucumber
½ avocado, cut in chunks
2 teaspoons liquid aminos
1 teaspoon lemon juice
2 tablespoons chopped parsley
1 small garlic clove, chopped
4 fresh basil leaves, torn
1 tablespoon chopped scallion

Avocado-Dill Soup 🌿

Soup • Dressing

This is a refreshing, cooling soup that is ideal on a hot summer's day. To thicken, add more avocado; to thin, increase the juice.

In a blender, combine the celery juice, cucumber, garlic, scallions, red pepper, dill, avocado, lemon juice and liquid aminos. Blend until smooth. Sweeten the soup with one teaspoon honey and blend in, if desired. Garnish with sprouts. Serves 1.

1 cup celery juice or cucumber juice
1 cucumber, peeled and chopped
1 small clove garlic, chopped
2 scallions, chopped
1 red pepper, chopped
1 tablespoon chopped fresh dill
1 avocado, cut in chunks
2 tablespoons lemon juice
½ teaspoon liquid aminos or pinch sea salt
Honey or maple syrup or stevia (optional)
Sprouts

Summer's Bounty Soup

Soup • Dressing

4 red peppers, juiced or
  puréed

1 medium cucumber,
  cut in chunks

1 scallion, chopped

1 clove garlic, chopped

3 tablespoons chopped fresh
  basil or other fresh herb

½ teaspoon dried oregano

Pinch sea salt

Dash lemon juice and liquid
  aminos and extra-virgin
  olive oil

½ cup chopped cucumber

1 chopped red pepper

8 medium mushrooms,
  thinly sliced

Filled with the flavors of summer, this attractive dish gives all the satisfaction of a savory Italian soup. If you're puréeing the peppers rather than juicing them, it's a good idea to strain them, although it takes a little extra time.

In a blender, combine the red pepper juice, cucumber, scallion, garlic, basil, oregano, salt, lemon juice, liquid aminos and oil. Blend quickly, leaving the soup chunky. Pour the soup into bowls and garnish with chopped cucumber, red pepper and sliced mushrooms. Serves 2–3.

For dressing: Omit the cucumber, red pepper and mushroom garnish.

Chilled Cucumber Soup

Soup • Dressing

1 large cucumber, peeled and
  cut in chunks

1 small clove garlic, chopped

¼ cup fresh mint or
  other fresh herb

3 tablespoons chopped onion

3 tablespoons lemon juice

½ teaspoon sea salt

This is a perfect hot weather soup—cool and refreshing. Once you liquefy the cucumber, add any fresh herbs or other vegetables you like. To thicken the soup, add avocado.

In a blender, combine the cucumber, garlic, mint, onion, lemon juice and salt. Blend until smooth. Taste and adjust the seasonings. Pour into a serving bowl. Chill before serving. Serves 1–2.

For dressing: Use as is, or substitute liquid aminos or tamari for the salt (start with one teaspoon), add ½ avocado, and use ¼ cup fresh basil in place of the mint.

Corn Chowder

When corn is in season, make up a large bowl of this delicious soup and watch it disappear! This recipe only takes a few minutes to prepare if you have the almond milk on hand. If you are not accustomed to eating raw food or if you have a delicate digestive system, take just a small serving—the soup contains a great deal of roughage.

In a blender, combine the corn, almond milk, avocado, cumin, minced onion and salt. Blend well. Pour the soup into serving bowls and garnish with a handful of corn kernels and some sunflower sprouts. Serves 4.

Variation: Replace the almond milk with grain milk.

4 cups fresh corn kernels (approximately 4 large ears)

2 cups almond milk (see recipe, page 28)

1 avocado, cut in chunks

1 teaspoon ground cumin

2 teaspoons finely minced onion

½ teaspoon sea salt

Corn kernels

Sunflower sprouts

Corn Chowder

Legume Controversy

Not all raw foodists think it's a good idea to eat raw peas and beans. Some people believe peas and beans should be cooked to destroy their natural toxins. For this reason and for palatability, you may want to consider blanching the sprouted peas in this recipe.

Sprouted Green Pea Soup
Soup • Purée • Sauce

6 tablespoons warm water

1 cup sprouted green peas, blanched (see note)

2 tablespoons chopped onion

½ teaspoon sea salt

1 tablespoon torn fresh basil or 2 tablespoons fresh mint

2 teaspoons diced red pepper (optional)

2 tablespoons grated cucumber (optional)

Fresh basil leaves and flowers (optional)

Clover sprouts (optional)

Dulse flakes (optional)

This is a fast, hearty soup that will retain most of the enzymes from sprouting. The trick to this soup is to work quickly. Since the peas will still be warm from blanching, you'll have a lovely thick, warm soup or a decorative purée. For a stunning culinary effect, swirl a dollop of it through one of the orange soups.

In a blender, combine the water, peas, onion, salt and basil. Blend until smooth. Pour into bowls. Garnish the soup with red pepper, cucumber, basil, clover sprouts or dulse flakes, as desired. Serves 1 as soup; 4 as dressing or purée.

Note: To blanch peas, place them in a 2-cup measure. Bring a pot of water to a boil, remove from heat and set aside for 1–2 minutes. Pour the hot water over the peas to cover. After 45–60 seconds, pour the water off.

Kohlrabi Soup
Soup • Purée • Sauce

1 kohlrabi globe, grated (approximately ¾ cup)

½ avocado, cut in chunks

1 teaspoon liquid aminos

1 tablespoon chopped parsley

Squeeze of lemon juice

3 tablespoons water (approximately)

A member of the turnip family, kohlrabi is sometimes called a cabbage turnip. It has a mild cabbage-like taste but is juicier. The purée will be white at first, but turns a rich, soft green with the parsley and avocado. If you enjoy a cabbage flavor, use this recipe as a soup base, a purée or a sauce. As a soup, serve it in individual bowls garnished with red pepper and sprouts or as a purée, use it to decorate plates. Challenge your friends to identify the ingredients in this soup—few will be able to!

In a blender, combine the grated kohlrabi with the avocado, liquid aminos, parsley, lemon juice and enough water to allow the blender to operate. Blend until the mixture is a thick purée. Serves 1.

Creamy Carrot-Asparagus Soup

Soup • Dressing • Sauce

This could be called the king of soups. The fiber in the asparagus creates a delightful texture and the tahini gives the soup a smooth quality. Do not use the woody ends of the asparagus; chop only the most tender part, about two inches from the end. (Vegetarian dogs are known to love the woody ends of the asparagus; they chew on them like a bone!)

In a blender, combine the carrot juice, asparagus, tahini, onion, liquid aminos and dulse flakes. Blend all the ingredients until smooth. Taste and adjust the seasonings. Yields approximately 1½ cups. Serves 1.

Variation: Heat the soup in the top of a double boiler or over very low heat until it is warm to the touch. For extra spice, stir in ½ teaspoon wasabi powder.

1 cup carrot juice

1 cup coarsely chopped asparagus, or more to taste

2 heaping tablespoons raw tahini or almond butter

1 teaspoon chopped onion, or more to taste

Liquid aminos, to taste

Dulse flakes, to taste

Basic French Dressing

Dressing • Marinade

Although you may think of French dressing as a sweet red dressing, in culinary circles, French dressing and vinaigrette are different words for the same thing. A variation of this recipe includes tasty bits of herbs and vegetables which add flavor and visual appeal.

In a small bowl, using a wire whisk or a fork, whisk together the lemon juice, oil and salt, until the salt dissolves. Add the liquid aminos, maple syrup and pepper. Yields ³/₄ cup.

Variation 1: Add 2 tablespoons each of minced parsley, red pepper, chives and shallots.
Variation 2: For a citrus-mushroom dressing, add 6 small, finely minced mushrooms, 2 tablespoons orange juice and 1 small clove garlic, pressed.
Variation 3: Substitute ground celery seed for the sea salt, and add 2 tablespoons chopped onion.

6 tablespoons lemon juice

6 tablespoons flaxseed oil or walnut oil

½ teaspoon sea salt

1 teaspoon liquid aminos

1 teaspoon maple syrup or equivalent stevia (optional)

Pinch pepper

Harvest Vegetable Soup

Soup • Dressing • Sauce

½ cup water
1 carrot, grated
1 stalk broccoli, stalk peeled
  and grated, florets chopped
1 small yam or
  sweet potato, grated
½ small onion, chopped
2 stalks celery,
  peeled and chopped
1 teaspoon liquid aminos
Sprouts
Dulse flakes

This nutritious and tasty orange soup contains antioxidants, chlorophyll and natural sodium. Dulse flakes add extra flavor and extra nutrition.

In a blender, combine the water and carrot; blend well. Add the broccoli; blend well. Add the yam; blend well. Add the onion, celery and liquid aminos. Blend until smooth. Serve in a bowl; top with sprouts and a sprinkle of dulse flakes. Serves 1.

For dressing: Add oil, spices and additional dulse to taste.

Harvest Vegetable Soup

Summer Tomato-Basil Soup 🌿

Soup • Dressing

Wait until summer when you can make this beautiful red soup from fresh, juicy, ripe organic tomatoes.

In a blender, combine the tomato purée, lemon, avocado, sprouts, basil, onion and garlic. Blend and pour into serving bowls. Top the soup with sprouts and basil flowers. Serves 2.

For dressing: Combine all the ingredients, including the onion and garlic. Add 1–3 tablespoons extra-virgin olive oil.

Note: To make the tomato purée: In a blender, break up the chopped tomatoes until you have a 3-cup yield. The tomato purée should be chunky not silky smooth.

3 cups tomato purée (6–8 medium tomatoes) (see note)
¼ lemon, peeled and seeded
1 avocado
Large handful of sunflower or buckwheat sprouts
2 tablespoons chopped fresh basil
1 tablespoon chopped onion (optional)
1 small clove garlic, chopped (optional)
Additional sprouts
Basil flowers

Bravo Brassica Soup 🌿

Soup • Dressing

The brassica, a genus of the mustard family, includes cabbage, kale, broccoli, cauliflower, radish, turnip and mustard. This soup works well with either broccoli or cauliflower.

See soaking instructions page 5. Blanch and peel the almonds, if desired (see page 5). In a blender, combine the almonds with the cucumber juice and garlic. Blend well. Gradually add the broccoli pieces and process until smooth. Add more water or juice if necessary to achieve desired consistency. Blend in the cumin, curry powder, lemon juice, liquid aminos and salt. Serves 2.

Variation: Replace the almonds with 1 avocado.

½ cup almonds, soaked 8–12 hours
1 cup cucumber juice or other light-colored juice
1 clove garlic, chopped
3–4 cups chopped broccoli or cauliflower (including stalks)
¼ teaspoon ground cumin
¼ teaspoon curry powder
1 tablespoon lemon juice
1 tablespoon liquid aminos
½ teaspoon sea salt

Winter Squash Soup 🌿

Soup • Dressing

1 tablespoon almond butter
4 tablespoons water
1 tablespoon liquid aminos
1 teaspoon flaxseed oil
½ cup grated zucchini
½ cup grated carrot
½ cup grated buttercup or other orange (winter) squash
½ scallion, chopped
1 tablespoon chopped cilantro
2 teaspoons sauerkraut (optional)
4–6 fresh basil leaves, chopped or other fresh herbs, to taste
Sprouts (optional)
Chopped vegetables (optional)
Chopped red pepper (optional)
Corn (optional)

Dark orange vegetables such as carrot and winter squash contain generous amounts of beta carotene and other carotenes, which are important antioxidants. If you're preparing this recipe for guests, top it with a dollop of Almond Whip (see page 123). Or, blend plain Almond Whip with lots of basil to make it a lovely green, then serve the soup with a dollop of white and a dollop of green. Pretty!

In a blender, combine the almond butter, water, liquid aminos, and oil; blend. Add the zucchini; blend. Gradually add the carrot and squash, blending until smooth. Add the scallion, cilantro, sauerkraut and basil and blend thoroughly. Let the soup sit for 10 minutes to allow the flavors to meld. Place a handful of sprouts and bits of chopped vegetables in a bowl and pour the soup on top. Garnish the soup with sprouts, chopped red pepper and corn. Serves 1.

For dressing: Omit the last 4 optional ingredients and increase the flaxseed oil to 1–2 tablespoons, if desired.

Fennel and Lemon Soup 🌿

Soup • Dressing • Purée

3 cups grated fennel
Water
1 teaspoon ground fennel seeds, or more to taste (see note)
1–2 tablespoons lemon juice
A few drops stevia

Fennel soup is a delightful and refreshing treat on a hot summer day. Serve as is, or with diced red pepper and sprouts. Drizzle the dressing or purée over vegetables or use it decoratively around the perimeter of a plate.

In a blender, combine the fennel with enough water to allow the machine to operate. Blend until smooth. Add the ground fennel seeds and lemon juice and blend until smooth. Add a few drops of stevia, to taste. Serves 2.

Note: To grind fennel seeds, place them in a clean electric coffee grinder and process them until powdered.

Premier French Dressing 🌿

The high percentage of polyunsaturates (Omega-3 fatty acids) in flaxseed oil enables it to bind well with liquids and emulsify for a thick, smooth dressing. This dressing will thin out if not served immediately, but it will taste just as good.

In a bowl, combine the oil, lemon juice, maple syrup and liquid aminos. Whisk with a fork or a wire whisk until the dressing becomes as thick as heavy syrup. Serves 1.

4 tablespoons flaxseed oil
2 tablespoons lemon juice
1 teaspoon maple syrup (optional)
1 teaspoon liquid aminos

Garlicky Marinade 🌿
Dressing • Marinade

This dressing is more acidic than the other French-style dressings and was designed primarily as a marinade. A quick fifteen to thirty minute soak in this marinade will give a "pickled" taste to most chopped vegetables.

In a small bowl, using a wire whisk or a fork, whisk together the lemon juice, oil and salt, until the salt is dissolved. Add the garlic, shallot, maple syrup, mustard, paprika, liquid aminos and pepper. Mix well. Yields ¾ cup.

6 tablespoons lemon juice
4 tablespoons flaxseed or walnut oil
1 teaspoon sea salt
2 cloves garlic, pressed
1 teaspoon minced shallot
1 tablespoon maple syrup or equivalent stevia
1 teaspoon dry mustard
1 teaspoon paprika
1 teaspoon liquid aminos
Pinch pepper

Wasabi Dressing 🌿
Dressing • Sauce • Dip

Wasabi is a hot horseradish root that grows in Japan. Its fiery horseradish-mustard taste lights up any dish. Wasabi can be purchased either as a green paste that comes in a little tube like toothpaste, or as a dry powder to which you add water. The powder is usually hotter.

If you like your food hot, hot, hot, the radish sprouts and wasabi in this recipe will set your mouth on fire. For a tamer version, use clover or alfalfa sprouts and a smaller amount of wasabi.

In a blender, combine the carrot juice, avocado, sprouts, tamari and wasabi. Blend thoroughly. Yields approximately 1½ cups.

1 cup carrot juice or carrot-celery juice
1 avocado, cut in chunks
½ cup radish or clover sprouts
2 teaspoons tamari
½ teaspoon wasabi powder, or more to taste

Zucchini with Pomodoro Sauce

Carrot-Avocado Soup ❧

Soup • Dressing

An old standby in raw cuisine, carrot soup is nourishing and easy to make. Even if you do not own a juicer, you can buy freshly made carrot juice at juice bars and at many health food stores.

In a blender, combine the carrot juice and avocado. Blend to desired consistency. Add the cumin, lemon juice, liquid aminos and garlic or shallot, if desired. Blend. Place a handful of sprouts and a selection of chopped vegetables in a bowl and pour the soup on top. Serves 1.

Variation 1: In place of, or in addition to the cumin, add 1 teaspoon grated ginger root.
Variation 2: Add ¼ cup torn-up dulse pieces, rinsed and ¼ cup clover, alfalfa or sunflower sprouts and blend.

1 cup carrot or mixed carrot and vegetable juice
½–1 avocado
Ground cumin, to taste
Lemon juice, to taste
Dash liquid aminos
Garlic or shallot, chopped (optional)
Sprouts
Chopped vegetables

Hearty Carrot Soup ❧

Soup • Dressing

Here is a richer and heartier version of carrot soup. Play with the herbs; perhaps a pinch of tarragon or mint would make your tastebuds happier!

See soaking instructions, page 5. In a blender, combine the almonds with the carrot and red pepper juices and blend until smooth. Add the garlic, ginger, parsley, liquid aminos and lemon juice. Blend until smooth. Put a handful of sprouts in two bowls and pour soup on top of each. Garnish with corn and additional alfalfa sprouts. Serves 2.

½ cup almonds, soaked 8–12 hours
1½ cups carrot juice
1 small red pepper, juiced
1 small clove garlic, chopped
½-inch (1 cm) piece ginger root (optional)
1 tablespoon chopped parsley or cilantro or other fresh herb
1 teaspoon liquid aminos
1 tablespoon lemon juice
Sprouts
Handful of corn kernels

Pomodoro ❧

Sauce

Serve pomodoro and pesto over slivered zucchini for a memorable summertime combination. For an intense basil flavor, place basil strips in the colander with the tomatoes. Or, add the basil just before serving for a less intense flavor.

In a colander, put the tomatoes and slivered basil. Drain for 2–3 hours. Place the mixture on a plate and toss with the salt and additional basil. Serves 2–3.

4–6 tomatoes, seeded and diced
¼ cup fresh basil, slivered
Pinch sea salt
Additional fresh basil, to taste

The Beet
Generation Borscht
Dressing • Soup • Sauce

1 red pepper, cut in chunks
½ lemon, peeled,
  seeded and chopped
1 tablespoon liquid aminos
1 cup grated beets
⅓ cup raw tahini
1 teaspoon paprika
Water

This earthy-tasting and thick, pink dressing will liven up any salad. To serve as borscht (beet soup), thin the dressing with beet juice or celery juice.

In a blender, combine the red pepper, lemon and liquid aminos; blend until smooth. Add the beets; blend. Add the tahini, paprika and enough water to achieve desired consistency. Yields approximately 1½ cups.

The Beet Generation Borscht

Fruity Dressing ❦

Dressing • Marinade • Sauce

This dressing is delicious served over chopped apples and currents. For proper food combining, serve this dressing with fruit.

In a bowl, combine the lemon juice, orange juice, mint, cumin and cayenne. Mix well. (The ingredients may also be placed in a jar with a lid and shaken until well blended.) Yields ½ cup.

¼ cup lemon juice
¼ cup orange juice
2 teaspoons chopped fresh mint
¾ teaspoon cumin
Dash cayenne

Orange-Tahini Dressing ❦

This delightful, light dressing only takes a few minutes to make. Its simplicity invites variation. Try adding 1–2 teaspoons tamari, or 2 teaspoons poppy seeds and ¼ teaspoon Chinese 5-spice powder.

Place the tahini in a small bowl. Using a spoon, gradually mix the orange juice into the tahini. Add the dulse, ginger, cinnamon, curry and salt. Yields approximately ½ cup.

2 tablespoons raw tahini
½ cup fresh orange juice
1 teaspoon dulse flakes
1 teaspoon grated ginger root
¼ teaspoon cinnamon
⅛ teaspoon curry powder
Pinch sea salt

Orange Sunset Dressing ❦

This is an unusual dressing because two whole lemons and two slices of onion are juiced along with the peppers or tomatoes. This results in a smooth, complex-flavored dressing. The oils in lemon rind are edible so for an intense lemon taste, add a quarter of the lemon rind to the juicer when you juice the lemons.

Place the tahini in a medium-sized bowl. Using a spoon, gradually mix the juice into the tahini, stirring until smooth. Stir in the salt and 5-spice powder. Yields approximately 2–3 cups.

¼ cup raw tahini
6 red peppers or 6 tomatoes, juiced
2 whole peeled lemons, juiced
2 slices sweet onion, juiced
¼ teaspoon sea salt
¼ teaspoon Chinese 5-spice powder

Sofrito 🌿
Soup • Dressing • Sauce

2 cups crushed, seeded
   tomatoes (see note)
1 clove garlic, chopped
2 tablespoons
   chopped onion
2 tablespoons
   chopped parsley
½ teaspoon ground cumin
Pepper to taste
1–2 teaspoons extra-virgin
   olive oil (optional)

Sofrito is a highly flavored vegetable base used in Hispanic soups and stews. This is an adaptation of a cooked recipe. Feel free to adjust the seasonings to suit your taste, adding basil and oregano for an Italian flavor; cayenne or hot sauce and cilantro for a Mexican one.

In a blender or food processor, combine the tomatoes, garlic, onion, parsley, cumin, pepper and oil. Blend briefly to combine the ingredients, leaving the soup chunky. Serves 1–2.

Note: You will need roughly 5 medium-sized fresh tomatoes. To seed them quickly and easily, cut them in half and scoop the seeds out with a teaspoon. It is not necessary to remove every last seed. To crush the tomatoes, place them in blender or food processor and pulse briefly.

Corny Cabbage Soup 🌿
Soup • Dressing

2 cups carrot juice
1½ cups fresh corn
1 cup chopped cabbage
2 tablespoons chopped onion
¼ cup torn-up dulse pieces,
   washed and lightly rinsed
1 teaspoon miso or
   2 teaspoons liquid aminos
1 cup sunflower or
   buckwheat sprouts
Cabbage and onion and corn

This rich, highly nutritious red soup tastes like a variation of corn chowder. Any kind of cabbage is good, but green cabbage is best. Because it comes from the sea, dulse sometimes contains tiny sea shells and bits of salt. Once you've torn and measured the dulse, wash it gently in cool water to rinse away these little ocean reminders.

In a blender, combine the carrot juice and corn; blend well. Add the cabbage; blend well. Add the onion, dulse and miso and blend until smooth. Place the sprouts in serving bowls; pour soup on top. Top with additional chopped cabbage, chopped onion and corn to taste. Serves 2–3.

Zippy Red Pepper-Ginger Dressing 🌿

Red pepper juice gives this dressing a lovely red color and a light, sweet flavor. If you are pressed for time, toss the peppers into the blender without juicing them. Chop them and put them into the blender a few pieces at a time, until the blades "catch" and liquefy them. This will result in a thicker dressing that contains bits of pepper skin, but it will cut your preparation time in half. Vary this recipe with a half cup carrot juice in place of the pepper juice.

In a blender, combine the red pepper juice, parsley, ginger and lemon juice. Blend well. To thin the dressing, add water. To thicken it, add ground flax seeds. Yields approximately ¾–1 cup.

Note: To grind flax seeds, place them in a clean electric coffee grinder and process them until powdered.

2 red peppers, juiced
¼ cup chopped parsley
1-inch (2.5 cm) piece ginger root, grated
2 teaspoons lemon juice
1–2 teaspoons ground flax seeds (optional) (see note)
Water (optional)

Fresh Pineapple-Ginger Dressing 🌿

Dressing • Marinade

Pour the dressing over fruit. To use as a marinade, soak fruit in the dressing for 15–30 minutes.

In a jar with a lid, combine the pineapple juice, ginger juice and sesame oil. Shake well. Yields 1 cup.

1 cup fresh pineapple juice
1 teaspoon fresh ginger juice
1 tablespoon sesame oil

Gomasio 🌿

When our macrobiotic friends make this recipe, they toast the seeds and the ground salt. Instead, we grind the sesame seeds and salt together, and keep them both raw. You can refrigerate or freeze any leftovers.

Traditionally, a mortar and pestle-like piece of equipment called a suribachi is used to make gomasio. First the salt is ground to a powder. Then the sesame seeds are added and ground until they crumble. This technique coats the salt with sesame oil for a distinct taste. If you do not have a suribachi or a mortar and pestle, make gomasio in an electric coffee grinder or a small food processor.

In a clean electric coffee grinder, grind the sea salt and sesame seeds together. Store the gomasio in a tightly covered container in the refrigerator for a month or more.

1 part sea salt
4 or 5 parts raw sesame seeds

Herb Vinaigrette

Party size

3 cups water

1½ cup lemon juice

1 cup liquid aminos

**¾ cup walnut,
    pumpkin seed, flax or
    extra-virgin olive oil**

1 cup chopped red onion

10 cloves garlic, chopped

½–¾ cup herbs

¼ cup chopped parsley

**2–3 teaspoons grated
    ginger root**

2 teaspoons cumin

1 teaspoon cayenne

Water

Family size

1 cup water

½ cup lemon juice

⅓ cup liquid aminos

**¼ cup walnut, pumpkin or
    extra-virgin olive oil**

⅓ cup red onion

3 cloves garlic, chopped

1¼ cup herbs

1 tablespoon parsley

**1 teaspoon grated
    ginger root**

½ teaspoon ground cumin

Pinch cayenne

Water

This recipe makes a large quantity for a party or to store in the refrigerator, where it will keep for up to a week. The flavor of this vinaigrette is dictated by your choice of herbs. Dill, cilantro or basil are all good choices.

For a thicker dressing add ½–1 avocado to the family-size dressing and 2–3 avocados to the party size. If you add the avocado, use the dressing within 24 hours.

In a blender, combine the water with the lemon juice, liquid aminos, oil, onion and garlic. Blend well. Add the herbs, parsley, ginger, cumin and cayenne. Blend until smooth, adding enough additional water to achieve desired consistency. The party size yields approximately 9 cups; the family size, 3 cups.

Oils and Raw Food

Great dressings depend on using the finest ingredients. Use only unrefined, cold-pressed nut and seed oils, not just because they taste wonderful and carry the flavor of food, but also because the body needs the essential fatty acids they contain. Eating only refined oils, which lack these essential fatty acids, will lead to nutritional deficiencies. In fact, all refined (heat-treated) oils are harmful to the body. The refining process creates trans-fatty acids which are the catalysts for all fat-related degenerative diseases.

The essential fatty acids Omega-3 and Omega-6, found in the highest concentration in flaxseed oil, are transformed by the body to hormone-like substances called prostaglandins. These fatty acids do not produce energy (calories) or store fat in the body like saturated fat, instead they have been shown to protect against heart disease, high blood pressure, arteriosclerosis, stroke and blood clots; increase the body's resistance to cancer tumors; provide relief from arthritis, asthma, pre-menstrual syndrome, allergies, skin conditions; and improve brain functioning, immunity and some behavior disorders.

Fats and oils, including nuts and seeds, also satisfy the appetite quickly and actually help to prevent overeating because it takes the body nine times longer to use up the calories from fat than it does from complex carbohydrates.

Use a tasty unrefined nut or seed oil on your salad, or grind the

Dressing Del Mar

Dressing • Sauce • Gravy

Eat some seaweed each day. Dulse is a source of protein, iron, chlorophyll, enzymes, vitamin A and the B vitamins. Kelp (or kombu) is known for its iodine, B vitamins and enzymes. They are both high in fiber, and contain important minerals from the sea.

When your meals do not include recipes that contain seaweed, sprinkle your food with dulse, kelp or other seaweed granules or flakes. If someone you know is trying to cut back on salt, give them a container of dulse granules—not only will it impart a naturally salty taste, but it will sneak some excellent nourishment into them as well!

In a blender, combine the red pepper, lemon, water, oil, dulse, garlic and kelp. Blend until smooth. Yields 1 cup.

1 red pepper, cut in chunks

1 lemon, peeled, seeded and chopped

½ cup water

¼ cup extra-virgin olive oil or flaxseed oil or walnut oil

3 tablespoons dulse flakes

1 clove garlic, chopped

1 piece of kelp (1 x 5 inches) (2.5 x 12.5 cm), rinsed and chopped

nuts and seeds into a powder and sprinkle it immediately over your salad for a tasty and nutritious meal that supplies 'good' fats. (Soaked and dehydrated nuts and seeds can be used.) Fats carry fat-soluble vitamins such as vitamins A, D and E. Serve oil with your vegetables to help make the vitamins and beta carotenes more bio-available to the body.

Hemp oil is now appearing in stores. This easily metabolized oil is a very balanced mix of all the essential fatty acids, unsaturated, mono-unsaturated and saturated fats. Hemp oil has a strong taste so mix it with flaxseed oil and extra-virgin olive oil for use on salads and vegetables.

Finally, avocados are another excellent source of 'good' fats. Although they do not provide essential fatty acids, avocados are full of vitamins and minerals and quickly satisfy the appetite.

Use a variety of healthy fats including unrefined, cold-pressed nut and seed oils, and fat-rich foods such as nuts, seeds and avocados to create great tasting, satisfying and nutritious meals.

Jeanne's Berry Dressing

Dressing • Sauce

4 strawberries, hulled
8–10 raspberries
2 teaspoons honey or
　1 tablespoon maple syrup
1 tablespoon extra-virgin
　olive oil or flaxseed oil
1 tablespoon lemon juice
1 teaspoon lemon zest
1 fresh basil leaf, chopped
Sea salt and pepper, to taste

This dressing is delicious when poured over a salad of endive, basil strips and strawberries. For proper food combining, serve this dressing with fruit.

In a blender, combine the strawberries, raspberries, honey, oil, lemon juice, lemon zest, basil, salt and pepper. Purée. Serves 1–2.

Lemon-Tamari Dressing

Dressing • Marinade • Sauce

2 tablespoons lemon juice
2 tablespoons tamari
½ teaspoon maple syrup or
　equivalent stevia, to taste
½ teaspoon grated ginger
　root
½–1 teaspoon sesame oil

This quick and simple dressing imparts a Chinese flavor to any salad or vegetable and can be made in just a few minutes.

In a small bowl, combine the lemon juice, tamari, maple syrup, ginger and oil. Mix well and serve. Serves 1.

Asian Sauce

Sauce • Marinade

4 tablespoons liquid aminos
　or tamari
1 tablespoon grated ginger
　root
1 tablespoon honey
Pinch cayenne
Pinch ground cumin
Pinch Chinese 5-spice powder

Use this sauce as a marinade for Chinese pea pods, sugar-snap peas, broccoli or any vegetable you want to give a Chinese flavor. This sauce will last several weeks in the refrigerator.

In a small bowl, combine the liquid aminos, ginger, honey, cayenne, cumin and 5-spice powder. Blend thoroughly. Yields 5 tablespoons.

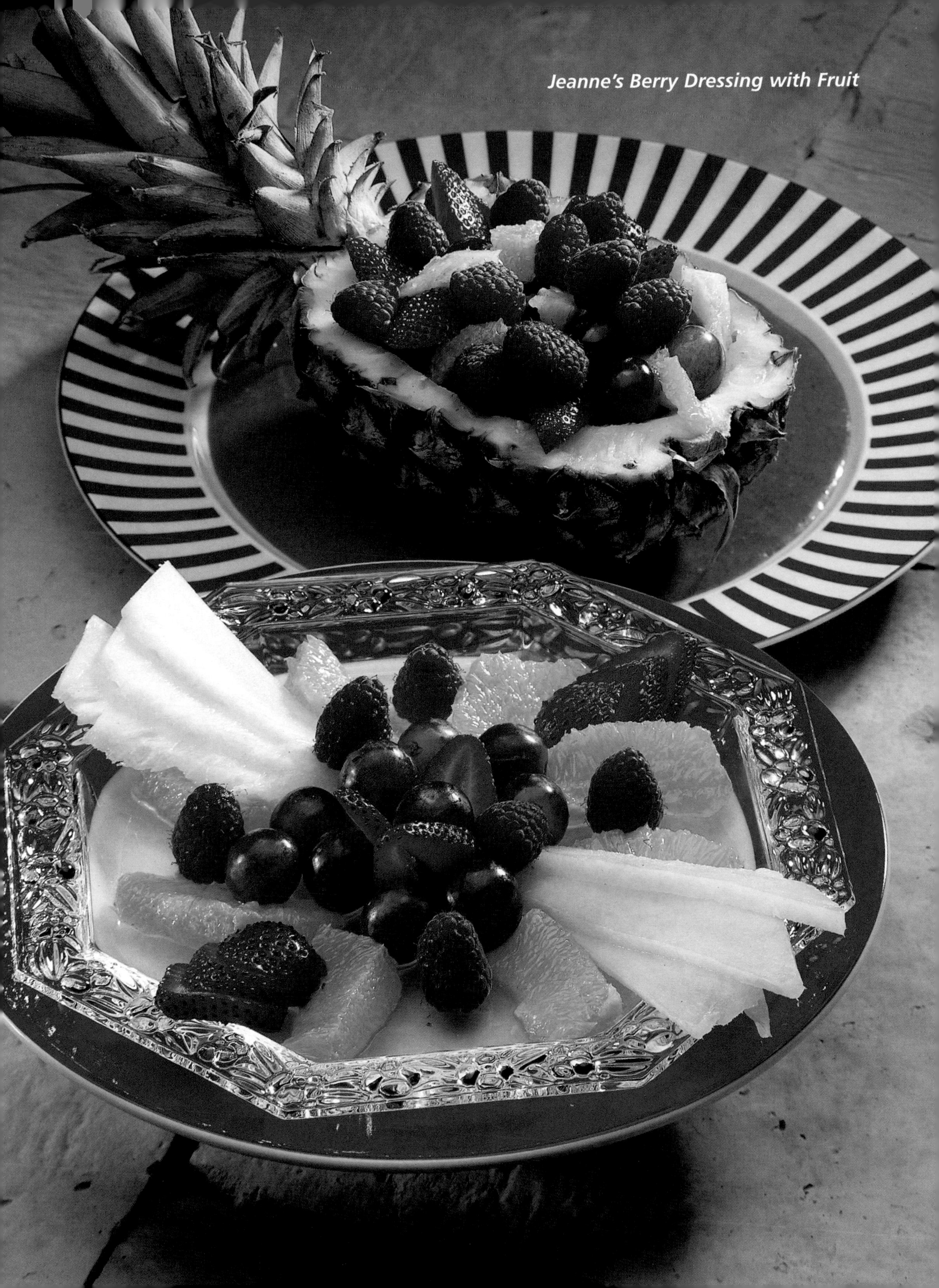

Jeanne's Berry Dressing with Fruit

Flax Seed Dressing

Dressing • Sauce

**2 tablespoons flax seeds,
  soaked 8–10 hours
  (see note)**

**1 cup carrot juice or mixed
  vegetable juice**

1 red pepper, cut in chunks

Dash cayenne

Dash liquid aminos

Flax seed is rich in lignan, a substance also found in whole grains to a much lesser degree. In fact, flax seed contains one hundred times more lignan than whole grains do. Researchers believe that lignan's anti-estrogen activity blocks the formation of colon and breast cancer.

Flax is also an excellent vegetarian source of Omega-3, an essential fatty acid that helps prevent heart disease. Flax contains a much higher amount of Omega-3 than fish oil. Flax seeds and flaxseed oil are both good sources of lignan and Omega-3.

Whole flax seeds are a good staple to have on hand. Ground in a coffee grinder or spice mill, they will thicken almost any food without altering its flavor, and the flaxseed meal is a nutty tasting and healthful addition sprinkled on salad. Grind only what you will be using, as flaxseed meal has a short shelf-life. On the other hand, whole flax seeds are protected by their hard outer shell and can be stored in a pantry.

Whole flax seeds, when eaten unchewed, will absorb up to thirty times their weight in water and become an excellent laxative. At some health institutes, flax seeds are often soaked in water overnight then drunk in the morning. To obtain the nutritional benefits of flax seeds, they must be ground.

The following recipe takes advantage of the nutritional benefits of flax seeds to yield a thick red dressing.

In a blender, combine the seeds and their soak water, carrot juice, red pepper, cayenne and liquid aminos. Blend until smooth. Refrigerate to let the flavors meld. Shake thoroughly before using. Use within 24 hours. If desired, add addional spices and herbs of your choice. Yields 1½–1¾ cups.

Note: To soak flax seeds, place them in a small jar or container and cover with ½ cup water. Leave them to soak in the refrigerator, covered or uncovered, for 8–10 hours. Do not pour off the water.

A Collection of Toppings

This is a collection of highly flavorful toppings; some come from around the world while others were specially developed to augment the flavor of raw-food recipes. If you used to love adding Parmesan cheese to your Italian dishes and salads, these recipes will have a special appeal for you. Experiment and create your own special tastes.

Gremolata

An Italian garnish. Use this tasty mixture to brighten up any dish.

In a small bowl, combine the parsley, zest and garlic. Mix well, pressing the mixture with the back of a spoon to release the oils from the zest. Sprinkle it over food just before serving. Or place it on the table in a small serving dish with a tiny spoon. The gremolata will keep in a tightly covered container in the refrigerator for several weeks.

¼ cup minced parsley

1 teaspoon grated lemon zest or orange zest or a combination

1 clove garlic, minced

Szechuan Zip

Szechuan peppercorns are not part of the pepper family. They have a distinctive, somewhat lemony, mildly hot flavor and can be found in Asian markets. Use this mixture to perk up salads or dressings with an Asian flair.

Using a suribachi, mortar and pestle, electric coffee grinder or a small food processor, grind the peppercorns until they are uniformly fine. Add the salt and grind until thoroughly mixed. This topping will keep indefinitely in the refrigerator, although it's best to make it in small batches to maintain the fresh pepper taste.

2 tablespoons Szechuan peppercorns

2 tablespoons sea salt

Flax Seed Topping

A salty topping that clings to the food because of the oil in the seeds.

Using a suribachi, mortar and pestle, electric coffee grinder or a small food processor, grind the salt until it is fine. Add the flax seeds and continue grinding until a uniform powder is formed. Store the topping in a tightly covered container in the refrigerator for 1–2 weeks.

½ teaspoon sea salt

¼ cup flax seeds

Asian Dressing ❦

Party Size

6 tablespoons raw tahini

1 cup water, or more to taste

¾ cup liquid aminos or tamari

¾ cup minced scallions

3 tablespoons flaxseed oil

3 tablespoons sesame oil

3–4 tablespoons honey

3 tablespoons grated ginger root

2–3 cloves garlic, pressed

¾ teaspoon Chinese 5-spice powder

½ teaspoon cayenne

½ teaspoon ground cumin

Family Size

2 tablespoons raw tahini

5 tablespoons water, or more to taste

4 tablespoons liquid aminos or tamari

¼ cup minced scallions

1 tablespoon flaxseed oil

1 tablespoon sesame oil

1 tablespoon honey

1 tablespoon grated ginger root

1 clove garlic, pressed

¼ teaspoon Chinese 5-spice powder

Pinch cayenne

Pinch ground cumin

5 tablespoons water, or to taste

This very popular dressing is delicious with Confetti Salad (see recipe, page 76) or any salad you want to have an Asian flavor. Since it keeps for several weeks in the refrigerator, make the party size recipe so that you always have some on hand. For the Party Size, make this dressing in a blender.

Heated, refined oils are not recommended for health reasons. However, if you are not following the Optimum Choice Raw recipes, toasted sesame oil in place of half to all of the unrefined sesame oil does enhance the flavor of Asian dressing.

Place the tahini in a large jar with a lid. Add the water gradually, stirring until the mixture is smooth. Add the liquid aminos, scallions, oils, honey, ginger, garlic, 5-spice powder, cayenne and cumin. Put the lid on the jar and shake until ingredients are blended. Taste; add additional water, if desired. Party size yields approximately 3½ cups; family size, 1 cup.

Peanut Information

Gado-Gado is an Indonesian dish traditionally made with peanuts. This raw-food adaptation uses almonds instead. A fungus called aflatoxin naturally occurs in the peanut crop and although the crops are inspected for it, a certain percentage is "allowed." Since aflatoxin is a proven carcinogen, it's a good idea to avoid peanuts. Also, peanut butter isn't made from raw peanuts; it is always produced from the roasted nut.

Gado-Gado 🌿

Dressing · Soup · Sauce · Gravy

Gado-Gado is a highly flavorful sauce that is wonderful slightly warmed and drizzled over almost any vegetable. Use the warm-to-your-finger-test: if you can't leave your finger in the sauce indefinitely, it's too hot and you are losing enzymes. Add dates if you want to sweeten your dressing (unless you are following Optimum Choice Raw recipes). Served as a soup, Gado-Gado is a rich, high-protein, high-fat meal. Serve it with something light such as a green salad tossed with lemon juice.

In a blender, combine the water, almond butter, lemon juice, tamari and honey. Blend well. Add the onion, garlic, ginger, oil, cayenne, and dates. Blend well, adding additional water if required to achieve the consistency of a smooth, thick soup. Taste and adjust the seasonings. Yields 2½ cups.

½ cup water
1 cup almond butter
Juice of 1 lemon
1 tablespoon tamari
1 tablespoon honey
2–4 tablespoons coarsely chopped onion
2 cloves garlic, chopped
1 tablespoon grated ginger root
1 tablespoon sesame oil
½–1 teaspoon cayenne pepper
2 dates (optional)

Indonesian Yum-Yum Dressing 🌿

Gravy · Dressing

This exotic salad dressing is also terrific on raw grated yam or grated yam that's been steamed for thirty seconds. (Although this is not an example of good food combining.) Eliminate the raisins if you are using only the Optimum Choice Raw recipes.

In a blender, combine the water, almond butter, raisins, liquid aminos, 5-spice powder, garlic and flax seeds. Blend well. Refrigerate. Yields ¾ cup.

Notes: To soak raisins, place in small jar or container with enough water to cover; soak for 20–30 minutes. To grind flax seeds, place in a clean electric coffee grinder and grind until powdered.

Variation: To make a sesame-coconut dressing: replace the almond butter with tahini; add 2 tablespoons coconut; and add an additional teaspoon raisins, ½ teaspoon Chinese 5-spice powder and small clove garlic.

½ cup water
3 tablespoons raw almond butter
2 teaspoons raisins (optional), soaked 20 minutes (see note)
1 teaspoon liquid aminos
½ teaspoon Chinese 5-spice powder
1 clove garlic, chopped
1 teaspoon ground flax seeds (see note)

Notmayo!

Dressing • Sauce • Spread • Dip

1 cup cashews, soaked 8–12 hours

⅓ cup water

1 lemon, peeled, seeded and chopped

3 tablespoons chopped onion

3 tablespoons chopped red pepper

1 clove garlic

1 tablespoon flaxseed oil or hazelnut oil

1 tablespoon fresh oregano or 1 teaspoon dried

2 teaspoons dulse flakes

2 teaspoons liquid aminos

½ teaspoon paprika

Pinch ground cumin

Pinch curry

This versatile recipe has endless variations, and it keeps well for several days. Use Notmayo! as a dip, a spread or a salad dressing. Thin it with a little bit of hot water to make a sauce that is wonderful over any of the pâté or loaf recipes. Or use Notmayo! to hold together your entrée pie crusts. Keep this dressing on hand to enhance your salads and to bind together leftovers for quick meals. Add additional seasoning to taste, or light this Notmayo! on fire with 1–2 tablespoons freshly grated horseradish.

Notmayo! is an excellent substitute for that cholesterol-laden, fat-sodden, raw-egg-based, vinegar- and sugar-filled other stuff.

For a healthier version, substitute almonds for the cashews. When using almonds, you will obtain a smoother Notmayo! if you blanch and peel them first.

See soaking instructions, page 5. In a blender, combine the cashews with water and blend until very smooth. Add lemon, onion, red pepper, garlic, oil, oregano, dulse, liquid aminos, paprika, cumin and curry. Blend, using additional water if necessary to achieve desired consistency. Yields about 1½ cups dressing.

Variation: Replace the water with up to 1 cup celery juice or any mixed vegetable juice, and add 3 tablespoons dehydrated mixed vegetables. If dehydrated vegetables are not available, use 2 tablespoons psyllium or ground flax seed to thicken the dressing.

Cashew Information

Cashews are a fascinating crop. They are grown in Viet Nam, India, Africa, Brazil and other tropical climates, and are members of the same botanical family as mangos, pistachios, poison ivy, poison oak and poison sumac! The cashew nut is completely encased by a fruit that is so toxic to the skin that touching it raises blisters. Traditionally, the just-picked cashew fruit was boiled in oil. Now, they are either soaked in water, then lightly roasted over a fire to release the acrid chemicals, or the whole fruit is quickly dipped into boiling oil, then removed and the nut extracted. These methods may be performed quickly enough that the heat does not go all the way through the fruit to the nut, but it is difficult to know for sure. Therefore, cashews are not considered to be truly raw. For this reason, they are not the best choice for a raw-food diet.

Cashews are included in this book because you can create delicious recipes with them. No other nut breaks down into such smooth sauces and dressings. But, cashews are meant only for occasional use, not as an everyday staple. If you are being strict in your food choices or are seriously ill and in the cleanse phase, do not use any cashews in your diet.

Try to use organically grown cashews. (See sources, page 207.) The rainforest preservation movement in Brazil has started to develop an organic cashew crop. Once the nuts are placed in tightly sealed tins, they are protected from any spraying at port of entry.

Sunflower Notmayo! ❦

Dressing • Sauce • Dip
Gravy • Spread

The delicous taste of pine nuts comes through in this lemony blend. If you prefer a more subtle pine nut taste or a less expensive recipe, increase the amount of sunflower seeds and decrease the amount of pine nuts, keeping the total amount of seeds and nuts the same.

In a blender, combine the water with the sunflower seeds, pine nuts, onions, scallions, lemon, liquid aminos, garlic, parsley, dulse, salt and cayenne. Blend until smooth. Add a bit more water if necessary to achieve the desired consistency. Yields approximately 2 cups.

Note: To grind sunflower seeds and pine nuts, place them in a clean electric coffee grinder and grind until powdered.

6 tablespoons sunflower seeds, ground (see note)
4 tablespoons pine nuts, ground (see note)
¾ cup water or any vegetable juice
2 tablespoons chopped onions
2 tablespoons chopped scallions
1 lemon, peeled, seeded and chopped
2 teaspoons liquid aminos
1 small clove garlic, minced
2 tablespoons chopped parsley
2 teaspoons dulse flakes
Pinch salt
Pinch cayenne

Vegan Aioli ❦

Spread • Sauce • Dip

This spread has a butter-like consistency and a very potent garlic taste—a little goes a long way. Spread some aioli on a nori sheet, add vegetables and roll up. Put a dab on dehydrated crackers. Toss in slivered vegetables and then add Pomodoro (see page 105). Serve as a condiment at the table. Aioli keeps well for several weeks tightly sealed in the refrigerator.

In a blender, combine the oil, garlic, pine nuts, and liquid aminos; blend for 1–2 minutes. Allow the flavors to develop for at least one hour before serving. Thin with water if desired. Yields approximately ⅓ cup.

Note: To grind pine nuts, place them in a clean electric coffee grinder and grind until powdered.

¼ cup extra-virgin olive oil
4 garlic cloves, chopped
3 tablespoons pine nuts, ground (see note)
1 teaspoon liquid aminos
Water (optional)

Hot Mustard Sauce

Sauce • Dip

1 teaspoon mustard seed
3 teaspoons water

Similar to the mustard sauce served in Chinese restaurants, this very hot dip is not for the fainthearted. It's good as an accompaniment to Sunny Roll-Ups (see page 156) or served with Asian Pâté (see page 139). If the sauce is too fiery for you, tame it with a half teaspoon of honey, blended well.

Place whole mustard seeds in a clean electric coffee grinder and grind until powdered. Put in a small dish. Gradually mix in water to achieve the desired consistency.

Summer Tomato-Basil Soup

Ginger-Lime Dressing

Dressing • Marinade • Sauce

This intensely flavored dressing also makes a great marinade. It's delicious over fruit, avocado or greens and is a good accompaniment to any meal with an Asian theme. Remember, it is always best to use fresh herbs in your recipes.

In a blender, combine the lime juice, oil, water, tamari, mint, cilantro, ginger, chili pepper, maple sprinkles, salt and pepper. Blend well. Yields approximately 1 cup.

¼ **cup lime juice**
¼ **cup sesame oil**
¼ **cup water**
2 **tablespoons tamari**
1 **tablespoon fresh mint**
1 **tablespoon fresh cilantro**
1 **teaspoon minced ginger root**
¼ **teaspoon dried red chili pepper, or to taste**
2 **teaspoons maple sprinkles or date sugar or equivalent stevia, or to taste**
1 **teaspoon sea salt**
Dash pepper

LJ's Carrot-Ginger Dressing

A zesty, refreshing and fruity Asian-style dressing that is equally good over plain greens or with a complex salad mix. Miso, popular in Japan, is made from fermented soybeans, whole grain and sea salt. Traditional miso is unpasteurized, and because it's naturally aged, it contains enzymes.

In a blender, combine the carrot juice, oil, miso, lemon and orange juices, ginger, honey, lemon and orange zests, tamari and pepper. Blend until smooth. Yields approximately 1 cup.

½ **cup carrot juice**
4 **tablespoons sesame oil**
3 **tablespoons white or yellow miso**
2 **teaspoons lemon juice**
2 **teaspoons orange juice**
1 **tablespoon grated ginger root**
1 **teaspoon honey**
½ **teaspoon lemon zest**
½ **teaspoon orange zest**
½ **teaspoon tamari**
Dash pepper

Tomatillo Sauce 🌿

1 cup finely diced tomatillos
   (3 or 4 tomatillos)
⅓ cup chopped cilantro
¼ cup minced onion
2 teaspoons fresh herbs such
   as oregano, basil, thyme
Liquid aminos, to taste
Cayenne, to taste
Maple syrup or stevia
   (optional)

Tomatillos are small, green, tomato-like vegetables with a dry outer skin or husk. This sauce is a tart, refreshing accompaniment to Mexican food. For a really simple sauce, just use one cup diced tomatillos, water to thin and a pinch of sweetener.

In a small bowl, combine the tomatillos, cilantro, onion, herbs, liquid aminos and cayenne. If the sauce is too tart, add maple syrup or stevia, to taste. Yields approximately 1½ cups.

Miso Mayo 🌿
Dressing • Sauce • Spread

3 tablespoons extra-virgin
   olive oil
3 tablespoons flaxseed oil
2 tablespoons lemon juice
2 tablespoons white or
   yellow miso
1 small garlic clove, pressed
½ teaspoon grated ginger
   root
½ teaspoon liquid aminos
¼ cup water (optional)

This recipe can be made thick like mayonnaise, or thinned with water and used as a dressing.

In a blender, combine the oils, lemon juice, miso, garlic, ginger and liquid aminos. Blend thoroughly. If necessary, add water to thin to the desired consistency. Yields approximately ¾ cup.

Basil-Garlic Dream
Dressing • Sauce • Dip

½ cup cashews,
   soaked 8–12 hours
½ cup water
⅓ cup chopped fresh basil
1 clove garlic, chopped
¼ lemon, peeled, seeded and
   chopped
1 teaspoon dried oregano
Pinch sea salt
Dash liquid aminos
Dash cayenne

To make this recipe thinner, add more water. To use it as a dip, reduce the amount of water. If you need to make it thicker, grind one tablespoon cashews or pine nuts in an electric coffee grinder and blend it all together. Use more basil, garlic or lemon to suit your own taste.

See soaking instructions, page 5. In a blender, combine the cashews with water and blend until smooth. Add the basil, garlic, lemon, oregano, salt, liquid aminos and cayenne. Blend, adding more water if necessary to achieve the desired consistency. Yields 1 cup.

Almond-Curry Dip

Dressing • Dip

Curry powder is a combination of spices. Different areas in India are noted for their unique curries and many cooks keep their beloved curry recipes a closely held secret to be passed from generation to generation. To vary the flavor of this recipe, use different juices, spices or herbs, or add some onion, or a half cup of chopped greens. To use this recipe as a dip, add enough almonds to achieve a thick consistency.

See soaking instructions, page 5. In a blender, combine the carrot juice, almonds, curry powder, liquid aminos and lemon juice. Blend thoroughly. Serves 4.

½ cup almonds, soaked 8–12 hours
1 cup carrot juice
1 teaspoon curry powder, or more to taste
Dash liquid aminos
Dash lemon juice

Almond or Cashew Whip ❦

Dressing • Sauce • Dip

Use this recipe instead of mayonnaise or as a base for creating a wide variety of tasty and colorful dressings. Make it green by adding herbs like parsley or basil, or yellow by mixing in turmeric, saffron or curry powder. Almond Whip is an Optimum Choice Raw recipe; Cashew Whip is not.

See soaking instructions, page 5. In a blender, place the nuts and enough water to allow the blender to operate. Blend, gradually adding enough water to achieve a smooth consistency. Yields 1½–1¾ cups.

Note: A smoother consistency can be obtained by peeling the almonds.

1 cup almonds or cashews, soaked 8–12 hours
¾ cup water

Red Salsa-Avocado Sauce ❦

Dip • Dressing • Sauce

This is a great-looking and tasting dip that's delicious with rounds of zucchini or celery pieces. Serve with Mexican-style food. If you like your food hot, replace the red pepper with a jalapeno or another hot pepper.

In a blender, combine the red pepper juice and garlic. Blend well; pour the mixture into a small bowl. Add the avocados, red pepper, onion, cilantro and lemon juice. Yields approximately 2½ cups.

2 red peppers, juiced
2 cloves garlic, chopped
2 avocados, cut in chunks
1 red pepper, finely chopped
4 tablespoons minced red onion
4 tablespoons finely chopped cilantro, or more to taste
Juice of 1 lemon

Natural Nut Dressing

Dressing • Gravy • Dip • Spread

1 cup water

½ cup sunflower seeds,
soaked 8–12 hours

¼ cup almonds,
soaked 8–12 hours

1 small clove garlic, chopped

1 tablespoon liquid aminos

1 teaspoon dried oregano

2 tablespoons fresh herbs
such as dill, basil or
tarragon (optional)

For optimum food combining, this high-protein dressing is best served with watery vegetables such as sprouted and leafy greens, cabbage, spinach, celery, zucchini, cucumber, summer squash and peppers. Avoid starchy vegetables like winter squashes, sprouted grains, legumes, yams and corn, which are better suited to a non-protein dressing. (For a more complete list, refer to the food combining chart, page 201.)

To make a dip or spread, reduce the amount of water to obtain a thicker mixture.

See soaking instructions, page 5. In a blender, combine the water with the sunflower seeds, almonds, garlic, liquid aminos, oregano and other herbs. Refrigerate. Yields 2 cups.

Variation: Replace the sunflower seeds with pine nuts, soaked 2–3 hours.

The Tahini Story

Tahini is simply liquefied sesame seeds, with nothing added, subtracted or refined. It has a consistency that's a bit thinner than peanut butter. Tahini is a high-quality protein containing all the essential amino acids. Since it is made from sesame seeds which are forty-five percent protein and fifty-five percent oil, it is rich in lecithin, vitamin E and calcium. Its high-alkaline mineral content makes tahini easily digestible for young children and people with digestive complaints, and it is a source of quick energy for active people and athletes. Tahini has a long shelf-life, probably due to its antioxidant properties but once opened, it must be refrigerated.

Tahini can be purchased raw. (See Sources, page 207.) Many health food stores carry only the roasted sesame tahini, but you can ask them to carry the raw tahini as it's made by the same manufacturers. In the process of grinding the whole seeds into tahini, reputable companies keep the temperature from the

Creamy Tahini Dressing

Dressing • Sauce • Gravy

This dressing will keep for seven to ten days. Vary the ratio of water to tahini to achieve the consistency you like. One part tahini to one part water results in a thick liquid.

For a milder taste, reduce the amount of onions, scallions, cumin, ginger juice or garlic. Vary the flavor of this dressing with basil, dill or oregano. Add dulse for a nutritious dressing.

In a blender, place the water and gradually add the tahini to blend. Add the lemon juice, liquid aminos, parsley, onions, scallions, garlic, cumin, ginger juice and cayenne. Blend until smooth. Add additional water if required to achieve desired consistency. Party size yields approximately 9–10 cups; family size, 4–5 cups.

Note: Make ginger juice by putting chunks of whole ginger root through a heavy-duty juicer with a juicing screen. Ginger juice will keep for 2–3 days in the refrigerator.

Party size
- 2½ cups water
- 2 cups raw tahini
- 1½ cups lemon juice
- 1 cup liquid aminos
- 2 cups chopped parsley
- 1 cup chopped onions
- ½ cup chopped scallions
- 10 garlic cloves, chopped
- 2 tablespoons ground cumin
- 2 tablespoons ginger juice (see note)
- 1 teaspoon cayenne
- Water

Family Size
- 1¼ cups water
- 1 cup raw tahini
- ¾ cup lemon juice
- ½ cup liquid aminos
- 1 cup chopped parsley
- ½ cup chopped onions
- ¼ cup chopped scallions
- 4 garlic cloves, chopped
- 1 tablespoon ground cumin
- 1 tablespoon ginger juice (see note)
- ½ teaspoon cayenne
- Water

friction in the grinding mechanism right around 100°F (38°C), which is well below the 118°F (48°C) it takes to kill enzymes. The jars are then immediately capped with a special lid that creates a vacuum. There is no need for pasteurization, or for the manufacturer to immerse the bottled raw tahini into boiling liquids or steam. You should be getting raw tahini that really is a raw-food product. (This same information applies to raw nut butters.)

Tahini is used throughout this book because of its healthful properties, pleasant taste and adaptability in recipes. At this point in time, it is also very economical. However, since tahini is a very labor-intensive crop, and as its popularity in North America is increasing, so too will its price. Currently tahini is only one-third the cost of almond butter, so if you've never used it, now is a good time to begin.

Instant Almond Gravy 🌿

Gravy • Dressing • Sauce

¼ cup almond butter or raw
  tahini

Water

1–2 tablespoons liquid
  aminos or tamari

Keep these simple ingredients on hand as your "emergency arsenal" for entertaining; to dress your salads quickly and easily; or, to pour on top of pâtés. Be sure to try any variations that appeal to you.

In a small bowl, blend the almond butter with enough water to create a creamy consistency. Add the liquid aminos. Yields ½–¾ cup.

Variation 1: Add a dash of cayenne, a pinch of Chinese 5-spice powder, a squeeze of garlic juice or ginger juice or any other seasonings, to taste.
Variation 2: Add 2 tablespoons white or yellow miso and 1 teaspoon maple syrup or honey.
Variation 3: Add 1 tablespoon miso and juice of 1 lemon.

Mock Sour Cream 🌿

Sauce • Dip • Spread

1 cup sunflower seeds,
  soaked 8–12 hours

½ cup chopped (peeled
  and seeded) cucumber

¼ cup celery juice

¼ cup chopped onion

½ lemon, peeled, seeded and
  chopped

1 teaspoon minced garlic

¼ teaspoon sea salt

1 tablespoon water, or more

Many raw fooders eat fermented foods because they are a source of enzymes. A popular recipe called "seed cheese," is a seed or nut pâté that is left out in the open air and allowed to ferment. A fermented liquid made from sprouted wheatberries helps speed up the process. If you'd like to experiment more with fermented seed cheeses, refer to any of the books by Ann Wigmore.

Fermenting is somewhat controversial because harmful bacteria can develop in fermented food, and people with compromised health have difficulty tolerating it. For this reason, Mock Sour Cream can be made with or without fermenting. For variety, add chopped chives or shallots.

Additional fermented recipes in this book are for sauerkraut, which historically has not had any bacteria problems when made properly. (See recipes, page 49.)

See soaking instructions, page 5. In a blender, combine the cucumber with the celery juice and liquify. Add the sunflower seeds and blend until smooth. Add the onion, lemon, garlic and sea salt; blend until smooth, adding enough water to achieve desired consistency. Refrigerate until needed or, for a more authentic "sour cream" taste, cover the container with cheese cloth and leave on the counter until slightly fermented. Depending on the temperature, this will take from 4–8 hours. Yields 1½ cups.

Guacamole for One 🌿

Dip • Dressing • Salad

Guacamole is a wonderful and simple way to prepare avocado. Under normal circumstances, people following a raw-food diet would typically eat two avocados a week. Someone who is underweight could consider eating more. Thin any guacamole recipe with water, lemon juice or vegetable juice and use it as a salad dressing.

In a small bowl, mash the avocado with a fork. Mix in the red pepper, scallion, celery, garlic, lemon juice, liquid aminos and cayenne. Taste and adjust the seasonings. Serves 1–2.

1 avocado, chopped
½ red pepper, chopped
1 scallion, chopped
1 celery stalk, chopped
1 clove garlic, minced
3 tablespoons lemon juice
½ teaspoon liquid aminos, or more to taste
Pinch cayenne

Guacamole for a Crowd 🌿

Dip • Dressing • Salad

If you want to vary this recipe, add an additional two cups of chopped vegetables. Use a variety of seasonal vegetables, if you like. A whole head of finely chopped cauliflower is particularly delicious.

In order to keep the guacamole from oxidizing and turning black, the pits are put back in the bowl with the guacamole!

In a food processor, process the avocados and the juice of 1 lemon until smooth. Add the red peppers, cilantro, onion, garlic, liquid aminos and cayenne. Pulse/chop until the vegetables are small, uniform pieces. Taste and add more lemon and liquid aminos if needed for taste and consistency. Serves 6–10.

8–10 avocados
Juice of 1–2 lemons
1–2 red peppers, cut in chunks
½ cup chopped cilantro
1 red or yellow onion, cut in chunks
2–3 cloves garlic, chopped
Liquid aminos or tamari or sea salt, to taste
Cayenne, to taste

Sesame Dulse 🌿

This topping adds a nutty, slightly salty flavor to any dish.

Using a suribachi, mortar and pestle, electric coffee grinder or a small food processor, grind the sesame seeds and dulse until they form a fine powder. Store the topping in a tightly covered container in the refrigerator for a month or more.

1 tablespoon sesame seeds
1 teaspoon dulse flakes or granules

Hot Red Pepper Sauce 🌿

Sauce • Dressing

2 medium red peppers, juiced

4 tablespoons chopped cilantro

2 tablespoons chopped parsley

1 tablespoon liquid aminos

½ teaspoon cayenne, or to taste

½ teaspoon chili powder, or to taste

Water (optional)

2 tablespoons ground flax seeds (see note)

The cayenne and chili powder give this dressing a touch of heat. If you like it really hot, step up the spices! If you don't own a juicer, purée the peppers in the blender. Straining the pepper juice to remove the little bits of pepper skin is a nice touch, but it is time–consuming and is not vital.

This sauce is delicious served over any of the pâtés or vegetable dishes in this book. For fun, place a tablespoon of the sauce in a contrasting-colored soup and swirl the color through with a spoon.

In a blender, combine the red pepper juice, cilantro, parsley, liquid aminos, cayenne and chili powder. Blend thoroughly, adding additional water if necessary to achieve desired consistency. Add flax seeds; blend well.

Refrigerate for several hours, to allow time for thickening. Reblend just before serving. Yields approximately 1–1½ cups.

Note: To grind flax seeds, place them in a clean electric coffee grinder and grind until powdered.

Variation: Replace the flax seeds with ½ cup almonds soaked in 1 cup water for 8 –12 hours.

Mole Sauce 🌿

2 small red peppers, juiced

1–2 tablespoons carob powder

½ teaspoon chili powder, or more to taste

½ teaspoon liquid aminos

½ teaspoon honey or equivalent stevia (optional)

1 tablespoon ground flax seeds (see note)

Carob works well as an alternative to chocolate, especially when combined with other flavors, as in this mole. Double this recipe to serve with Chili Rellenos for four (see recipe, page 146). If you wish, replace the ground flax seeds with three-quarters of a teaspoon of psyllium.

In a blender, combine the red pepper juice, carob powder, chili powder, liquid aminos and honey; blend until smooth. Add the ground flax seeds. Blend thoroughly. Refrigerate prior to serving. Reblend just before serving. Yields ¾–1 cup.

Note: To grind flax seeds, place them in a clean electric coffee grinder and grind until powdered.

Pesto Sauce 🌿

This traditionally flavored pesto is delicious served over julienned zucchini, spaghetti squash or sunflower sprouts. If the sauce turns out too garlicky for your taste, add additional pine nuts.

See soaking instructions, page 5. In a blender, combine the pine nuts, oil, garlic, basil, parsley and salt. Blend until very smooth. If the sauce is too thick, add a spoonful of warm water. Yields approximately ¾ cup.

2 tablespoons pine nuts, soaked 20 minutes
6 tablespoons extra-virgin olive oil
3 cloves garlic, chopped
6 tablespoons chopped fresh basil
1 tablespoon chopped parsley
Pinch sea salt

Spinach Pesto 🌿
Dressing • Sauce

A rich green dressing with the chlorophyll-packed nutrition of spinach and parsley and the flavor of pesto. If you prefer, use sunflower seeds in place of the pine nuts, remembering that they will need to soak 8–12 hours.

See soaking instructions, page 5. In a blender, combine the pine nuts with garlic and enough water for the blender to operate. Gradually add the spinach, parsley and basil, adding additional water as necessary to achieve a smooth consistency. Add the liquid aminos. Taste and adjust the seasonings. Yields 1½–2 cups.

1 cup pine nuts, soaked 2–3 hours
1 clove garlic, chopped
Water
1 cup torn spinach
1 cup chopped parsley
½ cup chopped fresh basil
1 tablespoon liquid aminos

Laura's Mint Pesto 🌿
Dressing • Sauce

This recipe works best with fresh mint. If you don't like mint, it's also good with the traditional basil. Toss the pesto with slivered vegetables or use it as a salad dressing. It is also delicious spread on slices of zucchini and served as an appetizer.

In a food processor, finely chop the pecans. Add the mint, lemon juice, garlic and salt and process until well blended. With the processor still running, slowly add the oil in a thin stream through the feeding chute. Continue processing the mixture until smooth. If necessary, thin the pesto with water. Yields ½ cup.

¼ cup pecans
4 tablespoons chopped fresh mint
Juice of ½ lemon
3 cloves garlic, chopped
Pinch sea salt
2 tablespoons extra-virgin olive oil

6 Entrées

By dispensing with the common practice of having a small lunch and a large dinner, you can make any of the recipes in this book at any meal. Many raw fooders eat protein-rich food at lunch because it takes longer to digest, and carbohydrate-based meals in the evening. Lunch, for example, might be Sunny Roll-Ups with a salad, while dinner could be Zucchini Zalad with some sprouts.

This chapter contains recipes made from denser foods such as nuts, seeds and grains. Always remember to soak nuts before eating so they become more digestible and easier for the body to convert into muscle and energy. The loaves, pâtés, burgers, mousse and more in this chapter are meant to be enhanced by a side salad and served with sprouts on, under, or next to them, even if the recipe doesn't expressly mention it.

Finally, before you make any of the recipes in this chapter, remember that if you need to thin foods like soups, dressings, pâtés or loaves, add juice or juicy vegetables like red peppers or cucumbers to the recipe. If you have something that needs to be thickened to hold its shape or to make it more attractive, psyllium, ground sunflower or flax seeds, or a handful of dehydrated vegetables will work wonders. Give the thickener some time to absorb moisture before you continue with the recipe.

Sun Garden Burgers

3 tablespoons flax seeds, ground (see note)

6 tablespoons water

1 cup carrot pulp (see note)

1 cup sunflower seeds, ground

½ cup finely minced celery

6 tablespoons finely minced onion

2 tablespoons finely minced parsley

2 tablespoons finely minced red pepper

2 teaspoons liquid aminos

These burgers are delicious served in a cabbage leaf bun. Fold a cabbage leaf over the burger with any condiments you like or cut a few squares of cabbage from the large leaves and place the burger in between them. Serve your burger on a plate with some yummy Marvelous Mushroom Gravy (see recipe, page 94.)

For a casual but gourmet presentation, place an artful squiggle of Sofrito Dressing (see recipe, page 108) on a plate. Top the dressing with mixed baby greens, sunflower and buckwheat sprouts. Place the burger in the center and add a dollop of Pomodoro Sauce (see recipe, page 105).

In a blender, combine the ground flax seeds and water; blend thoroughly. Immediately pour the mixture into a bowl and set aside. (Rinse the blender container immediately before the mixture left in it hardens and becomes difficult to wash out.)

In a medium-sized bowl, thoroughly mix the carrot pulp, sunflower seeds, celery, onion, parsley, red pepper and liquid aminos. Add the flax seed mixture and mix thoroughly. Add more water if necessary so that the mixture can be formed into patties. Form into six ½-inch (1 cm) thick patties. Place immediately in the dehydrator and dehydrate the burgers for 4–8 hours, leave them in the sun until warm or place them in a warm oven for 10–15 minutes. Makes 6 patties.

Note: To grind flax seeds, place them in a clean electric coffee grinder and grind until powdered. To make carrot pulp, put carrots through a heavy-duty juicer, using a juicing screen. Use the pulp in the recipe; drink the juice or reserve it for another use.

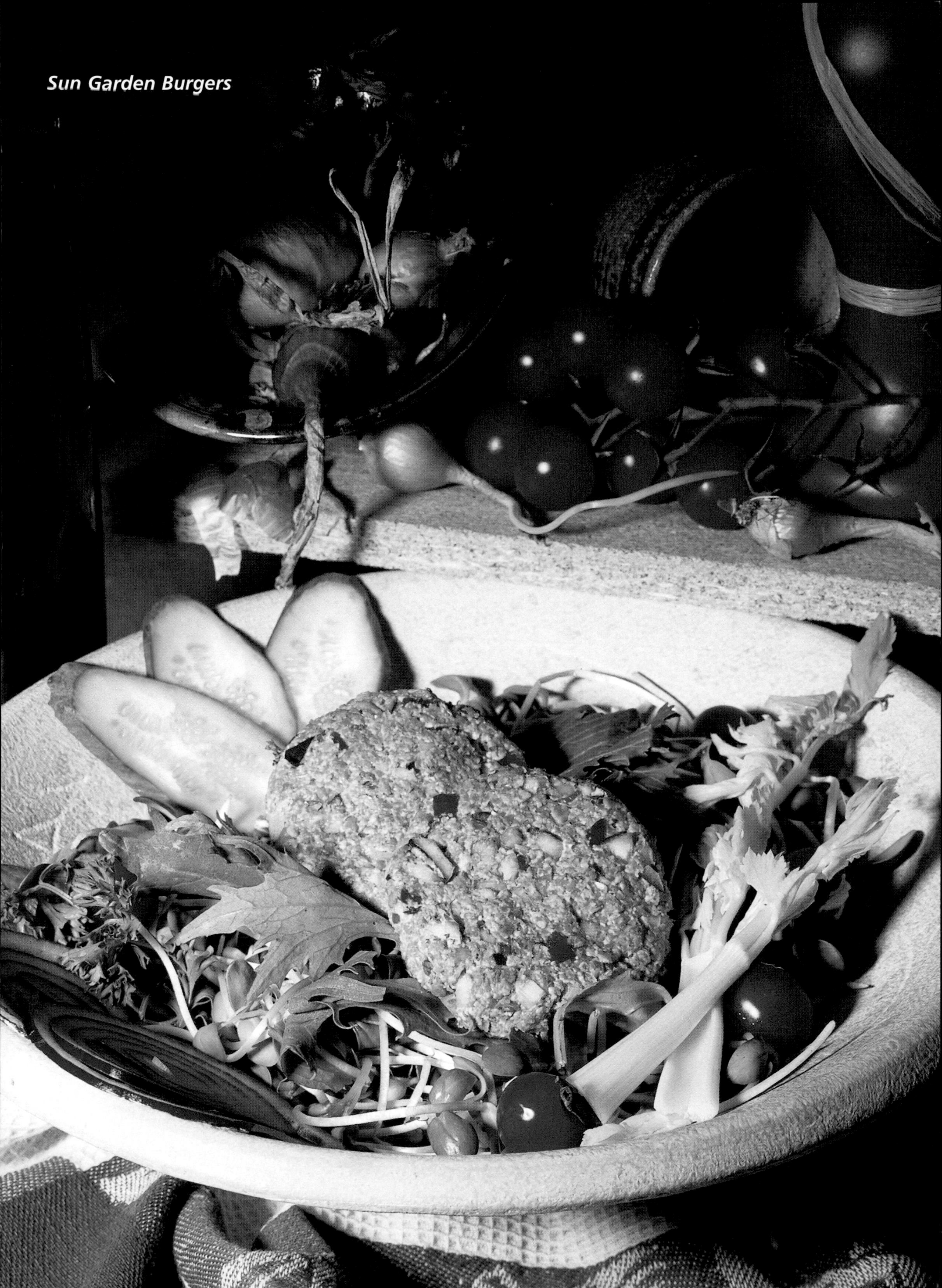
Sun Garden Burgers

Beta Burgers

2–3 medium yams, peeled and cut in chunks

1 cup sprouted wheat with ½-inch tail

½ cup chopped red onion

1 tablespoon mild miso

1 tablespoon dulse powder

These tasty burgers are called Beta Burgers because of the large amount of beta carotene in the yams. If you do not own a dehydrator and using the sun isn't possible, warm the burgers in a low oven for a few minutes until they are warm on the outside, or heat them for a few minutes in a frying pan over low heat. If you want to forget about dehydrating or warming, serve the burgers as they are, topped with some Marvelous Mushroom Gravy (see recipe, page 94).

You can substitute barley or other sprouted grains for the wheat.

Using a heavy-duty juicer with a blank screen, put the yams through the machine and into a large bowl. Make sure that you have at least three cups of ground yams. In a bowl, combine the ground yams with the sprouted wheat and onion; stir thoroughly. Put the yam mixture through the juicer. Be sure that the wheat is broken up (you may have to put the ingredients through the juicer again). Put the mixture in a bowl. Stir in the miso and dulse powder thoroughly. Form into burger-size patties and dehydrate until desired texture is achieved (4–6 hours). Makes 6 burgers.

Note: You can also make this recipe in a food processor. Using the grating attachment, grate the yams, then switch attachments to the S-blade, add the onions and sprouts, process thoroughly. Add the miso and dulse and process until well mixed.

Lentil Burgers

2 cups sunflower seeds, soaked 8–12 hours, sprouted 4 hours

1½ cups sprouted lentils

4 carrots, finely grated

1 small onion, cut in chunks

4 stalks celery, peeled and coarsely chopped

2–3 cloves garlic, chopped

2 scallions, chopped

4 tablespoons chopped parsley

4 tablespoons lemon juice

2 tablespoon liquid aminos or ½ teaspoon sea salt

1 tablespoon poultry seasoning

2 teaspoons fresh oregano (or 1 teaspoon dried)

Lentils belong to the legume family. Legumes possess a high amount of fiber which is considered an important factor in lowering cholesterol levels in the blood. Lentils also contain lignans and protease inhibitors, both of which slow cancer growth.

Sprouted lentils are always a delightful addition to any salad. Here they are presented in a burger, giving it bulk and fiber. The sunflower seeds hold the burger together.

These burgers are great served between cabbage leaves or on a plate covered with a warm mushroom gravy (see Marvelous Mushroom Soup, page 94) or smothered in Pomodoro (see recipe, page 105). Kids love to eat dehydrated burgers as finger food.

See soaking and sprouting instructions, page 194. In a food processor, combine the sunflower seeds, lentils, carrot, onion, celery, garlic, scallions, parsley, lemon juice, liquid aminos, poultry seasoning and oregano. Process until the ingredients are thoroughly mixed and broken into small bits. (Depending on the size of your food processor, you may have to process this recipe in batches.) Form the mixture into ½-inch (1 cm) thick patties. Dehydrate 8–12 hours or leave them in the sun or warm them in a very low oven. Makes 9–10 large patties.

Beta Burgers

Basic Pâté

Think of Basic Pâté as a "starter" recipe. Make up a batch then store it in your refrigerator, adding new ingredients during the week to give your meals taste and variety. (See Sunny Roll-Ups, page 156 and Asian Pâté, page 139.) Basic Pâté can be made from something simple, such as two or three cups of soaked sunflower seeds, or you can combine the tastes and textures of several nuts and seeds. When a pâté is allowed to ferment, it is called seed cheese.

The basic pâtés contain lemon and garlic to help preserve the food. The additional ingredients are up to you. Try raw tahini, onion, scallion, parsley or cilantro, shallot, garlic, ginger or ginger juice, cayenne, ground cumin, dulse, miso, sea salt and herbs. The possibilities are endless.

Basic Pâté

3 cups sunflower seeds, soaked 8–12 hours, sprouted 2–4 hours
1 cup lemon juice, or to taste
¼ cup liquid aminos, or to taste
Chopped garlic, to taste

Because soaked sunflower seeds are quite soft, you can use a food processor to make this recipe. You can also use a heavy-duty juicer with the blank screen. Do not make this recipe in a regular blender as you could burn out the motor. (Although one of the more powerful blenders would work—see equipment section, page 191, for recommendations.) See the recipe for Chili Rellenos, page 146, for directions for dehydrating pâté.

See soaking and sprouting instructions, page 194. In a food processor, process the sunflower seeds, lemon juice, liquid aminos and garlic until smooth. Store in a covered container in the refrigerator for up to 2 weeks. Yields 6–7 cups.

Variation 1: For Sunflower and Almond Pâté, replace 1 of the cups of sunflower seeds with 1 cup almonds, soaked 8–12 hours. Yields 5–6 cups.
Variation 2: For Basic Sunflower, Almond and Sesame Pâté, use 1 cup sunflower seeds, 1 cup almonds (soaked 8–12 hours) and 1 cup sesame seeds (soaked 8–12 hours, sprouted 2–4 hours). Yields 4–5 cups.

Working with Sunflower Seeds

If you are not ready to prepare the recipe immediately once the sunflower seeds have sprouted for the recommended amount of time, refrigerate them to stop the sprouting process. Oversprouted seeds will not have the best taste and texture for a pâté. Sprouted sunflower seeds will keep in a covered jar for several days if they have been well drained before refrigeration. Sunflower seeds keep longer, and the end results look better, if you remove the skins that float to the surface during soaking and sprouting. To do this, stir and rub the seeds with your hands during the final rinse. Fill the container with water to a level 6 inches (15 cm) higher than the seeds. Skim the skins from the surface of the water with a fine strainer. You can also fill the jar a few times while agitating the seeds, and as the skins float to the surface, drain them off.

Basic Pâté

Asian Pâté

Asian Pâté

If you have some Basic Pâté and some Asian Dressing on hand, then putting this dish together is a snap. It is light and refreshing and has a distinct Chinese flavor. Asian Pâté is a moist pâté that is suitable for stuffing vegetables or adding to salads, not for shaping into a loaf. It goes well with a salad of snap peas or snow peas and other Asian vegetables like bok choy, Napa cabbage and mung bean sprouts. Asian Pâté is also delicious stuffed in red peppers or in nori rolls. For variety, try the pâté with some cilantro, minced celery, chopped snow peas, chopped leeks and/or chopped shallots.

In a medium-sized bowl, combine the pâté, onions, parsley, pepper and enough of the Asian dressing to moisten and bind the ingredients. Mix well. Use an ice cream scoop to shape the pâté and serve it over a bed of sprouts. Serves 4–6.

3 cups Basic Pâté (or variation)
¼ cup finely chopped mild onions
¼ cup minced parsley
1 red pepper, finely chopped
Asian dressing, double recipe (see page 116)

Vegetable Pâté

Pâtés are often comprised of a high percentage of nuts. They can be difficult to digest and high in fat, so many people avoid them. This savory and attractive pâté contains only one cup of sunflower seeds. Its density comes from ground flax seeds and dehydrated vegetables which absorb moisture and add flavor. This tasty and crunchy dish is delicious spread on red or yellow pepper slices. The sunflower seeds in this recipe are not soaked.

Using a heavy-duty juicer with a blank screen, put the cauliflower, red pepper, squash, sunflower seeds, onion and parsley through the machine and into a large bowl. Stir in the dehydrated vegetables. Put the mixture through the juicer and into a bowl again. Stir in the flax seeds, shallot, parsley, liquid aminos, oil, olives, cumin, curry and coriander. Refrigerate the pâté for at least 1 hour. Stir the mixture, taste and adjust for seasoning. (The mixture continues to develop flavor from the dehydrated vegetables for some time.) Mold the pâté into the desired shape, cover with plastic wrap and keep refrigerated. Serves 8–10.

Note: To grind flax seeds, place them in a clean electric coffee grinder and grind until powdered.

1 small head cauliflower, cut in chunks
1 small red pepper, cut in chunks
1 small yellow squash, cut in chunks
1 cup sunflower seeds
¼–½ cup chopped onion
½ cup chopped parsley
1 cup mixed dehydrated vegetables
⅓ cup ground flax seeds (see note)
4 tablespoons chopped shallot or scallions
4 tablespoons chopped parsley
2–3 tablespoons liquid aminos
2–3 teaspoons flaxseed oil
8–12 green olives, chopped
1 teaspoon ground cumin
½ teaspoon curry powder
½ teaspoon ground coriander

Sunny Pâté 🌱

- **3 cups sunflower seeds, soaked 8–12 hours, sprouted 2–4 hours**
- **1 cup lemon juice**
- **½ cup chopped scallions**
- **¼–½ cup raw tahini**
- **¼ cup liquid aminos**
- **2–4 slices red onion, cut in chunks**
- **4–6 tablespoons coarsely chopped parsley**
- **2–3 medium cloves garlic, coarsely chopped**
- **½ teaspoon cayenne pepper, or more to taste**
- **1–2 tablespoons ginger juice (optional)**
- **1 teaspoon ground cumin (optional)**

Sprouted sunflower seeds are the most versatile of all the nuts and seeds. They are extremely digestible, easy to find and not nearly as expensive as nuts. And, because they sprout so easily, their nutrition is readily available to us. Sunny pâté is delicious in Sunny Roll-Ups (see recipe, page 156), stuffed in vegetables, thinned as a dressing, or placed atop a salad for a nutritious, high-protein meal. For a tasty and festive change of pace, dehydrate red peppers stuffed with Sunny pâté for 6–8 hours, see Chili Rellenos, page 146.

If your food processor is not large enough, make the recipe in batches. It can also be made by putting all the ingredients except the tahini and cayenne through a heavy-duty juicer, using the blank screen. Stir the tahini and cayenne in after the pâté goes through the juicer. Do not use a blender, unless it is a Vita-Mix-type machine.

Sunny pâté will keep for 10–14 days in the refrigerator, so you can make this recipe in quantity on the weekend and enjoy it all week.

See soaking and sprouting instructions, page 194. In a food processor, combine the sunflower seeds, lemon juice, scallions, tahini, liquid aminos, onion, parsley, garlic, cayenne, ginger juice and cumin and process until the mixture is a smooth paste. Taste and adjust the seasoning. The pâté will develop a stronger garlic taste in a few hours. Yields 7–8 cups.

Variation 1: Sunny Carrot Pâté: Replace 1 of the cups of sunflower seeds with 2 cups carrot pulp.
Variation 2: Almond-Tahini Pâté: Use soaked almonds in place of soaked sunflower seeds.

Vegetable Medley

- **1½ cups pâté (any kind)**
- **3 cups fresh corn kernels (approximately 3 large ears)**
- **7–8 carrots, cut into thin rounds**
- **3 stalks (peeled) celery, thinly sliced**
- **2 cloves garlic, minced**
- **2 large red peppers, chopped**
- **1 beet, chopped**
- **1 medium (peeled) yam, thinly sliced**
- **½ cup chopped yellow squash**
- **4 tablespoons chopped onions**
- **4 tablespoons chopped scallions**
- **3 tablespoons hulled sunflower seeds**
- **3–4 tablespoons fresh herbs (or 1–2 teaspoons dried) (optional)**
- **Lemon juice (optional)**
- **Liquid aminos (optional)**

This recipe was the result of experimentation with the Vegetable Supreme Loaf (see recipe, page 142). The chopped ingredients were lined up, ready to go into the juicer, but they looked so appetizing just as they were, that Vegetable Medley was born. This is a good dish for a potluck or to feed a large crowd.

Use the slicing attachment on your food processor or a mandoline to slice the carrots and yam very thin. Any type of pâté is fine.

In a large mixing bowl, combine the pâté, corn, carrots, celery, garlic, red pepper, beet, yam, squash, onions, scallions, sunflower seeds, herbs, lemon juice and liquid aminos. Mix well.

Serves 12–16.

Sunny Pâté, Sauerkraut and Sprout Salad

Hummus

2 cups chickpeas, soaked 12 hours, sprouted 48 hours
2–4 cloves garlic, chopped
½ cup water
¼–½ cup raw tahini
2 tablespoons liquid aminos
¼ cup lemon juice
4 tablespoons chopped parsley
2–4 tablespoons extra-virgin olive oil (optional)

Hummus originated in the Middle East and has now become a staple in many other parts of the world. You can find cooked versions of hummus in most health food and grocery stores. This is a raw version. If you find raw hummus difficult to digest, sprout the chickpeas (also called garbanzo beans or ceci beans) for twenty-four hours instead of forty-eight, and then steam them for 1 hour. (See sprouting chart, page 194.) Prepared this way, it would of course be considered a cooked food.

In a food processor, combine the chickpeas, garlic and water then pulse-chop until the chickpeas break down and the garlic is blended in. Add the tahini, liquid aminos, lemon juice and parsley. Process until the mixture is smooth, adding more liquid if necessary to achieve the desired consistency. Taste and adjust the garlic, lemon juice and liquid aminos. Serve hummus as a dip or on individual plates drizzled with olive oil. Serves 4–6.

Vegetable Supreme Loaf

1 ½ cups pâté (any kind)
3 cups fresh corn
7–8 carrots, coarsely chopped
3 stalks (peeled) celery, coarsely chopped
1–2 cloves garlic, chopped
2–4 cups seasonal vegetables, coarsely chopped
Lemon juice, to taste
Liquid aminos, to taste
Sea salt, to taste
3–4 tablespoons fresh herbs (or 1–2 teaspoons dried (optional))
Sunflower or flax seeds (optional) (see note)

This recipe varies with the seasons, which is why the ingredients list calls for two to four cups of vegetables. (And in the winter, when fresh corn is not available, you will need to substitute another vegetable.) Consider red peppers (limit to two because of high water content), zucchini, yellow squash, butternut squash, yams, sweet potatoes, beets, turnips, green beans, mushrooms, onions, scallions, spinach, broccoli and cauliflower.

In a large mixing bowl, combine the pâté, corn, carrots, celery, garlic and vegetables. Put the mixture through the juicer. Depending on the vegetables, you may want to put the mixture through the blank screen of your juicer twice to achieve the desired consistency. Place the mixture in a large bowl and add the lemon juice, liquid aminos, salt and herbs. Mix thoroughly.

Because some vegetables are juicier than others, you may need to use some thickening agents to achieve the right consistency for a loaf or pâté. Suggested thickeners include a handful of whole sunflower seeds finely ground and/or 2–6 tablespoons of whole flax seeds. For a different taste and consistency, add 1 cup or more of mixed dehydrated vegetables, allowing at least 1 hour for the vegetables to rehydrate. Stir the mixture thoroughly.

Form the mixture into a loaf. Serve with thinned Notmayo! (see recipe, page 118) or Sofrito Dressing (see recipe, page 108) as is, or in a pie crust. Serves 8–10.

Note: To grind sunflower or flax seeds, place them in a clean electric coffee grinder and grind until powdered.

Hummus

Faux Salmon

Faux Salmon

This attractive dish resembles salmon casserole. But we know it's not! Add more kelp, dulse or any other sea vegetables that you have on hand to increase the seafood flavor. For fun, press the mixture into a mold and unmold it onto a platter, surrounded with kale and parsley and topped with almonds or olives. This dish is elegant served with warmed Mushroom Gravy (see recipe, page 93), or Notmayo! (see recipe, page 118), thinned with a little warm water.

If you don't have carrot juice on hand, be sure to make it first (using a juicing screen); then change to the blank screen for the rest of the recipe.

See soaking instructions, page 5. Using a heavy-duty juicer, with a blank screen, put the almonds, carrots and onions through the machine and into a large bowl. Stir in the celery, parsley, scallions, lemon juice, kelp, dulse, liquid aminos and salt and mix thoroughly. Add enough carrot juice to achieve desired consistency. Shape the mixture into a loaf or place it in a pie crust. This mixture will keep for several days, covered, in the refrigerator. Serves 4–6.

2 cups almonds, soaked 8–12 hours

2 large carrots

½ cup coarsely chopped red onion

1½ cups minced celery

½ cup minced parsley

¼ cup minced scallions

¼ cup lemon juice

2 teaspoons kelp powder

1 teaspoon dulse powder or granules

1 tablespoon liquid aminos

Pinch sea salt

⅓ cup carrot juice, or more

Basic Entrée Crust

This is the basic formula for entrée pie crusts. (See pages 164, for dessert pie crusts.) Unlike traditional pie crusts that are empty calories made of refined white flour and filled with fat, this crust is a rich source of protein and fiber. While water is usually used to moisten the crust, you can change the flavor by using salad dressing or Notmayo!, although you may need to add a little more of the dressing to get the desired texture. For a thin crust, use two cups of nuts or seeds; for a thicker crust, use three cups.

See soaking instructions, page 5. For best results, after draining the nuts or seeds, dry them in the sun or with a dehydrator for 30–60 minutes or simply dry them with a towel. In a food processor, process the nuts or seeds until they are uniformly fine. Add the liquid aminos and pulse-chop. Add the water 1 tablespoon at a time just until the mixture holds together. Gradually sprinkle in psyllium while the processor is running. Press the mixture evenly into a pie plate with your hands. For a nice crisp texture, leave the crust in the sun for 1 hour or dehydrate for 30–60 minutes. Makes one 9-inch (22.5 cm) pie crust.

2–3 cups nuts and or seeds, soaked 8–12 hours

1 tablespoon liquid aminos

2–4 tablespoons water or juice or dressing

1 tablespoon psyllium, or more

Chili Rellenos 🦎

4 red peppers or Anaheim or
  Poblano peppers
2 cups Basic Pâté (see recipe,
  page 136)
½ cup finely minced carrots
½ cup minced celery
½ cup minced zucchini
½ cup minced onion
½ cup thinly sliced
  mushrooms
1 cup finely chopped cilantro
2 cloves garlic, pressed
2 teaspoons dried oregano
1 teaspoon cayenne, or more
  to taste
Lemon juice, to taste
Liquid aminos, to taste
Mole sauce
  (see recipe, page 128)
Mock sour cream
  (see recipe, page 126)

This delicious recipe is the centerpiece for a fabulous Mexican meal, described in the Special Occasion Menu (page 206). It's a little extra work because of its several components. The peppers are stuffed with a special pâté and topped with mole sauce and mock sour cream. Beautiful when served in multicolored peppers, this dish is dehydrated for 6–8 hours so the stuffing will be warm and the peppers are softened when you serve the meal.

Because green peppers are unripe, they are not recommended in this book. Vitamin-C-packed red peppers work well in this recipe, but use Anaheim or Poblano peppers if you want to be more authentic (they are usually green). Pick long thin peppers for authenticity.

Cut the peppers in half lengthwise and remove the seeds; set aside. In a large mixing bowl, combine the pâté, carrots, celery, zucchini, onion, mushrooms, cilantro, garlic, oregano and cayenne. Mix thoroughly. Add lemon juice and liquid aminos to achieve the desired taste and consistency. Stuff the peppers with the pâté. Dehydrate the stuffed peppers for 6–8 hours, removing them from the dehydrator right at serving time. Place the warm stuffed peppers on a serving platter or on indiviual plates. Drizzle a spoonful of mole sauce over each pepper and finish with a dollop of mock sour cream in the center. Serve the remaining mole sauce and sour cream on the side.

Deli Rye Thin Bread

4–5 cups sprouted rye with
  ½-inch (1 cm) tails
4–5 olives, chopped
1 tablespoon extra-virgin
  olive oil
1 tablespoon tamari
2 teaspoons caraway seeds
1 teaspoon dried oregano
Pinch sea salt

Caraway seeds and rye berries give this very chewy cracker the delicious taste of rye bread, New York deli-style. If you prefer to make live sprouted bread, double this recipe, form into a loaf and place it in the lowest temperature oven overnight, or form it into a 2-inch (5 cm) high loaf and dehydrate it.

In a food processor, combine the sprouted rye, olives, oil, tamari, caraway seeds, oregano and salt. Process thoroughly, frequently scraping down the sides of the processor until the berries are finely broken up and the mixture resembles a batter. In a dehydrator, spread the mixture thinly (less than ¼-inch (0.5 cm)) thick on solid liners. Top the mixture with additional caraway seeds. Pierce all over with a fork. When the mixture is dry enough, turn it over onto regular tray liners and continue to dehydrate. Break into serving-size pieces and store in an airtight container. Or, when almost dry, score the crackers with a knife at 2-inch intervals. When dehydrated, break along the scored lines. Makes approximately sixteen 2 inch by 3 inch (5 cm by 7.5 cm) crackers.

Chili Rellenos with Mole Sauce and Mock Sour Cream

Festive Stuffed Mushrooms

3 tablespoons sunflower seeds, soaked 8–12 hours

12 medium or 6 large whole crimini mushrooms

½ cup quartered crimini mushrooms, including stems

3 tablespoons chopped onions

2 tablespoons chopped cranberries, fresh or rehydrated dried

1 tablespoon chopped parsley

1 teaspoon poultry seasoning

Liquid aminos, to taste

Use the largest crimini or button mushrooms you can find. For double, triple or quadruple the recipe.

If you are lucky enough to get hot sun in your backyard, these lovely hors d'oeuvres will be softened and warmed in several hours. If you are using a dehydrator, it is best to make them one day in advance as the mushrooms tend to get a bit dry by the time the filling is nicely condensed and tasty. Simply cover them with clear wrap, refrigerate and by the next day they will be moist and delicious.

See soaking instructions, page 5. Place cleaned and stemmed whole mushrooms on a platter. In a mini-processor or a blender, combine the sunflower seeds, mushroom pieces, onions, cranberries, parsley, poultry seasoning and liquid aminos; process until thoroughly mixed. Stuff the mushrooms with the mixture. Dehydrate for 2–4 hours in the sun or the dehydrator. Serves 2–3.

Spinach Mousse

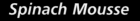

Spinach Mousse

The quintessential brunch food. Now that you are a raw foodist, it doesn't mean you can't serve traditional-style foods with the same delicacy of flavor as the high-cholesterol, egg-laden, fat-filled goodies we have all enjoyed in the past. This is the flavor of raw cuisine at its best. Once your palate has adjusted to the subtleties of food in the raw, you will never want to give up the benefits of a raw diet.

This delicious green mousse is very simple. If you want to keep it really light, dispense with the crust and serve it in 4 individual 6-ounce (30 g) ramekins. This recipe will fill a 9-inch (22.5 cm) pie pan including a crust.

This recipe calls for a large quantity of spinach. If you are using the packaged, pre-washed variety, be sure you are using an equivalent amount, by weight.

Spinach mousse looks beautiful decorated with paper-thin slices of mushrooms covering the entire top in a spiral pattern, topped in the center with a sprig of basil or parsley. If you're preparing a mousse for a party, you can make it in advance and store it in the refrigerator for one day, although it will lose some nutritional value. For a really large crowd, double or triple the recipe and make it in a large rectangular pan.

For crust: Make the pie crust using 2–3 cups almonds and 2–4 tablespoons water. Press the crust into a 9-inch (22.5 cm) pie pan; set aside.

For mousse: See soaking instructions, page 5. In a food processor, combine the spinach, tahini, pine nuts, lemon juice, mushrooms, salt and water; process thoroughly. The mixture will become an even green color. While the processor is still running, gradually sprinkle in the nutmeg, then the psyllium. Press the filling immediately into the pie crust. Decorate with mushrooms. Chill for at least 30 minutes before eating.

Note: Use 2 cups almonds for a thin crust; 3 cups for a thick one.

Crust

1 recipe Basic Entrée Crust (see recipe, page 145)

Mousse

2 tablespoons pine nuts, soaked 20 minutes
1 large bunch spinach (1 pound (500 g)), torn in pieces
¼ cup raw tahini
3 tablespoons lemon juice
3 cups sliced mushrooms, including trimmed stems
¾ teaspoon sea salt
5 tablespoons water
⅛ teaspoon nutmeg
1–2 tablespoons psyllium

Yam and Apple-Stuffed Mushrooms

12 small or 6 large whole
  mushrooms

12 small mushrooms, cut in
  chunks

3 tablespoons grated yam

2 tablespoons chopped
  onions

2 tablespoons chopped
  cranberries, fresh or
  rehydrated dried

2 tablespoons grated apple

¾ teaspoon poultry seasoning

Dash cayenne

Liquid aminos

Dash lemon juice

This dish has a wonderful holiday flavor. Triple or quadruple the recipe if you are serving it as an appetizer at Christmas or Thanksgiving.

Place the cleaned and stemmed whole mushrooms on a platter. In a mini-processor or a blender, combine the chopped mushrooms, yam, onions, cranberries, apple, poultry seasoning and cayenne and process until smooth. Add the liquid aminos and lemon juice, to taste, and to achieve the desired consistency. Stuff the mushrooms with the mixture. Dehydrate for 2–4 hours. Serves 2–3.

Variation: Stuff mushrooms with some Spinach Pesto (see recipe, page 129) and serve immediately, or dehydrate them.

Broccoli Mousse

Crust

1 recipe Almond Crust
  (see recipe, page 145)

Mousse

5 cups coarsely chopped
  broccoli florets and (peeled)
  stems

½ cup lemon juice

1 tablespoon liquid aminos

1 tablespoon water

2 cups sliced mushrooms

½ cup raw tahini

1 tablespoon chopped shallot

1 tablespoon chopped fresh
  dill (or 1 teaspoon dried)

2 teaspoons psyllium

For crust: Make the crust and press into a 9-inch (22.5 cm) pan; set aside.

For mousse: In a food processor, combine the broccoli, lemon juice, liquid aminos and water. Process until smooth. Add the mushrooms, tahini, shallot and dill. Process until the mixture is a thick purée. Gradually sprinkle in the psyllium while the machine is running. Press the mousse into the pie crust immediately. Refrigerate for at least 30 minutes or up to 24 hours before eating. Keep leftovers refrigerated. Makes one 9-inch (22.5 cm) pie.

Pizza-Kinda

Okay, it doesn't taste like anything you've ever eaten at a pizzeria. But it has some of the same characteristics as the gooey, cholesterol-laden, oxalic-acid-filled, yeasty, empty-caloried, saturated-fat-laden, zero nutrition, greasy, real pizza that we all know and used to love. For one thing, it is round. For another it has a crust. Only this crust is dehydrated sprouted grain, so it is good for you. It has toppings—so, when you prepare it, you can let your creativity run wild. It is tasty and fun to eat. Kids of all ages love it. It is a great party or picnic food. When you make the crust, make extras, if they are properly dehydrated, they will keep for some time carefully wrapped. Consider the following recipe as a guideline.

This is a plan-ahead meal. First you soak and sprout raw (hulled) buckwheat groats. Then you put them in a food processor, make your crust with the dough you've created, and dehydrate it in the sun or dehydrator.

Soak the raw hulled buckwheat groats for six hours and sprout them for twenty-four hours. Or follow the sprouting book of your choice, as the directions vary widely for hulled buckwheat. (See sprouting chart, page 194.) Stop the process when the majority of groats have a tail that is anywhere from just visible to ¼ inch (0.5 cm). Do you remember how to stop the process? You put the whole, drained jar in the refrigerator, and use the sprouts when you are ready.

To make pizza-kinda, there are two crust recipes to choose from and three toppings to try. Once you have made these recipes, you can invent your own crusts and toppings.

Basic Pizza-Kinda Crust ❦

2½ cups buckwheat groats, soaked 6 hours, sprouted 24 hours

⅓ cup extra-virgin olive oil

3–4 tablespoons herbs or spices, or more to taste

Liquid aminos

Be creative when adding flavorings—without them the crust will be quite bland. Add herbs such as dried basil and oregano, dried red chili peppers or sea salt.

See sprouting chart, page 194. Place the buckwheat groats in a food processor with the oil, spices and liquid aminos and process until a dough is formed. With a large spoon, drop the dough onto the solid liner of the dehydrator tray. Form four 7- or 8-inch (17.5 or 20 cm) rounds that are approximately ¼-inch (0.5 cm) thick. Dehydrate the rounds in the dehydrator or the sun until they are dry all the way through. Turn them after a few hours. Makes four 7- or 8-inch (17.5 or 20 cm) pizza crusts.

Herbed Pizza-Kinda Crust 🌿

1½ cups buckwheat groats, soaked 6 hours, sprouted 24 hours

1 cup chopped tomatoes, puréed and strained 30 minutes (see note)

2 tablespoons sunflower meal

2 tablespoons liquid aminos

2 tablespoons extra-virgin olive oil

2 tablespoons minced fresh basil

1 teaspoon minced garlic

1 teaspoon dried oregano

Sunflower meal is simply sunflower seeds that have been ground in a coffee or spice mill to a fine powder.

See sprouting chart, page 194. In a food processor, combine the buckwheat groats, tomatoes, sunflower meal, liquid aminos, oil, basil, garlic and oregano; process until a dough is formed. With a large spoon, drop the dough onto the solid liner of the dehydrator tray. Form four 6- or 7-inch (15 or 17.5 cm) rounds that are approximately ¼-inch (0.5 cm) thick. Dehydrate the rounds in the dehydrator or the sun until they are dry all the way through. Turn them after a few hours. Makes four 6- or 7-inch (15 or 17.5 cm) pizza crusts.

Note: To strain tomatoes, pour them into a sieve and drain them for the required time.

Tomato Topping for Pizza-Kinda 🌿

3 cups diced (seeded) tomatoes

1 small clove garlic, minced

Dried basil, to taste

Dried oregano, to taste

1 tablespoon dehydrated vegetables

Fresh basil, cut in strips

1–2 mushrooms, thinly sliced

2–3 tablespoons slivered vegetables

Chopped Greek olives (optional)

Dehydrated onion rings

Dehydrated pepper rings

In a food processor, place the tomatoes and process until crushed. Pour them into a strainer and drain the liquid for 5 minutes. Pour the drained tomatoes into a bowl, add the garlic, dried basil, oregano, dehydrated vegetables and ½ of the fresh basil. Allow the mixture to sit for 10 minutes to rehydrate the vegetables.

To assemble the pizza: Place ½ of the tomato topping on each crust. Add remaining fresh basil to taste, mushrooms and olives. Top with onion and pepper rings. Makes 2 pizzas.

Guacamole Topping for Pizza-Kinda 🌿

½ recipe Guacamole for One (see recipe, page 127)

1–2 mushrooms, thinly sliced

Greens

Sprouts

Dehydrated onion rings

Dehydrated pepper rings

Dulse flakes

To assemble the pizza: Pile half of the guacamole topping on each crust. Top with mushroom slices, greens, sprouts and dehydrated onion and pepper rings. Sprinkle with dulse. Makes 2 pizzas.

Pâté Topping for Pizza-Kinda

To assemble the pizza: Spread ¼ cup pâté on each crust. Top each with 1 cup of greens, pressing them gently into the pâté. Decorate with red peppers, onions, basil and mushrooms. Sprinkle liberally with dulse. Makes 2 pizzas.

Variation: For seed cheese pizza, let the pâté ferment in a jar covered with cheesecloth. Leave it on the counter for 4–8 hours.

½ cup pâté, any kind (see recipes, page 136–140)

2 cups mixed baby greens, torn

4 tablespoons chopped red peppers or tomatoes

4 tablespoons chopped onions

4 tablespoons basil strips

4 tablespoons sliced mushrooms

Dulse, to taste

Veggie Tartare

Traditional steak tartare is made of minced raw beef that is highly seasoned with bits of onion, capers, scallion and pepper. This vegetarian version is fun to eat since each person chooses his or her own condiments from a large platter set out on the table and mixes them into the Veggie Tartare. This unusual dish is a wonderful way to get your friends to "eat their salad."

Using a heavy-duty juicer with a blank screen, put the Vegetable Medley ingredients through the machine and into a large bowl. Stir in the ground flax seeds and refrigerate the mixture for at least 1 hour. The mixture should have a moist consistency. If it needs to be thickened, add a handful of ground sunflower seeds or additional ground flax seeds. If it needs to be thinned, add red pepper juice, lemon juice, water or liquid aminos, to taste.

Serve a mound of the mixture in the middle of each individual salad plate. Make an indentation in the top of the mound so guests can place the condiments of their choice. Serves 10–12.

Note: Suggested condiments include minced red onion, minced scallion, minced shallot, broccoli or radish sprouts, chopped green olives, chopped black olives, capers, sesame seeds or Gomasio (see recipe, page 109), Gremolata (see recipe, page 115), grated garlic, grated horseradish and chopped chives. Serve with liquid aminos or tamari, and sesame or other flavored oils.

Note: To grind flax seeds, place them in a clean electric coffee grinder and grind until powdered.

1 recipe Vegetable Medley (see recipe, page 140)

4–6 tablespoons finely ground flax seeds (see note)

Condiments (see note)

Sunny Roll-Ups 🌿

1 nori sheet

3–4 tablespoons Sunny Pâté
(see recipe, page 140)

3–4 green olives, sliced

Wasabi

2–3 pieces slivered red
pepper

3–4 pieces slivered carrot

Large handful clover or
alfalfa sprouts

Sunflower sprouts

Sunny Roll-Ups are made with square sheets of seaweed called nori, the nutritious green seaweed that Japanese restaurants use to make sushi and California rolls. Sunny Roll-Ups look just like sushi—the red pepper or carrot pieces show in the very center, making the dish a visual masterpiece. Even your most dedicated carnivore friends will love them! Once you've made them a few times, you will find preparing nori rolls very easy. You can buy nori at health food stores and Asian markets or through several mail order sources. (See Sources, page 207.) It is available toasted and raw; buy it raw.

Assemble the roll-ups as close to serving time as possible because the nori absorbs the moisture from the filling very quickly and can become a bit soggy. Once you are adept at making the nori rolls, your guests will love watching you assemble them.

Lay 1 sheet of nori on a clean cutting board or bamboo sushi mat. Place 3 or 4 tablespoons of the pâté along the edge of the nori nearest to you. Using a knife or a spatula, spread the pâté in a band that is almost as wide as the nori (stop within ½ inch (1 cm) of the left and right sides) and approximately 1½ inches (3.5 cm) deep. (The resulting band of pâté will be quite thick.)

Place a horizontal row of thinly sliced green olives down the middle of the pâté. Squeeze a thin, even line of wasabi down the middle of the pâté (it's hot, so use it cautiously). Place several pieces of slivered carrot or red pepper in rows next to the olives. Place a generous handful of clover or alfalfa sprouts on top (you can use more than you would believe possible; they will compress when you roll up the nori.) Finally, place a small amount of sunflower sprouts on top.

Now you are ready to roll. Starting with the end closest to you, lift the edge of the nori and roll it tightly over the pâté and vegetables. Pull the roll back toward you once or twice to compress the ingredients in the roll. Continue rolling until a tight cylinder is formed. (This gets easier with practice). If necessary, place a bit of water on the very end of the roll to seal it. Serves 1.

Note: Vary the Sunny Roll-Ups with Sunny Carrot Pâté or Almond-Tahini Pâté (see recipes, page 140).

Vegetable Nori Roll-Ups 🌿

Juice of 1 lemon
2 tablespoons liquid aminos
1 teaspoon extra-virgin olive oil or flaxseed oil
Dash cinnamon or cayenne (optional)
2 carrots, slivered
3 scallions, slivered
1 zucchini, slivered
1 daikon radish or cucumber, slivered
Alfalfa sprouts
Buckwheat and/or sunflower sprouts

This is a light, vegetable-only variation of nori rolls. It's great in the winter with root vegetables such as carrot, daikon radish, parsnip or butternut squash; or in the summer with zucchini, cucumber, carrot and scallion. Use what you have in the house along with some sprouts for a fun, quick, light meal. Vary the marinade according to your taste.

In a small bowl, combine the lemon juice, liquid aminos, oil and cinnamon or cayenne. Place the vegetables in a shallow pan and pour the lemon juice mixture over them. Marinate the vegetables for 15–30 minutes. Drain the vegetables thoroughly by tossing them in a colander or blotting them with paper towels. Arrange the marinated vegetables on nori sheets, top them with a lot of sprouts and roll them up. Makes 2–3 rolls.

Variation 1: Make the above recipe without marinating the vegetables, top them with sprouts and your favorite dressing. Roll up.
Variation 2: For a quick, simple meal, use sliced avocado and sprouts, top them with lemon juice and dulse, then roll them up.

Vegetable Nori Roll-ups

Walnut-Pumpkin Loaf

Pumpkin seeds are not just a by-product of Halloween jack-o-lanterns. They are one of the highest vegetarian sources of zinc, which is vital in healing and especially important for the male reproductive system. Pumpkin seeds are also an ingredient used in many herbal preparations to eliminate parasites. Pumpkins are grown primarily in China and Mexico and organic pumpkins are starting to become available. Pumpkin Seed Loaf is a dense and hearty nut pâté. For a more complex-flavored, lighter dish, see the variation below.

See soaking instructions, page 5. In a heavy-duty juicer, with a blank screen, put the pumpkin seeds, walnuts, yam, carrots and onion through the machine and into a large bowl. Stir in the seasoning, liquid aminos and lemon juice. Form into a loaf and serve surrounded by sprouts and greens.

Variation: Put Walnut-Pumpkin Loaf in a large bowl; set aside. In a food processor, place 2 stalks celery, chopped; 1 cup chopped parsley; 2 cups chopped mushrooms, 1 cup chopped seasonal vegetables of your choice; 2 cloves garlic, chopped and 2 teaspoons poultry seasoning. Pulse-chop until well mixed, then add to the Walnut-Pumpkin Loaf. Mix thoroughly. Add additional liquid aminos, lemon juice, water and seasonings for taste and desired consistency.

2 cups pumpkin seeds, soaked 4–6 hours

2 cups walnuts, soaked 4–6 hours or 2 cups almonds, soaked 8–12 hours

1 small yam or sweet potato, peeled and cut in chunks

2 carrots, cut in chunks

1 onion, cut in chunks

1 teaspoon favorite herb, or to taste

Liquid aminos, to taste

Lemon juice, to taste

Walnut-Pumpkin Loaf

Almond-Mushroom Loaf ❦

2 cups almonds,
soaked 8–12 hours
1 pound (500 g) crimini
1 medium onion, cut in
chunks
2 large carrots
3 stalks celery
1 garlic clove, chopped
2 cups chopped parsley
½ cup ground sunflower
seeds (see note)
2 tablespoons flaxseed oil
1 tablespoon liquid aminos,
or more to taste
Dash cayenne
Water

The mushrooms and ground sunflower seeds give this loaf a hearty, "meaty," taste. It is delicious spread on sliced vegetables, or you can serve this mixture as a dehydrated burger. Simply make ½-inch (1 cm) thick patties and dehydrate them for 4–6 hours. Serve with Marvelous Mushroom Gravy (see recipe, page 93).

See soaking instructions, page 5. Using a heavy-duty juicer with a blank screen, put the almonds, mushrooms, onion, carrot, celery, garlic and parsley through the machine and into a large bowl. Stir in the sunflower meal, oil, liquid aminos and cayenne. Add water if necessary to achieve desired consistency. Leave the mixture covered in the refrigerator for several hours to allow the flavors to blend. To control the consistency, add additional ground sunflower seeds to thicken or water to thin the mixture. Form the loaf into any shape on a platter. Serves 8–12.

Note: To grind sunflower seeds, place them in a clean electric coffee grinder and grind until powdered. Freeze any excess sunflower meal.

Red Pepper-Mushroom Mousse ❦

Crust
1 recipe Almond Crust
(see recipe, page 145)

Mousse
6 cups coarsely chopped red
pepper, juiced
2½ cups sliced mushrooms
¾ cup chopped fresh basil
½ cup raw tahini
3 tablespoons diced shallot
1 tablespoon lemon juice
1½ teaspoons dried oregano
¾ teaspoon sea salt
2 tablespoons psyllium

Red peppers have a very high water content so you may need to increase the amount of psyllium it takes to give the mousse a proper consistency. Once the psyllium has been thoroughly mixed in and the mixture has had time to set, it should be firm enough to cut with a knife and hold together on a plate.

For crust: Make the crust and press into a 9-inch (22.5cm) pan; set aside.

For mousse: In a food processor, combine the red pepper juice, mushrooms, basil, tahini, shallot, lemon juice, oregano and salt; process until smooth. Gradually sprinkle in the psyllium while the processor is running. Press the mixture into the pie crust immediately. Chill for at least 30 minutes or up to 24 hours before eating. Makes one 9-inch (22.5 cm) pie.

7 Desserts

Don't desert the dessert! You can have wonderful raw food desserts from apple or sweet potato pie to whipped toppings and hot carob sauce. While they are not always designed with food combining in mind, these desserts are far healthier than conventional sweets. Indulge in them occasionally, and treat your friends too.

Basic Dessert Crusts

Pie crusts can be casually thrown together or they can be made following carefully measured recipes. They always contain nuts or seeds, and something sweet such as maple syrup, dates or raisins. Often pie crusts contain ground psyllium seed husks to bind the ingredients. Recipes for four basic dessert crusts follow, as well as some variations

Basic Almond-Date Crust

1¼ cup almonds,
  soaked 8–12 hours

1 cup date pieces or chopped
  dates

1 tablespoon water

½ teaspoon vanilla (optional)

Dash cinnamon (optional)

2 teaspoons psyllium

This crust is infinitely variable—increase or decrease the ingredients according to your needs, add some sunflower seeds or use raisins in place of some or all of the dates. As long as you have a crust that will hold together as a knife slices through it and doesn't become soggy from the filling it holds, you have succeeded. If you want to economize, use date pieces, which are less expensive than whole dates.

See soaking instructions, page 5. After draining the almonds, dry them for 30–60 minutes in the sun or with a dehydrator, or simply dry them with a towel. In a food processor, chop the nuts until they are evenly ground. Add the dates and process until they are finely ground. Add the water, vanilla and cinnamon while processing. The crust must appear slightly damp and must hold together before adding the psyllium; add a small amount of water, if necessary. Gradually add the psyllium. Immediately press the mixture into an 8- or 9-inch pie pan. Dehydrate the crust for 1 hour, or leave it in the sun for 1–2 hours or in a warm oven for 20 minutes. Or, use the crust immediately. Makes an 8- or 9-inch (20–22.5 cm) pie crust.

Basic Pecan-Date Crust

1½ cups pecans

6 pitted dates, preferably
  medjools

Dash vanilla

Dash cinnamon

Water

This crust works equally well with walnuts. This recipe makes enough crust for a round layer-cake pan an eight-inch (20 cm) pie pan. To fill a larger pie pan (9 inches (22.5 cm) or more), increase the recipe by a third of a cup of nuts and two dates.

In a food processor, process the pecans until they are uniformly fine. Add the dates and process until they are fully blended and the mixture is sticky. Add the vanilla, cinnamon and enough water to hold the crust together. Press the mixture into an 8- or 9-inch (20–22.5 cm) pie pan. Dehydrate the crust for 1 hour or leave it in the sun for 1–2 hours or in a warm oven for 20 minutes. Or, use the crust immediately. Makes an 8- or 9-inch (20–22.5 cm) pie crust.

Basic Almond-Maple Crust

This delicate crust is good for soft fillings or frozen pies because it doesn't overwhelm the subtle taste or texture of the filling. Because the fillings are generally very rich, a small serving satisfies. Don't worry about getting the crust all the way up the sides of the pan. One cup will yield a very thin crust; two cups will be approximately the thickness of a traditional crust. Use two cups of almonds if you are using a nine-inch (22.5 cm) pie pan.

See soaking instructions, page 5. After draining the almonds, dry them for 30–60 minutes in the sun or with a dehydrator, or simply dry them with a towel. In a food processor, chop the almonds until they are uniformly very fine. Gradually add the maple syrup, using just enough for the almond meal to hold together. Sprinkle the mixture into an 8- or 9-inch (20–22.5 cm) pie pan and then gently press it into the bottom and up the sides. Makes an 8- or 9-inch (20–22.5 cm) pie crust.

1–2 cups almonds, soaked 8–12 hours

3–4 teaspoons maple syrup

Thick Dessert Crust

Most of the recipes in this book call for soaked or ground sunflower seeds. This recipe is an exception: the seeds go right into the recipe, unsoaked and without pre-grinding.

See soaking instructions, page 5. After draining the almonds, dry them for 30–60 minutes in the sun or with a dehydrator, or simply dry them with a towel. In a food processor, process the almonds until they are evenly chopped. Add the sunflower seeds and process until they are finely chopped. Add the raisins; process until they are blended in. Add the dates, a few at a time, until the mixture holds together and has a sticky dough-like consistency. Press into 9-inch (22.5 cm) pie pan. Dehydrate for 1 hour or leave in sun for 1–2 hours or in a warm oven for 20 minutes. Or, use the crust immediately. Makes a 9-inch (22.5 cm) pie crust.

Variation: For cookies, make any pie crust recipe (except for almond-maple), and thin it with a little orange or apple juice. Roll out the dough and cut it with a cookie cutter. Dehydrate.

3 cups almonds or pecans or walnuts, soaked 8–12 hours

1 cup sunflower seeds

1 cup raisins

1–2 cups dates, pitted

"The Best" Applesauce Pie

Crust

1 recipe Almond-Date Crust (see recipe, page 164)

½ cup almonds

½ cup dates

Water

Filling

10–12 apples (peeled and cored), cut in chunks

2 cups dates, pitted (medjool are the best)

1 cup raisins

2 teaspoons cinnamon

2 tablespoons psyllium

This pie rivals the most infamous cooked apple pie. Rich and sweet and aromatic with cinnamon, offer this pie to your skeptical friends—they will never believe that it's a raw pie.

For crust: Make the pie crust, increasing the almonds and dates by ½ cup each. Add additional water if required to hold the crust together. Press into a 9-inch (22.5 cm) pie pan; set aside.

For filling: In a heavy-duty juicer, using a blank screen, alternate putting the apples, dates and raisins through the machine and into a bowl. There should be at least 6 cups of applesauce mixture; if not, add more apples and put the mixture through the juicer again. For best results, transfer the mixture to a food processor and process until very smooth. Add cinnamon; process until mixed. With the processor running, gradually sprinkle in the psyllium; process until thoroughly mixed. Immediately pour the filling into the pie crust. Cover and refrigerate. Makes a 9-inch (22.5 cm) pie.

Variation 1: Substitute Thick Dessert Crust (see recipe, page 165) for the Almond-Date Crust.

Variation 2: For an apple tart, make a thick dessert crust (see recipe, page 165) and press it into a round tart pan or pizza pan. Make ½ the recipe for applesauce pie filling. Place the filling in the crust and top it with thinly sliced apples that have been dipped in lemon juice. Sprinkle with Sweet Dust Topping (see recipe, page 175).

Note: An apple-peeler-corer-dicer is a great little manual machine to quickly prepare the apples for this pie.

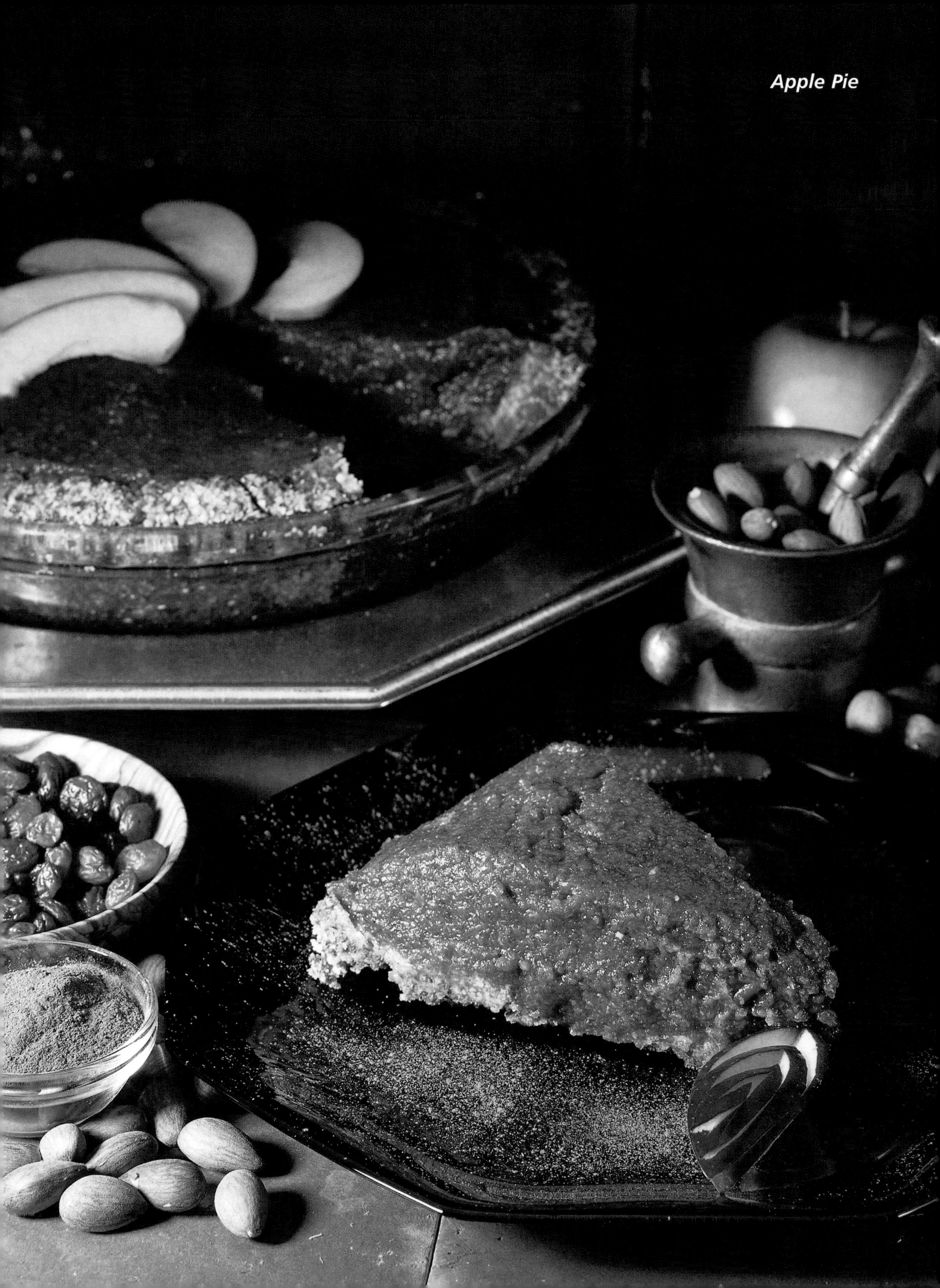
Apple Pie

Tropical Fruit Pie

Crust
1 recipe Thick Dessert Crust (see recipe, page 165)

Filling
2 cups sliced strawberries
2–3 papayas, cut in chunks
2–3 bananas, cut in chunks
Dash cinnamon
1 lemon, peeled, seeded and cut in chunks
Zest of 1 lemon
2 – 3 teaspoons psyllium
Assorted fruit
Lemon juice

Always use whatever fruit is seasonal and available for this pie. Tropical fruit pie with papayas and bananas is great but if you have to call your aunt in Australia to airship the papaya to you, maybe you should consider an apple pie instead!

This pie looks beautiful covered with fresh fruit. Decorate it with slices of papaya, some rounds of banana, sliced strawberries, whole raspberries or blueberries, little circles of pomegranate seeds—whatever is fresh, colorful and beautiful that day. To prevent darkening, dip the fruit in lemon juice before arranging it on the pie.

For crust: Make the pie crust and press into 9-inch (22.5 cm) pan; set aside.

For filling: Place the sliced strawberries in the crust. In a blender, combine the papayas, bananas and cinnamon and blend until the mixture is a smooth purée. Add the lemon and zest; blend until smooth. Sprinkle in the psyllium; blend until thoroughly mixed. Immediately pour the mixture over the strawberries. Chill until firm. Decorate with fruit that has been dipped in lemon juice. Makes a 9-inch (22.5 cm) pie.

Frozen Mango Pie

Crust
1 recipe Almond-Maple Crust (see recipe, page 165)

Filling
4–5 cups frozen mango chunks
¾ cup diced, dried apricots, frozen (optional)
½ cup diced, pitted dates or maple sprinkles or date sugar (optional)

For best results, use a heavy-duty juicer to make this recipe. If the mangoes are not very sweet, add a half cup diced pitted dates or maple or date sugar to sweeten. If mangoes aren't in season, look for frozen ones at your local supermarket or substitute sweet, ripe, frozen persimmons, papaya, sapote and/or cherimoya. The pie shell is optional; as long as you keep the pie frozen, you can serve it in wedges, without the shell.

The mangoes and diced fruit need to be thoroughly frozen. All the frozen fruit recipes work best when the bowl that catches the "ice cream" as it comes out of the juicer has been chilled in the freezer. Work quickly to obtain the best results with this recipe.

For crust: Make the pie crust and press into an 8-inch (20 cm) pie pan; set aside.

For filling: Using a heavy-duty juicer, with a blank screen, alternate putting the frozen mango chunks, dried apricots and dates through the machine and into a large bowl. Place the mixture in the crust. Freeze. Makes an 8-inch (20 cm) pie.

Variation 1: For a chunky effect, dice the apricots very small, and, instead of putting them through the juicer, simply stir them into the mixture just before pouring the filling into the pie shell.
Variation 2: Replace the frozen dried apricots with frozen dried mango slices.

Tropical Fruit Pie

Strawberry Pie

Crust

1 recipe Almond-Maple Crust (see recipe, page 165) or Almond-Date Crust (see recipe, page 164)

Filling

4 cups sliced strawberries

Binder

6 pitted dates, soaked 4–8 hours (reserve soak water)

2 cups quartered strawberries

Maple syrup or date sugar or stevia, to taste (optional)

4 teaspoons psyllium

This pie is made by piling the fresh, sliced fruit into the crust, then making a sweet, thick mixture called a binder and pouring it over the fresh berries to hold them together. Serve the pie with a dollop of Fluff Topping (see recipe, page 177). This recipe works equally well for blueberries, boysenberries, raspberries or a mixture of berries.

Use your favorite crust. Almond-Maple Crust is thin and delicate; Almond-Date Crust is thicker, sweeter and heartier.

For crust: Make the pie crust and press into a 9-inch (22.5 cm) pie pan; set aside.

For filling: Place the sliced strawberries in the crust.

For binder: See soaking instructions for dates, page 5. In a blender, combine the quartered strawberries with the dates and enough of the date soak water to achieve a thick purée. Taste and add sweetener, if required. While the blender is still running, gradually add the psyllium. When the mixture is very thick and smooth, immediately pour it over the strawberries in the crust, being sure to cover all areas of the pie. Using a spatula, smooth the binder around and into the berries. Refrigerate for at least 1 hour before serving.

Serve within 4 hours. Makes a 9-inch (22.5 cm) pie.

Peach Pie

Crust

1 recipe Almond-Date Crust (see recipe, page 164)

Filling

4 cups peeled and very thinly sliced ripe peaches

1 tablespoon lemon juice

Cinnamon, to taste

Topping

6 dates, soaked 30 minutes and pitted (reserve soak water)

2–3 very ripe peaches, peeled and roughly chopped

Maple sprinkles or date sugar or stevia, to taste (optional)

1–2 tablespoons psyllium

Use only very ripe peaches or the pie won't work. (Don't even think of trying this recipe with hard, unripened fruit.) They should be soft, fragrant and sliced very thin. Depending on the sweetness of the peaches, use more or less dates for the filling. For a peaches and cream experience, top the pie with Fluff Topping (see recipe, page 177).

For crust: Make the pie crust and press into a 9-inch (22.5 cm) pie pan; set aside.

For filling: In a bowl, toss the sliced peaches with lemon juice and cinnamon; set aside.

For topping: See soaking instructions for dates, page 5. In a blender, combine the chopped peaches with enough of the date soak water to allow the blender to operate; blend until smooth. Add the dates and enough soak water to achieve a smooth and thick consistency. Adjust for sweetness with the maple sprinkles. Add the psyllium; blend. Quickly pour the topping over the sliced peaches; mix thoroughly. Immediately pour the filling into crust. Refrigerate. Makes a 9-inch (22.5 cm) pie.

Variation: For a tart apple pie, replace the peaches with Granny Smith apples. For a sweeter apple pie, use Fuji, Jonagold or MacIntosh apples.

Yam Pie

Yam Pie

Crust

1 recipe Almond-date Crust (see recipe, page 164)

Filling

¾ cup dates, soaked 20 minutes, pitted and coarsely chopped

¼ cup raisins, soaked 20 minutes (reserve soak water)

½ cup pine nuts, soaked 5–10 minutes

6 small yams, peeled and cut in chunks

½ teaspoon cinnamon

½ teaspoon vanilla

⅛ teaspoon Chinese 5-spice powder

⅛ teaspoon garam masala or cloves or additional Chinese 5-spice powder

2 tablespoons psyllium

If you are wondering what recipe to prepare for friends who have not yet been introduced to raw food, wonder no more! This delicious pie is difficult to distinguish from its cooked cousin. It also freezes very well.

Let it thaw in the refrigerator. Because yams and sweet potatoes are available all year long (their harvest is July-August, but they keep in cold storage), this pie can be as big a hit in the fall as at a midsummer's party. Although you can make this pie with sweet potatoes, look for the deep orange yams, particularly the Garnet or Jewel varieties at your organic grocer. (This is a plan-ahead recipe that calls for soaking the almonds for the crust.)

For crust: Make the pie crust and press it into a 9-inch (22.5 cm) pie pan; set aside.

For filling: See soaking instructions, page 5. Soak the dates, raisins and pine nuts in three separate bowls. In a heavy-duty juicer, using a blank screen, alternate putting the yams, dates, raisins and pine nuts through the machine and into a bowl. There should be at least 4 cups; if not, add more yam and put the mixture through the juicer again.

Transfer the mixture to a food processor. Process thoroughly. Add the cinnamon, vanilla, 5-spice powder and garam masala. Process again. Be patient with processing; the smoother the better. Add a small amount of raisin soak water if the mixture is not very smooth after 3–4 minutes. (Add the extra liquid only if it is necessary; the pie should not be too wet.) When the mixture is smooth, gradually add the psyllium, while the processor is running. Pour the filling into the crust immediately. Refrigerate. The pie will be ready to eat within 1 hour. Serve with a dollop of Fluff Topping (see recipe, page 177). Makes a 9-inch (22.5 cm) pie.

Variation: For a more intense flavor, soak the fruit in the juice of 1 orange. Add 1 teaspoon orange zest to the yam mixture. Increase the existing spices by: ¼ teaspoon cinnamon, ½ teaspoon vanilla, ⅛ teaspoon Chinese 5-spice powder, pinch cloves, pinch sea salt.

Raisin Frosting

1 cup raisins, soaked 1 hour

1 cup apple juice

1 tablespoon flaxseed oil ½ teaspoon vanilla

Pinch cinnamon

1 teaspoon psyllium

A strong dose of sugar. Use this frosting to ice carrot cake or apple cookie supreme or put a thin layer on top of frozen banana or mango pie.

In a small bowl, combine the raisins and apple juice; let soak 1 hour; drain, reserving soak liquid. In a blender, combine the raisins with enough of the reserved soak liquid to allow the blender to operate; blend. When the raisins are very smooth blend in the oil, then the vanilla and cinnamon. Add the psyllium slowly. Blend thoroughly, then let the mixture thicken for 30–60 minutes in the refrigerator before using. Yields about ½ cup.

Banana-Coconut Creme Pie

This fabulous, make-ahead dessert is a great introduction to raw food as it tastes better than any "ice cream" pie made with dairy products. For best results, prepare and freeze the bananas, coconut and dates the day before you make the recipe.

For crust: Make the pie crust and press into a round layer-cake pan or an 8-inch (20 cm) pie pan; set aside.

For filling: In a heavy-duty juicer, using a blank screen, alternate putting the bananas, coconut and dates through the machine and into a chilled bowl. Quickly stir in the vanilla. Pour the mixture into the crust, smoothing the top with a spatula or the back of a spoon. Top with the coconut. Place the pie immediately in freezer. Keep the pie frozen until 15 minutes before serving, then place it in the refrigerator so that it softens enough to slice easily. Dipping the knife in hot water makes slicing easier. Makes an 8-inch (20 cm) pie.

Variation: for Carob-Coconut-Banana Creme Pie, quickly mix in ¾ cup carob powder just after the fruit comes out of the juicer. Mix in ¼ cup at a time. (Be careful to avoid inhaling carob powder; it is very fine and tends to become airborne.) Freeze. For utter decadence, frost with Raisin Frosting (see recipe, page 172).

Crust

1 recipe Almond-Maple Crust (see recipe, page 165) or Almond-Date Crust (see recipe, page 164)

Filling

6 frozen bananas
1 cup coconut, frozen
½ cup dates, chopped and frozen
1 teaspoon vanilla
2 tablespoons coconut

Lemon Pudding/Frosting

This dessert packs a wonderfully intense lemon flavor. To serve it as a frosting, thin it with additional lemon juice, if necessary. For best flavor, eat within four hours of preparation.

See soaking instructions, page 5. In a blender, combine the cashews and lemon juice; blend until smooth. Add the lemons and dates; blend until smooth. Taste for sweetness. Add additional dates or a little maple syrup, if necessary. Blend in the flaxseed oil. Eat within 4 hours of preparation. Serves 4.

1 cup cashews, soaked 8–12 hours
6 dates, soaked 8–12 hours and cut in chunks
Juice of 1 lemon
2 lemons, peeled, seeded and cut in chunks
1 tablespoon flaxseed oil

Banana Ice Cream

Ice Cream

For a delicious dessert, there is no need to get fancy with crusts and toppings; often the best approach is the simplest. Banana ice cream is easy and delicious. All you need is a heavy-duty juicer and an ample supply of frozen bananas.

Frozen mango chunks also make a delicious simple ice cream. Mix different frozen fruits to create tasty and attractive desserts. Try half banana and half mango. First put all the banana through the juicer, directing it into one side of a chilled bowl, then put through all the mango, directing it to the other side. The result is a beautiful orange and white mixture. Mix in a few frozen berries with the banana. Experiment with frozen sweet, ripe melon chunks which will make a sherbet-like frozen dessert. Have fun creating your very own assortment of healthier ice cream treats.

If you don't own a heavy-duty juicer, try making ice cream either in your blender or food processor. Add a bit of liquid such as apple juice to the frozen chunks or wait for the chunks to thaw a bit, then process or blend. While the result won't be as perfect as juicer-made ice cream, it will still be delicious.

Banana Ice Cream

Banana ice cream is a good reason to own a heavy-duty juicer. Keep a supply of ripe bananas in your freezer. Bananas are ready when the skins have brown spots on them and no trace of green. Peel the bananas first and freeze them in plastic bags.

1–2 ripe bananas, frozen

In a heavy-duty juicer, using a blank screen, process the frozen banana, catching it in a chilled bowl. Eat immediately. Serves 1.

Variation 1: Add frozen date bits or raisins or other fruit, or top the ice cream with carob sauce to make it a sundae.

Variation 2: For frozen Banana Pie, use 6–8 frozen bananas to fit a round layer-cake pan, or 8-inch (20 cm) pie pan. Top the pie with carob sauce or strawberries, then freeze.

Variation 3: For frozen Carob-Raspberry-Banana Pie, cover a frozen Banana Pie with puréed raspberries. Freeze. Pour a thick layer of carob sauce over the raspberry topping and freeze again.

Sweet Dust Topping

Similar to confectioner's sugar, this simple combination works well sprinkled on fruit or dusted over a dessert for a touch of sweetness.

4 tablespoons sesame seeds
1 tablespoon maple sprinkles
  or date sugar

In a clean electric coffee grinder, combine the sesame seeds and maple sprinkles and grind until powdered.

Apple Sorbet

2 cups applesauce (see note)

2 cups apple juice (approximately 4 apples)

2 tablespoons maple syrup or 2–4 dates, soaked 60 minutes

2 teaspoons lemon juice

This light and refreshing dessert takes a simple apple and makes it taste like something sinful. Use sweet apples. If you use tart apples, like Granny Smith, you may need to use a lot more maple syrup or dates to achieve the level of sweetness you want in a dessert. Try this recipe with peaches, kiwi, papaya, mango, plum, sapote or cherimoya.

In a blender or food processor, combine the applesauce, juice, syrup and lemon juice and blend until smooth. Taste and adjust for sweetness. Place the mixture in a shallow container with a lid and freeze, covered. Serve by scraping into curls with a soup spoon or ice cream scoop.

Note: To make applesauce, put 3–4 peeled apples through a heavy-duty juicer, using the blank screen.

Variation: For a special drink, add a scoop or two of Apple Sorbet to chilled, sparkling apple cider or apple juice.

Ice Cream Parlor Sauce

1 cup water

4 tablespoons raw tahini

4 tablespoons honey

¾ cup raw carob

½ teaspoon vanilla

Pinch sea salt

This sauce is reminiscent of the kind served by old-fashioned ice cream parlors; it is thin and chocolate-like. Carob is ground very fine so be careful not to inhale it while you work.

In a blender, place the water. Add the tahini 1 tablespoon at a time; blend after each addition. Add the honey 1 tablespoon at a time; blend after each addition. Add the carob ¼ cup at a time; blend after each addition. Add the vanilla and salt; blend. This sauce will keep for several weeks in the refrigerator. Yields 2 cups.

Date-Nut Logs

1½ cups dates, soaked 20 minutes, pitted

1 cup pecans or almonds or walnuts

1 cup coconut

1 teaspoon cinnamon

½ teaspoon vanilla

A nice sweet to have in the house for a snack, to bring to work or to pack in a school lunch box.

See soaking instructions, page 5. In a food processor, process the nuts until finely chopped. Add the coconut and briefly pulse-chop until mixed; add the cinnamon and vanilla. Add the dates a few at a time, processing until well mixed. Transfer the mixture to a large bowl and knead. Roll the mixture into finger-shaped 3-inch (7.5 cm) long logs. Roll in additional coconut. Refrigerate. The logs will keep in the refrigerator for up to 2 weeks, or longer in the freezer. Yields approximately 24 pieces.

Fluff Topping

Cashews have a natural sweetness; combined with dates, they are delectable. Soaked cashews will grind up into a very smooth fluffy topping that may be used in place of whipped cream or yogurt, and is superior to both. (Add the optional vanilla for a more "whipped cream" flavor.)

You can also use almonds, although they won't give up their mealy texture, no matter how much you blend. But they make a tasty topping and are the most nutritious nut. Using peeled almonds will result in a better texture for this recipe (see note).

Because of their softness and sweetness, medjool dates will give the best results, but khadrawi or honey dates will work, too. If you don't have time to soak the nuts and dates 8–12 hours, soak them for at least 4 hours.

See soaking instructions, page 5. In a small bowl, combine the dates with water to cover, plus 2 inches; place in refrigerator and let soak 8–10 hours.

Place the nuts in a blender. Grind the nuts, gradually adding date soak water until the mixture is the consistency of whipped cream. Add the dates one at a time. Blend until the mixture is smooth and creamy. Refrigerate. Fluff keeps well for up to 1 week. Yields 2 cups.

Variation: To make a rich Cashew–Date Frosting, blend the unsoaked cashews with enough water until the mixture is smooth, then add unsoaked dates 1 at a time until the desired thickness and sweetness are achieved.

Note: To peel almonds: After soaking and rinsing, place the almonds in bowl and pour very hot water (the equivalent of hot tap water) over the almonds to cover. Soak the almonds in the hot water for up to 1 minute; rinse with cool water. The skins should slip off when you pinch the end of the almond. Or, use almonds that have soaked for several days in the refrigerator, with daily water changes. After a few days, the skins can be peeled, although they don't come off as easily as with the hot water method.

1 cup of cashews or almonds or filberts, soaked 8–12 hours

4–6 soft pitted dates, soaked 8–12 hours (reserve soak water)

½ teaspoon vanilla (optional)

Fruit Dip or Pudding

Experiment with this recipe using whatever fruit is available and in season. With avocado and banana as a base just about any combination will taste delicious. Serve it as a fruit dip, a dessert pudding, or a breakfast dish.

In a blender, combine the banana and avocado; blend. Add the raspberries and strawberries gradually. Blend until smooth. Yields about ¾ cup.

Variation: For carob pudding, add 2–3 tablespoons carob powder.

1 ripe banana

½ ripe avocado

½ cup raspberries

4 strawberries

Mango Lime Parfait

Mango-Lime Parfait

A soft, cool and smooth dessert. For a strong citrus flavor, add one whole peeled lemon or lime to the blender in addition to the lemon or lime juice called for in the recipe. Before adding the dates, taste the mango mixture; you may not want to add too many if the mangoes are already sweet.

For crust: Make the pie crust using 1 cup of almonds. Do not press it into a pie pan; reserve the crust mixture in a bowl.

For filling: In a blender, place the mango pieces; blend until smooth. Add the juice, zest and dates; process until smooth. Be patient. Mango is a very fibrous fruit and you want to achieve smooth, pudding-like results.

Set out 4 parfait or wine glasses. Place some of the crust mixture at the bottom of each glass; add a layer of 3 or more tablespoons of the mango mixture; add another layer of crust. Repeat layers, finishing with the crust.

Variation 1: Substitute papaya or persimmon for mango.

Variation 2: Add another layer, consisting of thinly sliced kiwi fruit or strawberries.

Crust

1 recipe, Almond-Maple Crust (see recipe, page 165)

Filling

4 cups coarsely chopped mango (about 5 mangoes)

1 cup lime or lemon juice

1 teaspoon lime or lemon zest

4–8 dates, pitted and chopped

Sunflower Cookies

These cookies are sure to make a big hit with cookie lovers of all ages. Use a clean electric coffee grinder to grind up the sunflower seeds and pine nuts.

In a food processor, process the sunflower meal, pine nut meal and salt; add 6 dates, 1 at a time. When the mixture forms a ball, taste it for sweetness; add additional dates if necessary. When the dough is sweet enough, add the juice gradually until the mixture forms a thick dough. Roll the dough out thinly between two pieces of waxed paper. Cut into desired shapes. The cookies may be dehydrated for 8–12 hours, then frozen, or simply eaten as is.

Variation: Use 2 tablespoons maple sprinkles instead of the dates. Roll the dough into small balls and dehydrate or freeze.

1 cup sunflower seeds, ground

¼ cup pine nuts, ground

1 pinch sea salt

6–8 dates, pitted and chopped

1–2 tablespoons orange or apple juice

Apple Cookie Supreme

Cookies
2 cups hulled buckwheat groats, sprouted 12–24 hours

6 tablespoons maple syrup

4 tablespoons walnut oil

1 teaspoon cinnamon

1 teaspoon vanilla

Topping (per cookie)
2 teaspoons almond butter

1 teaspoon maple syrup

Thinly sliced apple or banana or strawberries or other fruit

Dash cinnamon (optional)

Here is an imaginative use of raw food ingredients with many possible variations. Because the cookies store well, all you have to do is add a topping at the last minute. Top only as many cookies as you will eat right away, otherwise the cookies will become soggy.

The base for this cookie is made from sprouted raw hulled buckwheat groats. Each cookie contains about two to three teaspoons of sweetened raw almond butter as a topping, so it is quite rich. You can freeze the base cookies, being sure to wrap and store them carefully as they are fragile. This is a plan-ahead recipe, as it calls for sprouting buckwheat groats (see sprouting chart, page 194).

For cookies: In a food processor, combine the sprouted buckwheat groats, maple syrup, oil, cinnamon and vanilla. Process until a dough is formed. On a dehydrator tray lined with a solid sheet, make approximately 18 3-inch (7.5 cm) rounds, 1/4-inch (0.5 cm) thick. Dehydrate them until dry throughout (12 hours or more).

Check every few hours and turn the cookies over when the top is dry. The cookies can also be dehydrated in the sun or, less desirably, in an oven that is intermittently warmed and shut off, maintaining the lowest possible heat. Refrigerate the cookies in an airtight container or freeze them.

For topping: In a small bowl, combine the almond butter and maple syrup. Spread the topping over each cookie. Top with apple slices. Sprinkle with cinnamon.

Variation: For topping, replace the maple syrup with 2 teaspoons honey, thinned with a little water if necessary, or 1–2 teaspoons maple sprinkles (also called maple granules) or date sugar. Or, use Raisin Frosting (see recipe, page 172) as a topping.

Carob Confection

1 cup almonds
1½ cups raw carob powder
2 tablespoons pine nuts
½ cup coconut
¼ cup plus 1 tablespoon honey
¼ cup plus 1 tablespoon water
Carob powder or coconut or ground almonds

Put these tasty confections in a pretty box, and bring them to the next dinner party you attend. These sweets are easily prepared in the food processor and they will keep in the refrigerator for two weeks.

In a food processor, process the almonds until finely chopped. Add the carob, pine nuts and coconut; process until mixed. Mix the honey and water together and add them gradually to the almond mixture while the processor is running. Process until the ingredients are well mixed and a dough is formed. Roll into balls. Roll the balls in carob or coconut or ground almonds (roll in some of each for a decorative platter of confections). Yields 24–30 pieces.

Carob Sauce

1 cup raisins, soaked 8–12 hours (reserve soak water)
8 dates, soaked 8–12 hours
4–5 tablespoons raw carob powder
½ teaspoon vanilla
2 tablespoons flaxseed oil

Carob is a healthier alternative to chocolate. Chocolate is approximately 23 percent fat, while carob is only 1 percent (unsaturated) fat. It is higher in sugar than chocolate, containing 48 percent sugar compared to 5 percent in chocolate. One tablespoon of carob contains 25 calories and some potassium and calcium, along with 1 gram of fiber. Also called St. John's fruit, it is commonly sold cooked, although it is also available raw.

In a small bowl, place the raisins and cover them with 1½ cups water. In a small bowl, place the dates with water to cover, plus 2 inches; soak the dried fruit for 8–12 hours. Drain, reserving the raisin soak water.

In a blender, combine the raisins and dates with enough of the reserved soak water to allow the blender to operate. Blend until smooth and thick, adding additional soak water if necessary to achieve desired consistency. Add carob; blend. Quickly blend in the vanilla and oil. For a warm sauce, just before serving, heat over a double boiler until warm to the touch. Yields approximately 1 cup.

Variation: For a quick one-portion sauce, moisten 2 tablespoons carob powder with enough maple syrup or honey to give you the sweetness and consistency you want. For a thicker sauce, add up to 1 teaspoon tahini. Or, mix equal amounts of carob powder and maple sprinkles or date sugar, then moisten with water.

Carob Confection

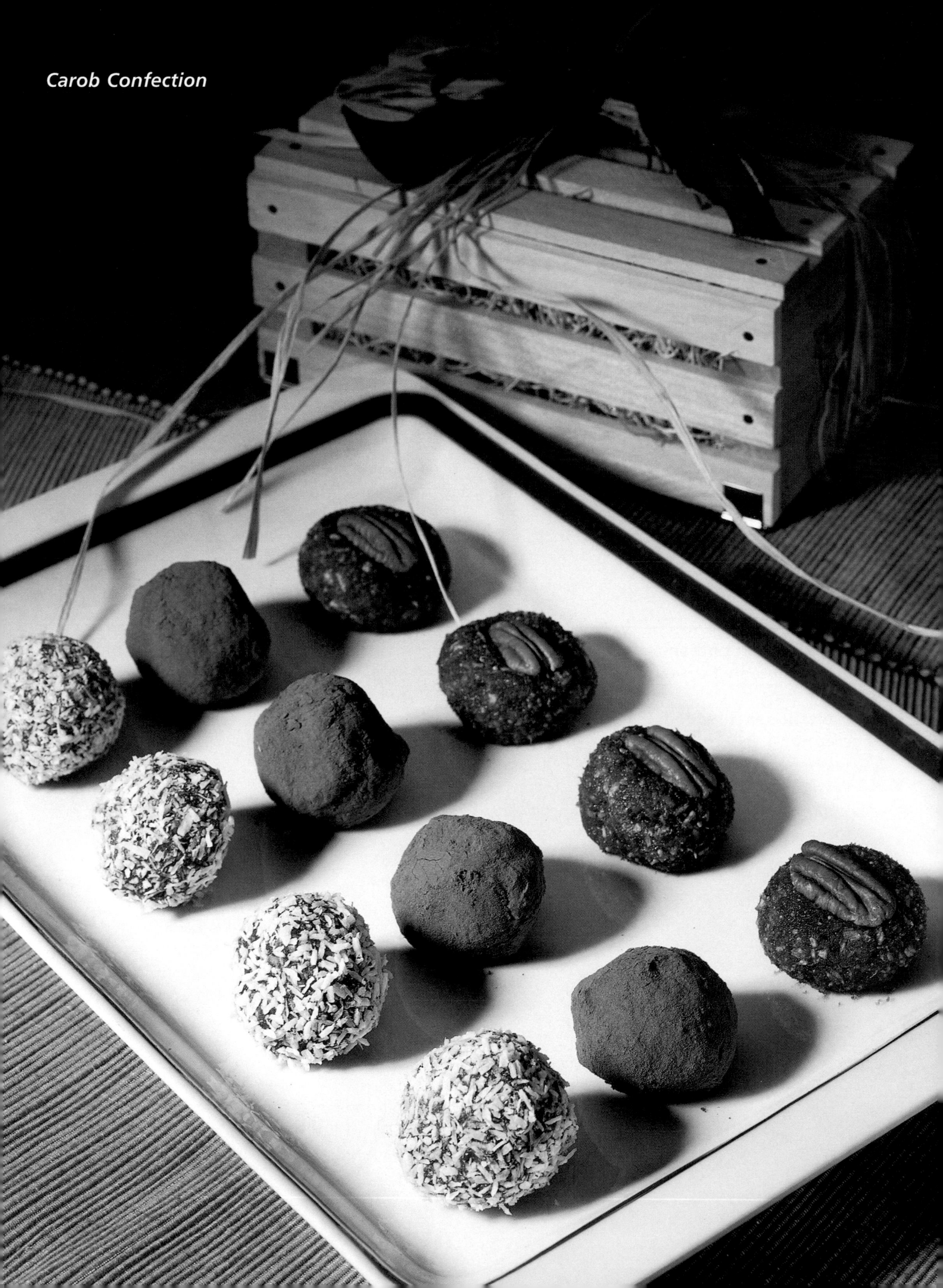

Halvah

1½ cup almonds
½ cup raw tahini
3 tablespoons honey
1 teaspoon vanilla
1 tablespoon plus 1 teaspoon
carob powder

Halvah is a candy popular in the Middle East, where it is usually made from ground sesame seeds. This recipe is far superior to the store-bought variety. For a lighter version, make this recipe with the almond pulp leftover from making almond milk. (Use the almond pulp the day you make it.)

In a food processor, place almonds and process until finely ground. Add the tahini, honey and vanilla; process thoroughly. Place ½ of the mixture in a bowl; set aside. Add carob to the remainder and process.

Press the plain mixture onto a plate or pan until it is ¼" (0.5 cm) thick (don't worry about filling the pan, just press the mixture to the correct thickness). Pat the carob mixture between your hands until it is approximately the same thickness. Place the carob mixture over the plain mixture. Press the two mixtures together to make a ½-inch (1 cm) thick, two-colored slab of halvah. Chill the halvah in the refrigerator for 1 hour or more, then cut it into bite-sized pieces and roll into little balls. Yields 20–24 pieces.

Variation: Omit the carob.

Energy Bars

1 cup walnuts or pecans
1 cup sprouted wheatberries
1 cup raisins
4 tablespoons shredded
coconut
2 tablespoons apple juice or
water (optional)
½ cup raisins or dates
(optional)

These dried fruit confections are less sweet than most because they contain sprouted wheatberries. They are more like an energy bar than a dessert. Take them on a hike or use them as a quick breakfast or snack. Try these recipes with other sprouted grains such as kamut, sunflower or barley. The coconut is optional in all the bars. Try several variations, using different nuts and fruits.

In a food processor, place the nuts and pulse them a few times to roughly chop them, then add the wheat berries, raisins and coconut. Process until a dough is formed, adding juice if necessary to achieve desired consistency. (Because this is a fairly dry mixture it has a tendency to stick to the blades. Watch it very closely in the processor, you may need to use a little liquid to keep the mixture moving.) Add additional rasins or dates for sweetness or consistency, if desired. Refrigerate. When the dough is cold, shape it into 3" x 1" x ½" (7.5 cm x 2.5 cm x 1 cm) bars. Roll in additional coconut. The bars will keep in the refrigerator for several weeks. Yields approximately 24 pieces.

Variation 1: For Pineapple-Walnut Bars, add to the recipe ½ cup dried pineapple that has been soaked 8–12 hours, ½ cup unsoaked raisins or dates and 4 tablespoons of coconut.
Variation 2: For Almond-Date Bars, use almonds in place of the walnuts.
Variation 3: For Apricot Bars, use almonds in place of the walnuts and 1 cup dried apricots (soaked for 4 hours) in place of the raisins.

Halvah

Orange-Date Dessert Bars

Crust
2 cups pecans or almonds or walnuts

1 cup oat flour (see note)

Dash cinnamon

4 tablespoons maple syrup

Filling
2 cups pitted, quartered dates (soaked 30–60 minutes in juice)

3 tablespoons water

Juice of 1 large orange

Zest of 1 large orange

An elegant dessert with a smooth, thick, sweet date filling surrounded by a crunchy, not-too-sweet crust. This is another "I can't believe it's not cooked!" recipe.

Remove the zest from the orange then juice it, not the other way around! Since the dates need to soak for thirty to sixty minutes, begin soaking them in the water and orange juice then prepare the oat flour.

For crust: Place the nuts in a food processor and process until coarsely ground. Add the oat flour then pulse to mix. Add the cinnamon, then the maple syrup, 1 tablespoon at a time, until the mixture holds together. If necessary, add additional water or more maple syrup. Lightly oil a 9-inch (22.5 cm) square pan. Press ½ of the crust into the bottom of pan; reserve the remaining ½ of the crust mixture.

For filling: In a small bowl, combine the dates with the water and orange juice; let them soak 30–60 minutes. In a food processor, combine the dates, soak water and zest; purée until smooth. Spread the date mixture over the crust. Crumble remaining ½ of crust over top. Press the mixture down with your hands or the back of a spoon to compress and smooth the top crust. Place the mixture in the sun for several hours or dehydrate it until the top is warm to the touch or place it in a warm oven for 10–15 minutes. Cut into bars. Yields approximately 30 bars.

Note: To make oat flour, place whole, raw oats in a clean electric coffee grinder (several tablespoons at a time). Grind until very fine, then place in a coarse sieve to sift out any hard bits. If you make more than one cup, put the remainder in a plastic bag and store it in the freezer. Rolled oats can also be used, although they are not raw; they are a heated and processed product.

Variation: Use dried apricots, apples, pears, pineapple, fig or peaches (soaked 4 hours) in place of the dates.

Orange-Date Dessert Bars

Very Carrot Cake

½ cup raisins, soaked
  20 minutes

½ cup dried apricots, soaked
  20 minutes

2 cups pecans or walnuts

2 tablespoons pine nuts

1½ cups coconut

1 teaspoon cinnamon

¼ teaspoon Chinese 5-spice
  powder

½ teaspoon garam masala or
  cinnamon

Pinch nutmeg

Pinch clove

6 cups carrot pulp

1½ cups date pieces or
  chopped dates

This tasty dessert makes enough to serve a crowd and keeps well for several days. Calling it cake is stretching a bit. It is dense and moist and chewy, more the consistency of fudge than cake. But whatever it is called, it will certainly satisfy your sweet tooth!

Make the carrot pulp while the fruit is soaking. Put the carrot juice aside for another recipe or drink it while you are working in the kitchen. Change from the juicing screen to the blank screen before proceeding with the rest of the recipe.

See soaking instructions, page 5. Soak the raisins and apricots in two separate bowls. In a food processor, combine the pecans and pine nuts; process until uniformly fine. Add the coconut and pulse a few times until mixed. Add the cinnamon, 5-spice powder, garam masala, nutmeg and clove and pulse until mixed; set aside.

In a heavy-duty juicer, using a blank screen, alternate putting the carrot pulp, raisins, apricots and dates through the machine and into a bowl. Knead this mixture with your hands until the ingredients are evenly combined. Add the nut mixture a little at a time, kneading it in. Firmly pack the mixture into a form pan or mold. This recipe is large enough to use several small molds or containers or put it in two 8-inch (20 cm) layer pans and make a layer cake with Raisin Frosting (see recipe, page 172). Yields 8 cups.

Dried Fruit Balls

1 cup dried apricots, soaked
  20 minutes

1 cup dates, soaked
  20 minutes and pitted
  (reserve soak water)

½ cup figs, soaked
  20 minutes

1 cup almonds or walnuts or
  pecans

½ cup coconut

30 extra almonds or walnuts
  or pecans (optional)

For a rich "chocolate"-type treat, add ¼–½ cup raw carob powder.

See soaking instructions, page 5. In a food processor, process the almonds until they are fine, but not a powder. Gradually add the apricots, dates, figs and coconut. Process until well mixed, using 1–2 tablespoons of soak water if necessary to create a doughy consistency. Refrigerate for several hours. Roll into small balls and press an almond into the top of each one. The balls will keep in the refrigerator for up to 2 weeks. Yields approximately 30 pieces.

Very Carrot Cake

Equipment

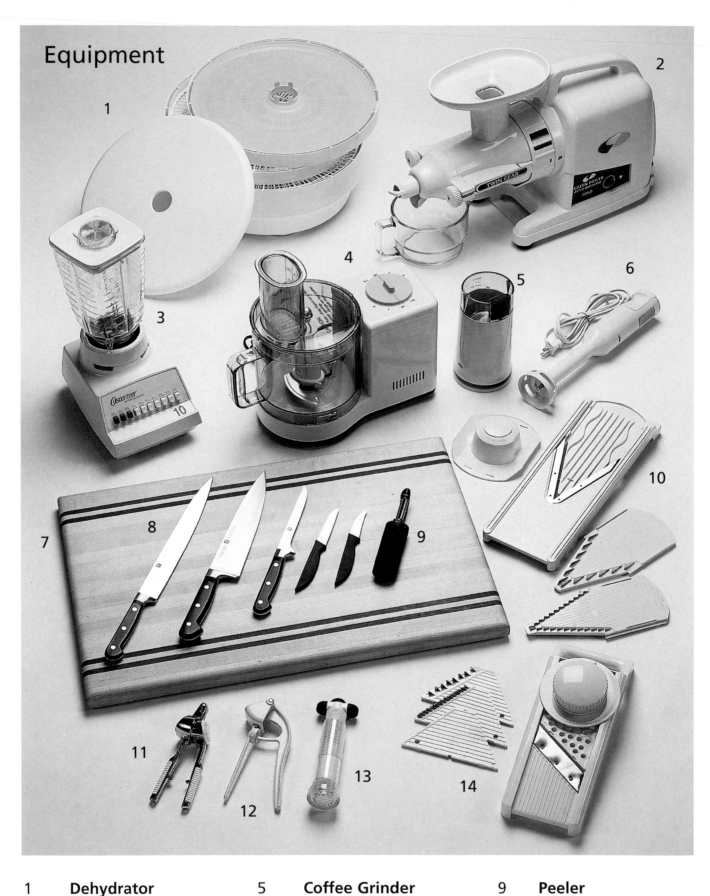

1	**Dehydrator**	5	**Coffee Grinder**	9	**Peeler**
2	**Juicer**	6	**Hand Blender**	10	**Mandoline**
3	**Blender**	7	**Cutting Board**	11-13	**Garlic Presses**
4	**Food Processor**	8	**Knives**	14	**Salad Shooter**

Appendix

Equipment List

Sharp knives: If you don't already own some, invest in a good set of sharp knives to make cutting vegetables fast and easy. It could make the difference between staying on a raw food program or not. You will need at least 1 paring knife and 1 large knife. Buy knives that can be sharpened at home!

Cutting board: There is a lot of controversy over whether wood or plastic is more hygienic. While plastic can go through the dishwasher, new evidence seems to suggest that wood has some special "disinfectant" properties. Whatever you decide, scrub the board until it is scrupulously clean each time you use it.

Blender: Make this one of your first purchases, after a grater and some sharp knives. An important piece of kitchen equipment, and relatively inexpensive, a blender is useful for purées, dressings, soups and more. Blenders are used when liquid is involved or soft smooth results are desired. For mixing large quantities of foods that are not liquid based, such as pie fillings, pâtés and loaves, a food processor is a better choice. The most important feature to look for in a blender is a strong motor. Often, older models are more powerful than more recent models. Many a newer model has had its motor burned out when attempting to blend soaked nuts or seeds. Garage sales are a great way to find an older blender with a powerful motor.

While you can function indefinitely with a traditional blender, the Vita-Mix brand is the ultimate in versatility, power and durability.

This powerful machine can blend or purée just about anything, including dry grains and nuts. This is an expensive machine and not essential. Buy one only after you already own the necessities: a good regular blender, a juicer, wheatgrass juicer and a good food processor.

Juicer: Perhaps the most of important piece of equipment you will buy. There are many juicers on the market but few that do an adequate job. Some juicers waste food, leaving behind a lot of wet pulp. Others heat up the juice from too much friction, damaging the delicate nutrients. Resist the temptation to buy a juicer from a department store or large discount store. To date, there are no juicers available from these sources that will serve you well.

There are several types of juicing machines. A centrifugal juicer expels the pulp into a basket as it spins. This type of machine does not do an adequate job of extracting the nourishment from the food and results in a lot of waste. Another type of juicer is a triturating or masticating machine that crushes the food, rupturing the cells and extracting high-quality nourishment. Slow-moving machines that use an augur do an adequate job, especially for wheatgrass. A meat grinder is an augur-type of machine. In fact, an old meat grinder will do a good job on wheatgrass if you happen to own one. Many years ago, Dr. Norman Walker invented the first excellent juicer, called the Norwalk. It is a combination augur and press. There are two steps involved, first passing the food through the augur, then placing the resulting pulp in a linen bag and pressing out

the remaining juice. The Norwalk process results in a very high quality of juice, but it is very time-consuming to use and a new Norwalk costs upwards of $2,000US, $3,000CDN.

Since the invention of the Norwalk, two more excellent types of juicers have been invented. A tried and true, trouble-free standby is the Champion. It is a masticating machine that will make juices, pâtés, ice cream, finely grated vegetables and more. The only thing the Champion cannot do is juice wheatgrass, certain herbs and other grasses. (Some distributors claim that the Champion will juice wheatgrass if you add a bit of water, but it doesn't do an adequate job because its friction creates heat that destroys the nutritional value of the wheatgrass juice.) The only changeable parts of a Champion are its filters. The blank is used for pâtés and ice cream, and the screen is used for juicing. By not using any filter at all, you can finely grate vegetables. Using the machine without any filter is not recommended by the manufacturer because when the blade is exposed, it can be very dangerous.

The newest juicer on the market is the Green Life machine, a simplified version of

the popular Green Power Juicer. It has a twin-gear design, where the food is pressed and crushed between the gears. It is expensive (more than twice the cost of the Champion) but it does all that the Champion does (except a fine grate) plus it will juice wheatgrass and all types of herbs and greens.

(Attachments for pasta making and other processes can be purchased separately.) It operates at a much lower speed than the Champion so it doesn't create heat from friction. Oxidation is further minimized by a feature that magnetizes the juice. The juice remains fresh much longer than with other juicers. If you are starting out with no equipment and are planning to use wheatgrass juice, it is worth the extra money to purchase either a Green Power or a Green Life machine. In the long run, you may save money because of the superior job it does extracting juice, thereby needing less produce.

There is another twin-gear design machine, actually the originator of the design, called the Angel Ultima. This machine is very highly rated as a juicer and wheatgrass juicer but it does not have the multi-purpose functions of a Green Power or a Champion. More expensive than the Green Power machine, the Angel Ultima would be useful as a juice-only, high-volume machine.

Wheatgrass juicer: To properly extract the juice from wheatgrass, an augur-type, slow-moving machine (or the twin-gear method as described above) is necessary to avoid creating heat from friction. If you own a juicer that doesn't work with wheatgrass, buy an inexpensive electric wheatgrass juicer, not a manual one (too much work!). A decent home-use wheatgrass juicer, such as the Miracle Wheatgrass Juicer, is less than $150US/$210CDN. An old meat grinder might work, as well as the Wheateena, which was once very popular for wheatgrass only. Keep your eyes open at garage sales!

Food processor: This multi-purpose machine saves a lot of time, especially when you are preparing food for a crowd. It comes with several blades that allow you to shred, grate and slice very quickly. But the most important feature is the steel blade, called the "S" blade, used for cutting, chopping and mixing. It makes all sorts of procedures virtually effortless—from chopping nuts to mixing all the ingredients for a pâté or loaf.

Salad shooter: Made by Presto, this small electric appliance slices and shreds very quickly and can be cleaned up fast. When working with the harder vegetables such as celery root, carrots, turnips and rutabagas it creates julienne-like pieces that are not mushy. This gadget is very useful for making tasty, creative salads.

Apple peeler-corer-slicer: A fun but non-essential gadget to have, this will help make apple pie a snap. Use it to peel, core and slice apples and vegetables like turnips very quickly.

Dehydrator: Dehydrators are used to partially or completely dry or warm food, while leaving the enzymes intact. Certain recipes for cookies, fruit leathers, stuffed vegetables, fruits, crackers, breads and many other items rely on the dehydrator for their texture, taste and shelf-life. Using a dehydrator can greatly expand your repertoire of delicious recipes, but it is not the first thing you need to buy.

The most important feature of a dehydrator is temperature control. Your dehydrator should also have a way to deliver the warm air as efficiently as possible so that your food will dry or warm evenly. The Excalibur 9 tray model is a good choice, as it gives you 15 square feet (4.5 square meters) of drying area, along with an efficient fan and a thermostat that allows you to set the temperature. It is also quite compact. The dehydrator comes with tray liners that resemble a plastic screen. Buy the solid liners, too, for cookies and fruit leathers. The Excalibur manufacturer calls them teflex liners.

Mandoline: This stainless steel, French-made piece of equipment can take the place of graters, cutting blades, salad shooters and a lot of hand-slicing, dicing and julienne. Professional chefs use the mandoline extensively to make short work of mounds of vegetables.

The mandoline is a rectangular piece of equipment with changeable blades that the food is drawn across, quickly cutting it into various shapes. Country fairs and kitchen equipment stores often sell inexpensive plastic versions. But, be warned that the mandoline is an extremely dangerous piece of equipment; its razor-sharp blades are not for the novice or the average home cook. However, if you are preparing large quantities of food and have skilled hands and a careful nature, a mandoline is a time-saving piece of equipment.

Garlic press: There are several different types on the market, all of which are capable of extracting small amounts of garlic, ginger or onion juice. Choose one that appeals to you.

Hand grater: The old standby grandma used to have still works just fine. The type that is just one flat piece of metal with several cutting sizes is good because you can work directly into a serving bowl. A hand grater can be indispensable when preparing food for one or if you do not own any other equipment.

Peeler: A high-quality, sharp vegetable peeler is essential.

Food mill, coffee grinder or spice mill: A small electric coffee grinder comes in very handy for grinding small quantities of nuts and seeds. Although you can grind nuts and seeds in a food processor, you can't always adequately work with small quantities in a processor, nor does a processor grind them as finely as a mill. An electric coffee mill will cost less than fifteen dollars and is perfect for a few tablespoons of nuts or seeds.

Growing Sprouts at Home for Fun and Good Health

(not to mention saving lots of money on your grocery bill)

There are two basic methods for growing sprouts: the water method and the soil method. With the water method, the sprouts are typically grown in a jar. The sprouts are soaked in water for a time, drained and then rinsed regularly until the sprout reaches its ideal length. Depending on the type of sprout used, this will take anywhere from one to five days. Examples of sprouts grown in this manner are alfalfa, clover, fenugreek, pea, broccoli, radish, onion and mung. Once the sprouts reach their most desirable stage, you can slow their growth by refrigerating them. Sprouts will keep in the refrigerator for some time with occasional rinsing and draining.

The soil method of growing sprouts begins the same way but the little sprouts are then transferred to soil in a nursery flat or cafeteria tray and grown indoors until the sprout/vegetable is ready. This process takes anywhere from five to fourteen days. The most important sprouts grown in this manner are wheatgrass, sunflower sprouts and buckwheat lettuce.

Several grains and seeds are grown using both methods. Wheat, spelt, barley, kamut and similar grains can be grown in a jar to

Sprouting Chart

Item to be Sprouted	Method	Amount	Soaking Time	Sprouting Time
Adzuki Bean	Jar	½ cup	12 Hours	3–5 Days
Alfalfa Seed	Jar	3 tablespoons	5 hours	3–6 days
Almond	Jar	3 cups	overnight (8–10 hours)	Most often used soaked only- can be sprouted 1–2 days
Amaranth	Jar	1 cup	3–5 hours	2–3 days
Barley (hulless variety)	Jar	1 cup	6 hours	12–24 hours
Barley-unhulled, for grass	Soil—see Wheatgrass	2–2½ cups per flat	—	7–10 days
Broccoli seed	Jar	2 tablespoons	8 hours	3–4 days
Buckwheat, hulled	Jar	1 cup	6 hours (no longer)	1–2 days
Buckwheat, unhulled	Soil—see Wheatgrass	2–2½ cups per flat	—	7–9 days
Cabbage seed	Jar	1 tablespoon	4–6 hours	4–5 days

yield a small sprout for raw cereal and in recipes such as tabouli. They are also grown in soil for their grass.

You must use unhulled sunflower seeds (also called in-shell) in order to obtain the delicious soil-grown 4-inch (10 cm) long green sunflower sprouts. Once the seeds have soaked and sprouted a tiny tail in a jar or bucket, transfer them immediately to the soil. They will be ready in 5–8 days. You can obtain a small sprout using the jar method with hulled sunflower seeds. Soak the seeds overnight, then sprout them from four to twelve hours. Hulled, sprouted sunflower seeds are extremely easy to grow and are an important item in raw food preparation. They cost little to grow, provide valuable nutrition and have a delicious flavor.

Use the chart below as a guideline. For more comprehensive directions about sprout growing, read a book devoted solely to the subject (see Bibliography, page 215).

You may occasionally encounter a batch of seeds that does not sprout. Not all seeds are viable. Your seeds can go through a lot of hands before you receive them. For example, in the case of most oats, they are steamed after harvest to prevent rancidity. The life force in the grain has been killed, so that they will keep, inert, on the shelf for an indefinite period of time. Sometimes the seeds you buy are old, or have been in an overheated environment, have been exposed to moisture, or are a difficult variety to sprout. If you consistently find your seeds aren't sprouting, and you have tried a few different methods (soaked for less time, etc.), it may not be your technique. It could be the seed. It's important to find a good source for viable seeds. If your seeds don't sprout, tell your source, perhaps they can advise you. Since they buy by the ton, a reliable source tests each batch of sprouting seeds prior to purchasing them. What should you do with your seed or grain that is not viable? Feed it to the birds or squirrels, or give it to someone who will be cooking it, and look for another source.

Special Instructions	Estimated Yield	Length at Harvest
Rinse 2–3 times a day	4 cups	½"– 1½" (1 cm – 3.5cm)
Grows rapidly in warm climates; 'green' in indirect sun on last day	3–4 cups	1"–2" (2.5cm– 5cm)
Will keep in refrigerator up to 5 days—change soak water daily	4 cups	0–⅛" (up to 0.25 cm)
Rinse 3 or more times a day	3 cups	0–¼" (up to 0.5cm)
Difficult to obtain viable hulless variety for jar sprouting.	2½ cups	0–¼" (up to 0.5cm)
Follow instructions for Wheatgrass	—	—
Rinse 2–3 times a day. 'Green' in indirect sun last 1–2 days.	2 cups	1"–2" (2.5cm– 5cm)
For best results, rinse every 30 minutes for the first few hours.	2 cups	⅛"–½" (0.25cm–1cm)
Follow instructions for wheatgrass.	—	—
Rinse 2–3 times a day, shaking vigorously.	1½ cups	1"–2" (2.5cm– 5cm)

Item to be Sprouted	Method	Amount	Soaking Time	Sprouting Time
Clover	Jar	3 tablespoons	5 hours	4–6 days
Fenugreek	Jar	4 tablespoons	6 hours	2–5 days
Garbanzo Bean (also called chick pea or Ceci bean)	Jar	1 cup	12–48 hours	2–4 days
Kale seed	Jar	4 tablespoons	4–6 hours	4–6 days
Kamut	Jar or soil	—	—	—
Lentil	Jar	¾ cup	8 hours	2–3 days
Mustard seed	Jar	3 tablespoons	5 hours	3–5 days
Oats, hulled (unhulled for oat milk only)	Jar	1 cup	8 hours	1–2 days
Onion seed	Jar	1 tablespoon	4–6 hours	4–5 days
Pea	Jar	1 cup	8 hours	2–3 days
Pea (Pea Shoot)	Soil—see Wheatgrass	—	—	10–14 days
Pinto Bean	Jar	1 cup	12 hours	3–4 days
Pumpkin	Jar	1 cup	6 hours	1–2 days
Quinoa	Jar	1 cup	3–4 hours	2–3 days
Radish	Jar	3 tablespoons	6 hours	3–5 days
Rye	Jar	1 cup	6–8 hours	2–3 days
Seseame seed, hulled*	Jar	1 cup	8 hours	—
Sesame seed, unhulled*	Jar	1 cup	4–6 hours	1–2 days
Spelt	Jar	1 cup	6 hours	1–2 days
Sunflower, hulled	Jar	1 cup	6–8 hours	less than one day
Sunflower, unhulled	Soil—see Wheatgrass	2–2½ cups per flat	—	5–8 days
Teff	Jar	1 cup	3–4 hours	1–2 days
Wheat (for sprouts)	Jar	1 cup	8–10 hours	2–3 days
Wheatgrass—(Red winter wheat is the most commonly used variety)	Soil	2 cups per nursery flat	Soak in Jar or bucket for 8–12 hours. Important to Transfer sprouts to damp soil prior to reaching ¼"(0.5cm).	Place empty flat on top of seedlings. Leave alone. In 2–3 day spouts will lift up the top tray. Harvest between day 8 and10. Second growth possible, but not a sweet or as nourishing. Directions vary according to climate.

Estimated yield: these are rough approximations, there are too many variables to be accurate.
*Hulled sesame seed: will not sprout. Soak for 8 hours prior to using.
*Unhulled sesame seed: will sprout, good for sesame milk, strain very carefully. As sprouts, hulls are irritating to digestive tract for some people.

Special Instructions	Estimated Yield	Length at Harvest
Grows rapidly in warm climates, 'green' in indirect sun on last day.	3–4 cups	1"–2" (2.5cm– 5cm)
Becomes bitter if left to grow past one inch.	2½–3 cups	1"–2" (2.5cm– 5cm)
Soak longer for easier digestion. Rinse often.	3– 3½ cups	½"– 1" (1 cm – 2.5cm)
Rinse 2–3 times a day.	3–4 cups	¾"–1" (1.5cm–2.5 cm)
Follow instructions for wheatgrass.	—	—
Grows rapidly in warm climates. Rinse often. Use whole, unbroken, unsplit lentils.	3–4 cups	½"– 1" (1 cm – 2.5cm)
'Green' in indirect sun on last day.	3 cups	½"– 1½" (1 cm – 3.5cm)
Rinse 3 times a day. Buy unsteamed. Difficult to sprout; usually to use soaked only.	1 cup	0–⅛" (up to 0.25 cm)
Rinse 3 times a day	1½–2 cups	1"–2" (2.5 cm– 5 cm)
Refrigerate at ½"(1cm). Will keep 7–14 days if rinsed and drained regularly.	2½ cups	½"– 1" (1 cm – 2.5 cm)
Follow instructions for Wheatgrass.	—	4"–7" (10 cm–17.5 cm)
Rinse 4 times a day or more.	3–4 cups	½"– 1" (1 cm – 2.5 cm)
May not grow a sprout. Okay to use after soaking only.	1½–2 cups	0–⅛" (up to 0.25 cm)
For better taste-rinse 5–6 times prior to soaking.	3 cups	0–½" (up to 1 cm)
Rinse often and drain well. Needs air circulation. 'Green' in sun on last day.	3–4 cups	¾"–2" (1.5 cm–5 cm)
2 rinses a day. Do not leave in an overly warm environment.	3 cups	½"–¾" (1cm–1.5cm)
Soak 8 hours, no sprouting.	1½ cups	will not sprout
Rinse 4 times a day.	1½ cups	0–⅛" (up to 0.25 cm)
Use in recipes in place of wheat	—	0–¼" (up to 0.5cm)
Skim off skins after soaking.	2 cups	¼"– ½" (0.5 cm –1cm)
Follow instructions for Wheatgrass.	—	—
—	2½–3 cups	0–⅛" (up to 0.25 cm)
Grows rapidly in warm climates.	2–3 cups	¼"–¾" (0.5cm–1.5cm)
Days 3–8 water but do not soak the soil. Allow sprouts ample light to green. Put outdoors in the day during warm weather, or use a grow light or southern exposure window. Harvest before second set of leaves emerge. Cut and store in refrigerator; keeps 5–7 days.	—	—

Unless otherwise indicated, all jar sprouts should be rinsed 2 or 3 times a day. Directions: Fill jar with water. Swish vigorously, drain, repeat. All jar sprouts should be inverted in a dish rack or similar rack while sprouting. All jar sprouts require air circulation while sprouting and are best covered with screening, cheesecloth, or special sprouting lids.

Seasonal Buying and Storage Chart

Crop	Season	Origin	Best Variety	Best Storage	Shelf Life
Alfalfa seed	fall	Canada, US	—	cool dark pantry	1 year*
All beans	fall	US	—	cool dark pantry	2 years or more*
Almond butter, raw	late September	California	varied	refrigerator	4–6 months
Almonds, shelled	late September	California	Nonpareil	freezer, refrigerator	6 months
Apples, dried	October	Washington State	Delicious	Refrigerator, cool dark pantry	harvest to harvest
Apricots, dried	late July	California	Blenheim	refrigerator, cool dark pantry	harvest to harvest
Buckwheat, hulled (Kasha)	late September	US	—	refrigerate	6 months
Buckwheat, unhulled	late September	US	—	cool dark pantry	1 year*
Cashews	all year	Brazil, India, Africa, Vietnam	—	freezer, refrigerator	6 months
Cherries, dried	late July	California	Bing	refrigerator, cool dark pantry	harvest to harvest
Dates, all	September	California	Medjool, honey khadrawi	refrigerator, freezer	one year
Fenugreek	fall	Canada, US	—	cool dark pantry	1 year*
Figs, dried	October	California	Calimyrna Back Mission	freezer, refrigerator, cool dark pantry	harvest to harvest
Filberts, shelled	November	Oregon	—	freezer, refrigerator	6 months
Flax seed	fall	Canada, US	—	pantry	1 year*
Flax oil	fall (processed all year)	Canada, US	—	refrigerator/freezer	4 months from processing date
Grain	late September	US	—	cool dark pantry	1 year*
In shell nuts	see variety	see variety	—	cool, dark pantry	harvest to harvest*
Macadamias, shelled	December	California, Hawaii	—	freezer, refrigerator	6 months
Mango, dried	all year	tropics	fiberless	cool dark pantry	one year
Olive oil	November–December	California, Mediterranean	—	cool dark pantry, refrigerator	harvest to harvest
Olives	November–December	California, Mediterranean	—	cool dark pantry, refrigerate after opening	1 year
Pears, dried	October	California	Bartlett	cool dark pantry	harvest to harvest
Pecans, shelled	November	Georgia	—	freezer, refrigerator	6 months
Persimmons, dried	late October	California	Fuyu	cool dark pantry	harvest to harvest

Seasonal Buying and Storage Chart

Crop	Season	Origin	Best Variety	Best Storage	Shelf Life
Pine nuts (pignolias), shelled	all year	Portugal, China	—	freezer, refrigerator	6 months
Prunes, dried	September, October	California	Ashlock	freezer, refrigerator, cool dark pantry	harvest to harvest
Pumpkin, hulled	fall	China, Mexico	—	refrigerate	6 months
Raisins	September, October	California	Monukka or Thompson	refrigerator, cool dark pantry	harvest to harvest
Raw oats	late September	US	—	freezer, refrigerator	6 months
Red clover seed	fall	Canada, US	—	cool dark pantry	1 year*
Sesame oil	all year	Mexico, Guatemala, El Salvador	—	cool dark pantry	Harvest to harvest
Sesame tahini, raw	all year	Mexico, Guatemala, El Salvador	—	refrigerator	6 months
Sesame, hulled	all year	Mexico, Guatemala, El Salvador	—	refrigerator	6 months
Sunflower, hulled	fall	Minnesota, Kansas, Nebraska	—	refrigerator	6 months
Sunflower, in shell	fall	Minnesota, Kansas, Nebraska	—	cool dark pantry	1 year*
Walnuts	October	California	—	freezer, refrigerator	6 months
Wheat	late September	US		cool dark pantry	1 year*

* Conservative estimate. Under proper conditions they will last much longer.
All nuts in the shell will last much longer than harvest to harvest if stored in a cool area.
All unhulled grains and seeds will last much longer than harvest to harvest if stored in a cool area.
All hulled nuts and seeds have a shorter shelf-life, and are best stored in the refrigerator or freezer.

Information courtesy of SunOrganic Farm.

About Food Combining

The theory of food combining is based on the fact that each type of food requires different lengths of time, different enzymes and different pH balances (the degree of acidity or alkalinity of the digestive juices) for proper digestion. Some foods, like nut and seed proteins, require an acid environment. Other foods, such as starches (winter squash, yams) and acid fruits (oranges, pineapple), break down more easily in an alkaline environment. Combining foods that require different digestive environments causes indigestion (gas, constipation, diarrhea, nausea, bloating, fatigue) and results in incomplete digestion.

Incomplete digestion forces the body to spend energy creating more digestive enzymes (and even white blood cells), thereby robbing it of the energy it needs to create tissue-building, metabolic enzymes.

Many people say that watermelon gives them indigestion. Since watermelon digests in only 20-30 minutes, when it enters a stomach filled with slower digesting food, it gets held up in its digestive process and ferments. This fermentation causes gas and discomfort. However, watermelon eaten on an empty stomach does not create digestive distress, and because of its rapid transit, the stomach is free to digest other foods within half an hour. As a result, one of the food combining rules is: Eat melons alone.

To combine foods properly, follow these guidelines:

1. Drink liquids alone. Drink at least 20 minutes prior to meals, not at the meal itself since liquids dilute the digestive juices.
2. Eat melons alone. Wait 30 minutes before consuming anything else.
3. Eat fruits alone. Lemons or lemon juice are the only exception to the rule. Both go well with all food and act as a preservative.
4. Do not combine acidic fruits with sweet fruits (e.g., oranges and dates).
5. Do not combine proteins and starches (e.g., nuts and yams).
6. Do not combine fruits and vegetables.
7. Do not combine too many different types of foods.

That sounds like a lot of "do nots" but, in practice, food combining is not very difficult.

Note that summer squashes, zucchini, peppers and cucumbers are botanically classified as fruit, but based on experience and the history of food combining, they are treated as vegetables. Tomatoes are also classified as a fruit, and, according to Dr. Herbert Shelton, a famous natural hygienist, tomatoes should either be eaten alone or combined with non-starchy vegetables and proteins. (Some of the health Institutes do not serve any tomatoes and do not feel that they combine well with vegetables or proteins.) Most people have no problem with these 'fruit-vegetables,' however, if you do notice digestive problems, stop combining them with vegetables and eat them alone or in combination only with each other. The avocado is also botanically classified as a fruit. However, in accordance with common usage, avocados combine easily with all foods except proteins and melons.

Not everyone agrees that food combining is an important issue. Renowned nutrition expert Dr. Gabriel Cousens believes that if you eat primarily enzyme-rich raw food, the food will digest itself making food combining rules unnecessary. Dr. Cousens feels that digestive difficulties arise from overeating, even the most nutritious foods. In his opinion, food combining principles are much more relevant when food is cooked because then the body must work harder to manufacture the necessary digestive enzymes.

Food Combining Groups

Proteins

Digestion Time: Approximately 4 hours

Beans (all)*	Brazil nuts	Pine nuts
Nut/Seed-based soups*	Cashews	Pinons (pignolias)
Nut/Seed dressings*	Chickpeas (garbanzo)	Pistachios
Nut/Seed milks*	Filberts (hazelnuts)	Poppy seeds
Nut/Seed pâtés*	Flax seeds	Pumpkin seeds
Nuts (all)*	Green coconuts	Sesame seeds
Soaked nuts and seeds*	Lentils	Soybeans
Sprouted nuts and seeds*	Macadamia	Sunflower seeds
Almonds	Pecans	Walnuts

*Note: Soaked and sprouted proteins combine best with other foods and are more easily assimilated by the body than nuts, seeds and beans that have not been soaked and/or sprouted.

Starches

Digestion Time: Approximately 2–3 hours

Sprouted grains*	Dried legumes	Rice
Sprouted legumes*	Dried peas and beans	Rye
Sprouted peas and beans*	Flours (all)	Spaghetti squash
Acorn squash	Grains	Sweet Potatoes
Amaranth	Hubbard squash	Teff
Barley	Millet	Wheat
Breads (all)	Oats	Winter squash
Buckwheat	Potatoes	Yams
Butternut squash	Pumpkin	
Cereals (all)	Quinoa	

*Note: Soaked and sprouted peas, beans, legumes and grains combine best with other foods and are more easily assimilated by the body than peas, beans, legumes and grains that have not been soaked or sprouted.

Low Starch-Content Vegetables
Digestion Time: Approximately 2–3 hours

Beets	Parsnip
Carrots	Peas
Celeriac (celery root)	Rutabaga
Corn	Turnip
Jerusalem artichoke	

High Water-Content Vegetables (Non-Starchy)
Digestion Time: Approximately 2–3 hours

Alfalfa sprouts	Clover sprouts	Mint
All leaf lettuces	Collard greens	Mizuna
All sprouted greens	Crookneck squash	Mung bean sprouts
Arugula	Cucumbers	Mustard greens
Asparagus	Daikon radish	Okra
Beet greens	Dandelion greens	Onions
Bok choy	Dill	Parsley
Broccoli	Edible weeds	Pea Greens
Brussel sprouts	Endive	Peppers (red, yellow, orange)
Buckwheat lettuce	Escarole	Radish sprouts
Cabbage	Fennel	Radishes
Cabbage sprouts	Fenugreek sprouts	Scallions
Cauliflower	Fresh herbs	Sorrel
Celery	Garlic	Spinach
Chard	Green beans	Summer squash
Chicory	Jicama	Sunflower greens
Chinese cabbage	Kale	Turnip greens
Chives	Kohlrabi	Watercress
Cilantro	Leeks	Zucchini

Fruit-Vegetables
Digestion Time: Approximately 2–3 hours

All summer squash	Pepper
Crookneck squash	Tomatoes
Cucumber	Zucchini

Melons
Digestion Time: Approximately 15–30 minutes

Cantaloupe	Muskmelon
Casaba	Persian
Crenshaw	Watermelon
Honeydew	

Acid Fruits
Digestion Time: Approximately 1–1½ hours

Apples (sour)	Kumquats	Pomegranates
Cherries (sour)	Lemons	Raspberries
Cranberries	Limes	Star fruit (carambola)
Grapefruit	Oranges	Strawberries
Grapes (sour)	Pineapples	Tangerines
Kiwi	Plums (sour)	Ugli fruit

Sub-Acid Fruits
Digestion Time: Approximately 1½–2 Hours

Apples (sweet)	Cherimoya	Mangoes
Apricots	Cherries (sweet)	Nectarines
Berries (most)	Fresh figs	Papaya
Blackberries	Grapes (most)	Peaches
Blueberries	Guavas	Pears
Boysenberries	Huckleberries	Plums (sweet)

Sweet Fruits
Digestion Time: Approximately 3–4 hours

All dried fruits	Persimmons
Bananas	Raisins
Dates	Sapote

Note: Avoid dried fruits and dates until the maintenance phase, then use them sparingly.

Exceptions: Avocados combine well with all foods except protein and melons (digestion time: 2 ¾ hours). Tomatoes are best eaten alone. During the maintenance phase, combine them with watery vegetables and proteins. Lemons and lemon juice combine well with all foods. The juice of fruits and vegetables generally can be combined (carrot/apple juice).

Three-Week Menu Plan

Week 1

	Breakfast	Mid-AM	Lunch	Mid-PM	Dinner
Monday	Watermelon or Green Drink*	Green Drink*	1 or 2 Sunny Roll-Ups with Sprout salad	Green Drink	Zucchini Zalad Sprouts
Tuesday	Watermelon or Green Drink	Green Drink	Faux Salmon Basic Hippocrates Mix Lemon-Garlic Dressing	Green Drink	Guacamole for One in red pepper cups Sprouts and greens Premier French Dressing
Wednesday	Watermelon or Green Drink	Green Drink	Green Drink	Green Drink	Green Drink
Thursday	Watermelon or Green Drink	Green Drink	Corny Cabbage Soup Sprout Salad Instant Almond Dressing	Green Drink	Vegetable Chop Suey Sprouts Ginger–Lime Dressing
Friday	Watermelon or Green Drink	Green Drink	Broccoli Mousse Sprout Salad Gado–Gado Dressing	Green Drink	Confetti Salad, sprouts Asian Dressing (made without tahini)
Saturday	Oranges and grapefruit	Green Drink	Asian Pâtè in pepper halves, served on a bed of sprouts	Green Drink	Summer Squash Provençale Assorted sprouts
Sunday	Melon— honeydew, cantaloupe or Persian	Green Drink	Hearty Carrot Soup Finocchio Salad Premier French Dressing	Green Drink	Sprouted rye salad Sunflower/buckwheat sprouts

*See directions for the Green Drink and watermelon juice in the Juice chapter.
Consume sprouts, dulse and/or other seaweed at every lunch and dinner. Consume sauerkraut several times a week. Serve protein meals at lunch to allow time for proper digestion. Serve predominantly complex carbohydrates at dinner.

Week 2

	Breakfast	Mid-AM	Lunch	Mid-PM	Dinner
Monday	Watermelon or Green Drink	Green Drink	Sun Garden Burgers Spinach and Mushroom Salad Citrus–Mushroom Dressing	Green Drink	Stuffed Avocado Delight Julienne of Carrot and Zucchini Greens and Sprouts
Tuesday	Watermelon or Green Drink	Green Drink	Vegetable Medley (make ½ recipe) Sprouts	Green Drink	Long Tail Rye Salad Basic Hippocrates Mix Premier French Dressing
Wednesday	Watermelon or Green Drink	Green Drink	Green Drink	Green Drink	Green Drink
Thursday	Watermelon or Green Drink	Green Drink	Summer Bounty Soup Sprouted Salad Sunflower Notmayo!	Green Drink	Gazpacho Salad Sprouts Garlicky French Dressing Sunny Corn Crackers
Friday	Watermelon or Green Drink	Green Drink	Popeye's Secret Ensalada Sprouts	Green Drink	Pea Soup (warmed) Confetti Salad Sprouts
Saturday	Oranges and grapefruit	Green Drink	Spinach Mousse Sprouted Salad, Greens Natural Nut Dressing	Green Drink	Corn 'n' Cabbage Salad Sprouted Salad, Greens Sauerkraut
Sunday	Melon— honeydew, cantaloupe or Persian	Green Drink	Harvest Vegetable Soup Sprouts Creamy Tahini Dressing	Green Drink	Curried Winter Squash Basic Hippocrates Mix Lemon and oil

Week 3

	Breakfast	Mid-AM	Lunch	Mid-PM	Dinner
Monday	Watermelon or Green Drink	Green Drink	Sunflower-Almond Nori Rolls Ensalada Vinaigrette	Green Drink	Deli Rye Thin Bread Asian Salad Asian Dressing (made without tahini)
Tuesday	Watermelon or Green Drink	Green Drink	Creamy Carrot-Asparagus Soup Sprout Salad Orange-Tahini Dressing	Green Drink	Cabbage Roll-ups Sprouts and Greens
Wednesday	Watermelon or Green Drink	Green Drink	Green Drink	Green Drink	Green Drink
Thursday	Watermelon or Green Drink	Green Drink	Carrot Sunny-Roll Ups Sprouts and Greens Hot Mustard Sauce	Green Drink	Over the Rainbow Salad sprouts French Dressing
Friday	Watermelon or Green Drink	Green Drink	Veggie Tartare with assorted condiments	Green Drink	Ensalada Red Salsa Avocado Dressing Sauerkraut
Saturday	Oranges and grapefruit	Green Drink	Bravo Brassica Soup Rainbow Salad Vinaigrette	Green Drink	Slivered Veggie Chop Suey Asian Dressing Sprouts
Sunday	Melon— honeydew, cantaloupe or Persian	Green Drink	Vegetable Supreme Loaf (½ recipe) Marvelous Mushroom Gravy Sprouts and Baby Greens	Green Drink	Warmed Beta Bergers Cole Slaw Sprouts and Greens

Gourmet Raw Cuisine

Special Occasion Menu Suggestions

Nori Roll Delight

Summer Tomato–Basil Soup
Wild Greens Salad with Tamari
  Dressing
Sunny Roll-Ups
  (Exotic Sunflower Pâté and assorted
  condiments nestled in a Nori Roll)
Zucchini Zalad
Mango–Lime Parfait

Asian Flavors Dinner

Warmed Gado-Gado Soup
Vegetable Chop Suey on Sprouts and
  Greens with Ginger–Lime Dressing
Asian Pâté in Red Pepper Cups
Hot Mustard
Very Carrot Cake

Faux Traditional

Baby Greens with Herb Vinaigrette
Warmed Marvelous Mushroom Soup
Festive Stuffed Mushrooms with
  Cranberries
Veggie Tartar Plate with Assorted
  Condiments
Sweet Potato/Yam Pie

An Elegant Brunch Buffet

Fresh Fruit Salad Bowl
Confetti Salad with Asian Dressing
Tureen of Corn Chowder
Spinach Mousse served with warmed
  Marvelous Mushroom Gravy
Apple Sorbet
Orange-Date Dessert Bars

Mexican Dinner

Warmed Marvelous Mushroom Soup
Chilled Organic Baby Greens with
  Premier French Dressing
Chile Rellenos with Mole Sauce and
  Mock Sour Cream
Guacomole and Red Salsa Avocado
  Sauce
Chopped Zucchini Mexicano
Frozen Carob Raspberry Banana Pie

Sources

This section is designed to help you find the items you need to be a raw fooder. For the most up-to-date sources, visit this author's website at: www.rawgourmet.com. There will be ongoing new recipes and support information. You can also email the Raw Gourmet at: RawGourmet@aol.com. For those who are not using the Internet, feel free to write the Raw Gourmet at:
P.O. Box 4133
Carlsbad, CA 92018-4133

Food

SunOrganic Farm
Box 409
San Marcos, CA 92079
Phone: 888-269-9888 (toll-free)
Fax: 760-510-9996
sales@sunorganicfarm.com

SunOrganic Farm is a mail-order catalog business that caters to raw fooders. They carry all the organic seeds, nuts and grains mentioned in this book. They personally test all the sproutable items for viability. They also carry an extensive line of dried fruits, dehydrated vegetables, dates, maple sprinkles and syrup, date sugar, oils, raw almond butter, raw tahini, olives, carob, bee pollen, herbs, spices, teas and more. For those of you who are not one hundred percent raw they have non-wheat pastas and beans and grains, plus some organic condiments and products.

Living Tree Community Foods
P.O. Box 10082
Berkeley, CA 94709-5082
Phone: 800-260-5534
          510-526-7106
Fax: 510-526-9516
www.livingtreecommunity.com

Living Tree Community is a mail-order catalog business that caters to raw-fooders. This organization supports family farmers and currently carries organic almond butters, other nut butters and all the organic nuts mentioned in this book. They also carry a large line of dried fruit including kiwi slices, sun-dried tomatoes, medjool dates, kalimyrna figs and much more. They ship worldwide.

Gold Mine Natural Food Co.
7805 Arjohns Drive
San Diego, CA 92126
Phone: 800-475-FOOD (3663)
Fax: 858-537-9830
www.goldminenaturalfood.com
email: sales@goldminenaturalfood.com

Goldmine Natural Food Company is a mail-order catalog business that caters to our macrobiotic friends. They have a fine selection of the seaweeds used in this book, high-quality sea salt, miso, tamari, oils, dried mushrooms, agar, kuzu and more. For those who are not one hundred percent raw they also supply non-wheat pastas and many flavorful items to spice up your food, along with other natural products.

Diamond Organics
Highway 1
Moss Landing, CA 95039
Phone: 888-ORGANIC (674-2642)
Fax: 888-888-6777
info@diamondorganics.com
www.diamondorganics.com

Diamond Organics offers year-round shipping of organic produce, including wheatgrass, many types of sprouts, fruit, vegetables, greens, herbs, flowers and roots. They feature vegetables, fruits and greens for juicing.

In the UK:

The Fresh Network
PO Box 71, Ely, Cambs,
CB6 3ZQ, UK
Phone: 0870-800-7070
Fax: 0870-800-7071

The Fresh Network is the UK source for books, equipment and information, also serving parts of Europe. They sponsor many raw food events throughout the year and publish a quarterly subscription magazine.

The Soil Association

Bristol House
40-56 Victoria Street
Bristol, England BS1 6BY
Phone: 0117-314-5000
Fax: 0117-314-5001
info@soilassociation.org

The Soil Association publishes a yearly directory of organic suppliers for the UK (Scotland, Wales, England, Northern Ireland). It is listed by county/unitary authority. It also offers an extensive list of companies offering nationwide delivery.

Sprouts and Sprouting Supplies

Sproutpeople®

19581 Viking Ave. NW
Poulsbo, WA 98370
Toll-free: 877-6887 (877-SPROUTS)
Phone: 360-779-1885
Fax: 360-779-1887
www.sproutpeople.com

The Sproutpeople carry a wide selection of organic seeds and sprouting supplies. They are happy to give advice, also.

Super Sprouts, Inc
Living Foods Resource Center

720 Bathurst Street
Toronto, Ontario M5S 2RV
Phone: 416-977-7796
Fax: 416-977-8929

Super Sprouts offers a juice and salad bar, including fresh wheatgrass juice. They grow sunflower, buckwheat, wheatgrass and hydroponic sprouts and hold frequent lectures and classes on raw food topics. They also carry books and equipment. Wholesale and retail prices. Home delivery by request.

Sunflower Farms

12033 Woodinville Dr. #22
Bothell, WA 98011
Fax: 425-488-5652

Sunflower Farms ships buckwheat lettuce, sunflower greens, wheatgrass and pea greens, all certified organic by the state of Washington. They also have a mix that is available seasonally.

Healthy Green Wheatgrass

912 East 28th Avenue
Vancouver, BC V5V 2P2
Phone: (604) 879-2280
Healthy Green Wheatgrass grows the soil-grown sprouts: buckwheat, sunflower and wheatgrass. They offer home delivery in the Lower Mainland and will ship to locations within one day away by bus. They will try to honor special needs and requests.

Juicing Machines

The Champion Juicer

This machine has withstood the test of time. It is a real workhorse. You can juice with it, make pâtés, grate, purée and make ice cream from frozen fruit. However, you cannot juice wheatgrass with a Champion. If you are juicing wheatgrass, you need to use a separate machine.

Distributor:
The Raw Gourmet

Toll Free: 888-316-4611
nomi@rawgourmet.com
www.rawgourmet.com

The Green Star Juicer –
Twin Gear Technology

This machine does it all. It is expensive but if you can afford it, it's worth it. You can juice with it, make all the pâtés, ice creams and purées, and you can use it to make wheatgrass juice. Recently, the manufacturer of the Green Power Juicer has introduced this more compact and affordable model. It is a great performer. The Green Life and Green Star Juicer do everything the Green Power Juicer did, all the attachments necessary for juicing come with it and it has a considerably longer warranty. All attachments for Asian specialities such as mochi are included.

Distributor in the USA:
The Raw Gourmet

888-316-4611
nomi@rawgourmet.com
www.rawgourmet.com

Distributor in Canada:
Alpha Health Products Ltd
7434 Fraser Park Drive
Burnaby BC V5J 5B9
Toll-free: 800-663-2212
Phone: 604-436-0545
Fax: 604-435-4862
contacts@alphahealth.ca
www.alphahealth.ca

The Miracle Wheatgrass Juicer

A small electric juicer, not designed for commercial use, but more than adequate for home use. A manual wheatgrass juicer is hard work to use. Purchase a manual juicer only if you do not have electricity.

Distributor:
The Raw Gourmet
888-316-4611
nomi@rawgourmet.com
www.rawgourmet.com

Blenders

K-Tec Champ

The Premier Home Blender!

K-TEC is the innovative leader in the commercial blender market. This same engineering genius goes into their home use blender, the Champ HP3™. Computer controlled blend cycles make perfect smoothies or soups with one-touch operation. No old fashioned knobs, switches, or dials to wear out or struggle with cleaning. Its half-gallon capacity GE Lexan™ (break resistant) jar is lightweight and easy to clean. Pre-programmed blending cycles direct a powerful 3-peak horsepower motor to change speeds and times, automatically assuring perfect blending consistency – making any blending task a breeze. Complete 8 year warranty on machine and lifetime warranty on coupling and blade for home use. The K-tec can blend frozen bananas into smoothies or large chunks of carrot into soups. Easy on, easy off lid with no need for a plunger type tool to mix ingredients. For daily raw food prep, the K-tec is essential for smooth results and fast preparation.

Distributor:
The Raw Gourmet
888-316-4611
nomi@rawgourmet.com
www.rawgourmet.com

Dehydrators

The Excalibur

Your dehydrator must have a temperature control. Otherwise, it may overheat the food and kill the enzymes. Choose from several models, ranging from 4 trays with 4 square feet (1.2 square meters) of drying area to 9 trays with 15 square feet (4.5 square meters) of drying area.

Distributor: The Raw Gourmet
888-316-4611
nomi@rawgourmet.com
www.rawgourmet.com

Living-Food Retreats

Ann Wigmore Institute
P.O. Box 429
Rincon, Puerto Rico 00677-0429
Phone: 787-868-6307
Fax: 787-868-2430
wigmore@coqui.net
www.annwigmore.com

Creative Health Institute
918 West Union City Road
Union City, MI 49094
Phone: 517-278-6260
Fax: 517-278-5837
info@creativehealthinstitute.us
www.creativehealthinstitute.us

Hippocrates Health Institute
1443 Palmdale Court
West Palm Beach, Florida 33411
Phone: 561-471-8876
Fax: 561-471-9464
Reservation Line: 1-800-842-2125
info@hippocratesinst
www.hippocratesinst.com

The Optimum Health Institute
6970 Central Avenue
Lemon Grove, CA 91945
Toll Free: 800-993-4325
Phone: 619-464-3346
Fax: 619-589-4098
optimun@optimumhealth.org
www.optimumhealth.org

OR:

Optimum Health Institute
Rt. 1 Box 339-J Cedar Lane
Cedar Creek, TX 78612
Toll Free: 800-993-4325
Phone: 512-303-4817
Fax: 512-303-1239
ohi@totalaccess.net
www.optimumhealth.org

Helpful Kitchen Tools

Saladacco (Spiral Slicer)
Mandoline-Plus

Distributor:
The Raw Gourmet
888-316-4611
nomi@rawgourmet.com
www.rawgourmet.com
email: rawgourmet@aol.com

The saladacco (spiral slicer) is a manual kitchen tool that turns zucchini, carrot, yam, beet, parsnip and other hard vegetables into long thin strands, like spaghetti or angel hair pasta. Some of the strands are 3 or 4 feet long! It also makes decorative spiral slices. This is a popular item because it adds a new dimension to raw food cuisine and is inexpensive. See a picture and further description at: www.rawgourmet.com/saladacco.

The Raw Gourmet also distributes the Mandoline-plus, which enables you to rapidly create thin slices and three different size julienne strips. The saladacco and the mandoline-plus are available wholesale and retail.

Toss n chop

Distributor:
The Raw Gourmet
888-316-4611
nomi@rawgourmet.com
www.rawgourmet.com

This time-saving manual item is part scissor, part salad tong.
It replaces knife, cutting board and other prep equipment in the making of a salad. Simply place all ingredients for your salad including dressing components, carrots, onion, celery etc., in a bowl and toss and chop for a quick and easy salad. Rather than painstakingly chopping each item by hand, you toss and chop all at once, with no mess to clean up.

Nut Milk and Sprout Bags

Distributor:
The Raw Gourmet
888-316-4611
nomi@rawgourmet.com
www.rawgourmet.com

The amazing nut-milk and sprout bag has many uses. Blend water and nuts, then squeeze through bag to quickly make nut or seed milk. It also can be used as a sprouting bag. It can even be used as a traveling juicer, by blending veggies or fruits, then squeezing through the bag. Two sizes: large and small for all your sprouting and nut-milk needs.

Videos

The Raw Gourmet Videos

Distributor:
The Raw Gourmet
888-316-4611
nomi@rawgourmet.com
www.rawgourmet.com

Raw food preparation classes by the author of The Raw Gourmet, Nomi Shannon.

Three videos are available: Volume 1: *Start Your Day the Healthy Way* features fruits, juicing, smoothies, puddings and cereals. Volume 2: *Making Meals Out of Nuts and Seeds* features entrees like mock salmon loaf, pate, roll-ups, burgers, stuffed peppers, nori rolls, chile rellenos neat balls and gravy and more. Volume3: *Palate Pleasing Recipes for 4-400* features recipes for home and banquets. How to multiply a recipe. See traditional tasting foods made raw like spaghetti, marinara sauce, pesto sauce, spinach mousse, lasagne. See the saladacco and mandoline-plus demonstrated. All videos include plating ideas and recipes. Great companion to The Raw Gourmet book.

Grocery Guide

The symbol * denotes items suggested for an initial shopping list.

Note: All food should be organic if possible.

Adzuki beans: Also called aduki beans. A legume, for sprouting in a jar.

Agar: A natural jelling and thickening agent made from seaweed.

Alaria: See Wakame.

Alfalfa seed*: A small legume, for sprouting in a jar.

Almond butter (raw)*: A good alternative to peanut butter and a convenient item for quick recipes.

Almonds, raw (shelled)*: Keep refrigerated or frozen to prevent rancidity.

Apricots, dried: Buy the unsulphured variety. Keep them refrigerated or frozen for longest shelf-life.

Arrowroot powder: Used as a thickening agent.

Barley, hulless variety: Used for sprouting in a jar. Often difficult to find.

Basil: Fresh basil is always preferable, but keep some dried basil stored as a staple. Store dried basil in the freezer to maximize freshness.

Buckwheat whole (unhulled): For soil-grown sprouted greens, commonly referred to as buckwheat lettuce.

Buckwheat, whole, raw (hulled): Also called groats. For sprouting in a jar, using as a cereal and for dough. When toasted it is called kasha.

Caraway seed: These seeds lose their flavor quickly. Store them in the refrigerator or freezer to prolong their life.

Carob, raw: A powder ground from pods of the carob tree (St. John's fruit); it is a good substitute for chocolate. Available raw.

Carrots: Carrots are important for juicing and their pulp is the base of several recipes.

Cashew, pieces or whole: Their sweet, smooth properties make them excellent for toppings and dressings. Cashews are not considered a true raw food, so they are for occasional use only.

Cayenne pepper*: A stimulating and warming herb made from grinding the small hot cayenne pepper; it is as beneficial for health as it is tasty.

Chickpeas: Also called garbanzo or ceci beans. Extremely popular in the Middle East, these legumes are used for sprouting in a jar.

Chinese 5-spice powder: An aromatic blend of cinnamon, cloves, fennel seed, star anise and Szechuan peppercorns. It gives an unmistakably "Asian" flavor to any dish.

Cilantro: Also called Chinese parsley and fresh coriander. Looks like pale parsley, adds a familiar "Mexican" and "Asian" flavor to recipes.

Cinnamon: Essential for apple pie. Buy it ground.

Clover seed*: A small legume, for sprouting in a jar.

Coconut: Buy unsweetened, organic, unpasteurized shredded coconut.

Cumin: A pungent, strong-flavored spice that aids digestion. Buy it whole or ground.

Curry powder: A mixture of up to 20 spices, most commonly including: cardamom, coriander, cumin and turmeric. It loses its pungency quickly so buy it in small amounts.

Dates*: The three best varieties for raw food preparation are medjool, khadrawi and honey.

Date mash: Useful for large-scale food preparation. Sold by the bucket.

Date pieces: An economical substitute for most recipes calling for whole dates.

Date sugar: Made from dates only. It is heated in the process so it is not considered a raw food.

Dehydrated onion rings (home-made): Easy to make and good for salads and pizzas.

Dehydrated vegetables: Available singly or a variety. Excellent for flavoring and thickening food.

Dehydrated red pepper rings (home-made): Easy to make and good for salads and pizzas.

Dulse: A popular and delicious seaweed. Buy large pieces and granules or flakes.

Fennel Seeds: The seeds have a licorice-like flavor, are good as a seasoning and aid the digestive process.

Fenugreek seeds: A small legume for sprouting in a jar. The seeds are extremely beneficial to the lymph system.

Flax seeds: These seeds are used as a thickener. Flax seeds are high in beneficial oils. They are ground and used in beverages and sprinkled on salads. They have important therapeutic qualities.

Garam masala: "Garam" is the Indian word for "warm," and "masala" means mix. This traditional mixture of spices (for which there are dozens of variations) is meant to impart warmth and an exotic flavor to food.

Garbanzo beans: *See* Chickpeas.

Garlic*: Always buy fresh garlic—avoid both the powders and the pre-peeled garlic in jars. Besides having a wonderful flavor, fresh garlic has important therapeutic qualities.

Ginger*: Fresh ginger root is always recommended. Keep a piece in the refrigerator, and one in the freezer where it will last many months.

Herb blend: Because you can't always have fresh herbs available, keep your favorite dried blend in the freezer to prolong its life and preserve its flavor.

Hazelnuts: Also called filberts. Keep them frozen or refrigerated.

Herbs: Always use fresh herbs, when available. Try basil, oregano, dill, tarragon, chives, mint and/or cilantro.

Hijiki: A black, thread-like seaweed, imported from Japan.

Honey: Some people prefer not to use honey as it comes from an animal. Buy raw, unfiltered honey from a local beekeeper.

Kelp: This nourishing seaweed is also known as kombu. Buy granules and/or large pieces.

Kuzu: Also known as kudzu. A natural jelling and thickening agent, made from a root that grows wild in Japan.

Lemons*: Buy the fresh fruit only. Lemons are used extensively to flavor and preserve food.

Lentils*: A legume, for sprouting in a jar. Purchase whole (not split) lentils. They are available in many colors; green and red are the most common.

Liquid aminos*: The manufacturer claims this is a non-heated, non-fermented, non-pasteurized soy product, similar in taste and appearance to soy sauce. Liquid aminos are used as a flavoring in place of salt. The most common brand is Bragg's Liquid Aminos.

Maple sprinkles: A granulated sugar substitute made from pure maple syrup. They are not a raw food. Also referred to as maple granules.

Maple syrup: Used for sweetening. Although maple syrup is a natural product, it is not a raw food.

Miso: Used as a salt replacement or seasoning, miso is a thick paste made from soybeans, grain and sea salt. There are many types available. Generally, the darker the miso, the stronger the flavor. Buy unpasteurized, naturally aged miso which contains enzymes.

Mung beans: A medium-sized legume, for sprouting.

Nama shoyu: Traditional unpasteurized Japanese soy sauce. Many raw fooders insist on this product as it is raw. However all soy sauce is made with wheat, which is not recommended on a raw food diet, except in the form of sprouted wheat or wheatgrass. If you want a non-wheat, unpasteurized product use tamari or Bragg's liquid aminos.

Nori sheets*: Popular green seaweed that comes in square sheets. Used in Japanese restaurants to make sushi. Buy it raw, not toasted.

Nutmeg: A spice with a warm, spicy and sweet aroma that is useful for desserts.

Oat groats, raw*: Be sure to buy unsteamed oats for cereal flour and raw food recipes.

Oils: Best choices are flaxseed, extra-virgin olive, grapeseed, walnut, pumpkin, hazelnut, pistachio, almond and hemp. Always buy cold-pressed, unrefined oils and store them in dark glass bottles to avoid damage from the sun. Flora manufactures pumpkin oil, almond oil, walnut oil and flaxseed oil. Omega manufactures flaxseed oil, hazelnut and pistachio oils. Barlean manufactures flaxseed oil.

Olives, Greek: Buy sun-dried, salt-cured olives.

Olives, green: Usually soaked in lye, then salt brine. Although they are not heated, there are probably few living enzymes left in green olives.

Onion, dehydrated: Fresh mild onion, such as Spanish, is the best choice. Dehydrated onions lend an interesting flavor to food.

Oregano: Fresh oregano is a summer treat, dried lends an "Italian" flavor to food. The dried variety, which should be stored in the freezer, is more pungent.

Paprika: Ground mild chili. Use it for flavor and color. Store it in the freezer.

Parsley: A nourishing green for juicing and raw food recipes.

Peas, dried (whole): A legume, for sprouting in a jar or soil.

Pecans, shelled: Used for crusts and pâtés. Store in the freezer or refrigerator to prevent rancidity.

Pine nuts: Also called pignoli and pinons. A soft, white nut used primarily for sauces. Pine nuts come from the pine cone of the pinon tree, in the American southwest. They are also grown in China and Portugal. They have an exceptionally short shelf-life; always store them in the freezer.

Pizza seasoning: A pre-made blend of popular Italian herbs made by Frontier Herbs.

Prunes, dried: Store them in the refrigerator.

Psyllium: The husks of psyllium seeds are ground to a powder and used in raw cuisine as a thickener. Buy only a very finely ground powder with no ingredients added, or finely grind coarser husks in the blender.

Pumpkin seeds: Buy only raw seeds. They are commonly available via mail-order.

Pumpkin pie spice: A blend of spices to give that "pumpkin pie" taste.

Radish seeds: For sprouting in a jar. Radish seeds will add "bite" to your meals.

Raisins: Thompson or Monukka varieties are best. "Golden" raisins have usually been chemically bleached.

Red chili pepper, dried: A pinch of these crushed, dried red chili flakes and seeds will add flavor without too much heat for most palates.

Red clover seeds*: A small legume, for sprouting.

Red peppers: An important source of vitamin C. Green peppers, which are not ripe, are not used in raw cuisine.

Rye: A grain, for sprouting in a jar. They are used in salads and for dough.

Scallions: Also called green onions or spring onions.

Sea salt: Choose a reputable source so you know that it is unadulterated, pure sea salt. Much salt is stripped of all its natural minerals which are later added back chemically.

Seaweed*: There are many types of seaweed. Begin stocking your pantry with dulse pieces, nori sheets and dulse and kelp granules. Maine Coast sea vegetables brand makes inexpensive shakers of various seaweeds to sprinkle on food. Buy 1 of each flavor and use them generously.

Sesame seed, hulled: For sprouting in a jar. They are used in many recipes.

Squash: Summer squashes, such as crookneck and pattypan, have thin, edible skins and soft seeds; winter squashes, such as acorn, butternut and hubbard, have hard, thick skin and seeds.

Stevia*: A natural sweetener made from a

flower that is far sweeter than sugar. Stevia comes in liquid and powder.

Sunflower seeds, raw (hulled)*: For sprouting in a jar. An important staple used in many recipes.

Sunflower seeds, in shell: For soil-grown greens. Buy either black or striped.

Tahini, raw*: A butter made from ground sesame seeds. A good alternative to nut butters and to grinding sesame seeds. Highly nutritious and economical, it is used in many recipes.

Tamari*: A wheat-free soy sauce. Unpasteurized; no alcohol added.

Turmeric: A strong-flavored, aromatic, yellow spice. It is considered therapeutic.

Wakame: Also called alaria. This highly nutritious seaweed is not only good for you, it imparts a delightful flavor to foods. It is usually sold in large pieces.

Walnuts, raw (shelled): Store them in the refrigerator or freezer to prevent rancidity.

Wasabi: This Japanese horseradish paste comes in a tube or a jar, or you can buy it as powder and reconstitute it. It's available at Asian markets.

Water*: Pure water is absolutely essential for drinking and for all food preparation, including soaking sprouts and washing vegetables. A high-quality, reverse-osmosis unit installed in your kitchen is the best idea. Alternately, you can use a water distiller. Beware of "store-bought" water in plastic jugs. Often the water is not what the label says it is, and it could have been in the plastic container for a long time.

Wheatberries, hard red winter variety: For growing wheatgrass or sprouting in a jar.

Wheatberries, spring variety: For sprouting in a jar. Use wheatberries in recipes and as cereal.

Zucchini*: Known as courgettes in the United Kingdom.

Bibliography

Airola, Paavo. *Juice Fasting*. Health Plus Publishers: Phoenix, AZ, 1971.

Anderson, Jean, M. S. and Deskins, Barbara. *The Nutrition Bible*. William Morrow and Company: New York, 1995.

Anderson, Richard. *Cleanse and Purify Thyself*. Dr. Richard Anderson, ND, 1988.

Belsinger, Susan. *Flowers in the Kitchen*. Interweave Press: Loveland, CO, 1991.

Blauer, Stephen. *The Juicing Book*. Avery Publishing Group, Inc: Garden City Park, NY, 1989.

Braunstein, Mark M. *The Sprout Garden*. The Book Publishing Company: Summertown, TN, 1993.

Clement, Brian R. with DiGeronimo, Theresa Foy. *Living Foods for Optimum Health*. Prima Publishing, 1996.

Cousens, Gabriel. *Conscious Eating*. Vision Books International: Santa Rosa, CA, 1992.

Gibbons, Euell. *Stalking the Good Life*. David McKay Company: New York, 1971.

Gibbons, Euell. *Stalking the Wild Asparagus*. David McKay Company: New York, 1962.

Gursche, Siegfried. *Healing With Herbal Juices*. **alive** books: Burnaby, BC, 1993.

Howell, Edward. *Enzyme Nutrition: The Food Enzyme Concept*. Avery Publishing Group: Wayne, NJ, 1985.

Jensen, Bernard. *Tissue Cleansing Through Bowel Management*. Bernard Jensen Publications: Escondido, CA, 1981.

Kulvinskas, Viktoras. *Survival Into the 21st Century*. Omangod Press: Wethersfield, CT, 1975.

Malkmus, George H. *God's Way to Ultimate Health*. Hallelujah Acres Publishing: Eidson, TN, 1995.

Meyerowitz, Steve. *Juice Fasting and Detoxification*. The Sprout House: Great Barrington, MA, 1984.

Robbins, John. *Diet for a New America*. Stillpoint Publishing: Walpole, NH, 1987.

Robbins, John. *May All Be Fed*. William Morrow and Company: New York, 1992.

Romano, Rita. *Dining in the Raw, Cooking With the Buff*. Prato Publications: Italy, 1993.

Rosengarten, Jr., Frederic. *The Book of Edible Nuts*. Walker Publishing Company: New York, 1984.

Santillo, Humbart. *Food Enzymes, The Missing Link to Radiant Health*. Hohm Press: Prescott Valley, AZ, 1987.

Shelton Herbert. *Food Combining Made Easy*. Willow Publishing: San Antonio, TX, 1997.

Szekely, Edmond Bordeaux, ed. *The Essene Gospel of Peace*. Book One, International Biogenic Society, USA, 1981.

Walker, Norman W. *Colon Health: The Key to a Vibrant Life*. Norwalk Press, 1979.

——— *The Vegetarian Guide to Diet and Salad*. Norwalk Press, 1995.

——— *Fresh Vegetable and Fruit Juices*. Norwalk Press, 1970.

Wigmore, Ann. *The Hippocrates Diet and Health Program*. Avery Publishing Group: Wayne, NJ, 1984.

——— *The Wheatgrass Book*. Avery Publishing Group: Wayne, NJ, 1985.

——— *Why Suffer?* Avery Publishing Group: Wayne, NJ, 1985.

Index

*Page references to photographs are set in **boldface**.*

alive Natural Health Guides

alive BOOKS

Look for the full series at your local health food store, nutrition centre or bookstore. Call 1-800-663-6580, or visit www.alive.com for more information.

self help information

Liver Cleansing Handbook
Poor diet and lifestyle have devastating effects on the liver. Eating natural foods and detoxifying your liver will benefit you mentally, emotionally and physically.

Nature's Own Candida Cure
Some yeasts are beneficial to the body, others cause chronic illness. Health can be regained, and candida controlled, through natural methods.

Natural Relief from Asthma
Non-existent 100 years ago, asthma now affects millions. Learn asthma's causes, and how to obtain relief successfully and naturally.

Osteoarthritis
Natural treatments for osteoarthritis, the most common form of joint disease. Change your dietary habits for prevention and reversal.

Fighting Fibromyalgia
Conventional medicine offers no cure, but there are many things you can do to relieve the discomfort. Discover what natural strategies and treatments can do for you.

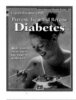

Prevent, Treat and Reverse Diabetes
Improve Type I diabetes with proper eating; the major cause of Type II diabetes is poor/wrong nutrition. Control and reverse both types with natural treatments.

Rheumatoid Arthritis
The natural approach addresses the underlying systematic problems. Learn about diet, supplements, antioxidants and alternative therapies.

Attention-Deficit Disorder
Alternative therapies for learning disorders, ADD, ADHD, hyperactivity and dyslexia. Natural alternatives to stimulants and antidepressant drugs.

healing foods & herbs

Fantastic Flax
Flax is healthy, economical, and ultra-rich in fibre, protein, beneficial fats, vitamins and minerals. Add flax seeds and oil to your diet with breakfast, lunch and baking recipes.

Evening Primrose Oil
A safe, effective treatment for eczema, premenstrual syndrome, menopause, depression, migraines and more. Learn the special benefits of this yellow flower's rich oil.

Cranberry
Used for treating and preventing bladder infections and many other ailments for centuries. Western and natural doctors recommend and rely on its healing effectiveness.

Papaya - the Healing Fruit
More vitamin C than oranges, and more vitamin A than carrots. How to incorporate this nutritious fruit into your health regime.

Sprouts
A live and nutritious source of energy, vitality and health. How to buy seeds, grow your own sprouts, and use them in easy, healthy recipes.

Health and Healing with Bee Products
Benefit from bee pollen, propolis, honey and royal jelly, thanks to honey bees. The ultimate "nutraceuticals" for hundreds of conditions from hair loss to arteriosclerosis.

Whole Foods for Seniors
It is never too late to reverse wrong eating habits and incorporate whole foods into your diet. Relief for heartburn, acid reflux, high blood pressure, diabetes and more.

Enzymes
Are you suffering from a lack of energy, mental weariness, metabolic disorders, or poor circulation? Eating enzyme-rich foods can help prevent these and many other conditions and improve your quality of life.

Chef's Healthy Pasta

Healthy, natural, easy-to-make recipes for whole-grain pasta, vegetarian meals. Familiar flavours and exotic ingredients.

Chef's Healthy Salads

Create and enjoy healthy, delicious salads every day. Discover flavourful, tasty dressings featuring natural, unrefined oils.

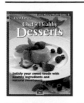

Chef's Healthy Desserts

Healthy alternatives to commonly-used, harmful ingredients. Discover delicious, "to-die-for", guilt-free desserts.

Healthy Breads with the Breadmaker

Wake up to the fresh taste and wonderful aroma of fresh-baked bread. Practical info and advice on baking healthy, great-tasting bread.

Good Fats and Oils

Easy to understand information, including the differences between good fats and bad fats. Learn the health benefits, and how to use these oils in the kitchen.

Super Breakfast Cereals

Whole grains provide a natural set of nutrients your body is programmed to metabolize. How to buy, store and prepare whole grains. Great recipes too!

Making Sauerkraut

Sauerkraut eliminates disease-causing bacteria and reintroduces friendly bacteria. Lactic acid-fermented foods contain potent enzymes that boost metabolism.

Health Hazards of White Sugar

Refined sugar and artificial sweeteners pose danger. Nature's own, unrefined sweeteners are full of vitamins and minerals.

Smoothies and Other Scrumptious Delights

Finally a collection of over 50 recipes for naturally healthy mouth watering smoothies. Easy to prepare for people on the go. Loved by the whole family!

Juicing for the Health of it!

Benefit from the healing power of juices in new, simple, effective ways. Use organic fruit and vegetables to treat acne, angina, high blood pressure, insomnia and more.

Natural Alternatives to Vaccination

Many parents choose not to vaccinate their children because of the side effects and dangers of vaccination. Learn about inmune boosting strategies and natural supplements.

Healing with Water

Feel younger, stronger and more alive with the liquid of life - water. Developed 100 years ago by Father Sebastian Kneipp, this at-home hydrotherapy eases poor circulation, heart problems, stress and more.

Supplements for Natural Body Building

Natural ways to build your body without life-threatening steroids. 10 supplements for body-builders and those who want to look and feel their best.

Menopause - Normally and Naturally

Middle age for women can be worry-free, active and healthy. Learn about good nutrition, nutritional supplements and herbal remedies.

Good Digestion

Nutrition is so much more than simply what we eat. Easy-to-understand information on how digestion actually works.

Sauna - The Hottest Way to Good Health

A European tradition for cleansing and detoxifiying. Enjoy normalized blood pressure, improved immune function, reduced stress and more.

Choosing the Right Fats

This book dispels myths about fat, such as: fats make you fat. Essential fats in the oils of freshly pressed olives and the oils of various freshly pressed nuts, seeds and pumpkins have life giving properties.

Nature's Best Heart Medicine

Learn new scientific discoveries to quickly reduce your risk of a heart attack, even if you've already suffered one. You'll find lots of simple advice on how to incorporate foods and supplements rich in fantastic flavonoids into your daily diet.

Best sellers and favourites from the *alive* library

Look for *alive* books at your local health food store, nutrition centre or bookstore. Call 1-800-663-6580, or visit www.alive.com for more information.

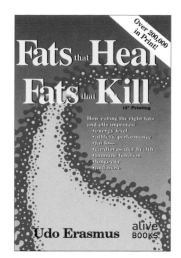

Fats that Heal Fats that Kill
Udo Erasmus
480 pages, softcover
over 200,000 in print

allergies
Disease in Disguise
Carolee Bateson-Koch DC ND
294 pages, softcover

Dagmar von Cramm
240 pages, softcover with French flaps

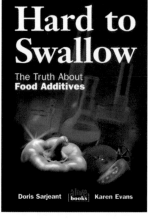

Doris Sarjeant, Karen Evans
332 pages, softcover

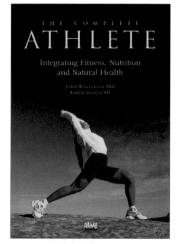

John Winterdyk PhD,
Karen Jensen ND
320 pages, softcover

Rudolph Breuss
114 pages, softcover

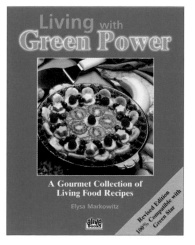

Elysa Markowitz
172 pages, hardcover

Jeanne Marie Martin
445 pages, hardcover